AUSTRALIAN CYCLING CHAMPIONS

130 YEARS OF

BICYCLE RACING

By Warren Beaumont

**PLATEAU
PUBLISHING**

First published in 2021

by Plateau Publishing
Wentworth Falls, NSW Australia 2782
PO Box 232 Wentworth Falls, NSW 2782
www.plateaupublishing.com

A catalogue record for this
work is available from the
National Library of Australia

ISBN: 978-0-646-83413-9

Beaumont, Warren, Australian Cycling Champions
- 130 years of bicycle racing

Cover and internal design by PGH Publications and
Warren Beaumont.
Printed in Australia by Ligare Books, Riverwood, NSW.

CONTENTS

Penny Farthing Bicycle Club, (c.1885) Launceston. From the Collection of the Queen Victoria Museum and Art Gallery, Launceston, Tasmania.

Cycling party riding safety bicycles at Government House, Melbourne, 1896. Photo courtesy State Library Victoria.

Penny Farthing bicycle with rider, 1880, collected
by Pretyman family. Courtesy of Libraries Tasmania.

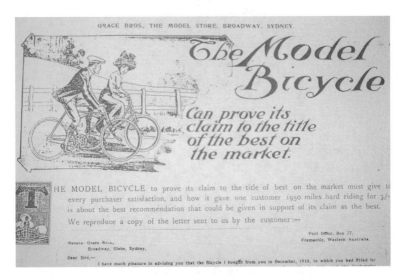

Advertisement for The Model Bicycle (safety) from Grace Bros
catalogue, Grace Bros, Broadway, Sydney, 1912.
The Mens and Ladies' models were priced at six pounds.

Cyclists with safety bicycles, Jenolan Caves, NSW, 1900.
Courtesy Jim Fitzpatrick's The Bicycle and the Bush.

Robert Walne was the Australian Professional 10 Mile Champion in 1900.
This photo during racing at the Melbourne Cricket Ground.
Photo courtesy the AusCycling Victoria History Archive,
Carmellotti/Holgate collection.

INTRODUCTION

Australians were quick to take up cycling on the high wheeler or 'ordinary' bicycle in the late 1870s and amateur bicycle clubs formed for touring or racing around the country from the 1880s. In 1884 the first Intercolonial Cycling Championships was held, while the first national amateur track championships ran from 1888. When the smaller chain-driven safety bicycle appeared from 1887, professional track cycling became hugely popular.

The Austral Wheel Race in Melbourne (1887) and the Sydney Thousand (1903) were the world's richest handicap track cycling races, while the Austral became known for race fixing and gambling scandals. Australia's cyclists were among the best in the world and in 1899 Ben Goodson placed in the world 100km track championship.

The Melbourne to Warrnambool started in the 1890s and is the world's second oldest one-day race. Hubert Opperman won four Warrnambool fastest times and was known for his long-distance road performances including winning the Paris-Brest-Paris non-stop 1200 miles race.

Jack Hoobin won our first world amateur road championship in Belgium in 1950, while Clyde Sefton's silver at Munich in 1974 was our first Olympic road medal.

Australia's Amateur Road Championships started in 1928 (1978 for women), National Professional Road Championships in 1950 and open National Road Championships in 1993. Victoria's Sun Tour began in 1952 and the Tour Down Under in 1999. These and the national track championships contributed to the success of our top men and women at major international events.

Australia's road cycling champions also took on the gruelling Tour de France. Hubert Opperman placed 12th in 1931; Phil Anderson was the first non-European to wear the leader's Yellow Jersey in 1981 and placed fifth in 1982; Cadel Evans was our first Tour winner in 2011; while Ritchie Porte placed third in 2020.

Women road cyclists were featured in newspapers and magazines from the 1890s when they set long distance road records riding safety bicycles. Among the trailblazers was Sarah (Mrs E.A) Maddock, the first woman to ride from Melbourne to Sydney in 1894.

Our top women's road cyclists raised the profile of Australian road cycling from the 1980s. Liz Hepple placed second in the Tour de France Feminin and Kathy Watt had a breakthrough gold medal road race win at the 1992 Barcelona Olympics. Australian women road champions continued to win major races and medals internationally including Oenone Wood, Sara Carrigan, Katrin Garfoot, and current stars Chloe Hosking and Amanda Spratt.

From 1905, Australia's track champions moved to the USA in one of the greatest migrations in the history of sport, where Alf Goullet and Alf Grenda set the world record in the six-day race. Bob Spears won the world professional sprint title in 1920, Dunc Gray won gold in the 1000m time trial at the 1932 Los Angeles Olympics, while Russell Mockridge claimed two gold medals at the 1952 Helsinki Olympics.

Our international track cycling champions from 1970 who won world championships included Gordon Johnson, John Nicholson, Danny Clark, Gary Sutton, and Dean Woods. More recently they were followed by great track champions such as Shane Kelly, Ryan Bayley, Cameron Meyer and Matthew Glaetzer.

In 1988 our women track cycling champions competed at their first Olympic Games and among our most successful at the world championships, Olympics and

Commonwealth Games are sprinters Michelle Ferris, Anna Meares, Kaarle McCulloch and Stephanie Morton, and endurance champions Katie Mactier, Amy Cure, Annette Edmondson, and Ashlee Ankudinoff.

Behind the success of many of our top road and track cycling champions were local cycling clubs and the Australian Institute of Sport, while mentorship and coaching from former greats and experts often made the difference between success and failure at the national and world championships, Olympic and Commonwealth Games, and European tours and classics.

Australia's cyclists have competed on the world stage since the 1890s and are one of the world's top road and track cycling nations with a top four to five UCI nation ranking. They have the capabilities to continue this great cycling legacy, despite the challenges and disruption caused by the coronavirus in 2020 and 2021.

AUTHOR

Warren Beaumont is a Blue Mountains, New South Wales-based journalist, who wrote for cycling and sports trade magazines in the 1980s to early 1990s such as National Cycling, Freewheeling, Push-On Cycling, Sports & Leisure Retailer and Sports Link, and was an active recreational and touring cyclist for 35 years.

The author researched cycling history and interviewed Australia's past champion cyclists in the 1980s-1990s and from 2017 the book took shape through further research, interviews and attending major cycling events.

In the book the author charts the history of road and track racing in Australia from the late 1880s to 2020 and highlights the national and international performances of a large number of our road and track cycling champions.

Don Walker winning the 5 Mile Commonwealth Stakes at the
MCG in 1902; and with officials after his win.
Photos courtesy the AusCycling Victoria History Archive,
Carmellotti/Holgate collection.

1867. Mr. W. A. George of Goulburn started building a Velocipede bicycle design and that same year, Sydney entrepreneur Joseph Pearson is believed to have conducted velocipede or 'boneshaker' races at the Albert Street Ground in Redfern.

1868. The velocipede riding craze swept through Europe in 1867-68 and velocipede riding became popular with men and women on the streets of Melbourne in 1868. The first velocipede bicycle was typically made of cast-iron with metal-rimmed wheels and wooden spokes, using treadle 'pedal' cranks attached to a larger front wheel. It was also known as 'the boneshaker' as it was quite uncomfortable to ride.

1869. Australia's first recorded bicycle race over two miles was held at the Melbourne Cricket Ground in 1869, attracting 12,000 spectators but only three competitors. Our first bicycle club the 'Boneshakers' formed in Melbourne in 1869. The Boneshakers rode velocipedes for touring and racing until around 1875 when the first high wheelers or 'ordinary' bicycles were imported.

1870-1892. The ordinary was a superior and lighter racing machine, developed in England from 1870, also called the 'penny farthing' and the high wheeler. It was notoriously difficult to mount the saddle and dismount, as the saddle was over a metre high. The increased speed if offered was offset by the frequency of accidents while riding the ordinary bicycle.

The ordinary bicycle featured large front driving wheels of 56 to 60 inches diameter and small rear wheels of 20 to 22 inches diameter. The ordinary became extremely popular for racing as it offered great advances in metal strength, comfort, and speed. The weight of racing machines soon dropped to around 25 pounds.

The ordinary gave bicycle enthusiasts a new outlet for recreation, long distances could be covered, and bicycle touring clubs started up across the country. The cost of buying an ordinary ranged from six to 20 pounds, putting it out of the reach of many average wage earners.

1874. James Starley designs the tangent-spoked wheel for the Ariel high wheeler.

1878. Bicycle touring clubs started up across the country and the Melbourne Bicycle Club formed in 1878. Club members dressed in club colours and met at several appointed places, all mounted on the high wheelers. They would pedal out to a resort, often 10, 15 and 30 miles distant and the Saturday morning newspapers listed details of touring runs.

1879-80. In England in 1879, Henry John Lawson patented a bicycle with a basic chain drive system connected to the rear wheel.

The Sydney Bicycle Club was inaugurated in 1879 and like the Melbourne club, had an impetus to race bicycles. The Sydney club's first race was held at the Cricket Association Ground in May 1880 when high wheelers were raced for the first time in Sydney.

1880s. Other amateur bicycle clubs formed in South Australia, Brisbane, Goulburn, Dubbo and in Tasmania. The Brisbane Bicycle Club held its first meeting at the Bellevue Hotel in 1881 with novelty races on high wheelers in the Botanic Gardens. Melbourne was the centre of the first cycle racing boom and the high-wheeler bicycle became popular. The Melbourne Exhibition Ground became the citadel of cycle racing and was the venue for Australia's first six-day bicycle race in 1881. The Launceston bicycle club formed in March 1883 and conducted touring and racing events.

1883. The first amateur group in New South Wales was established in August 1883. It was called the New South Wales Cyclists Union and by March 1891 had 21 clubs affiliated with a membership of 567.

1884. The Melbourne Bicycle Club conducted Melbourne's first full racing programme at the Cricket Ground in 1884. That same year the first Intercolonial Cycling Championships were organized and conducted in Sydney and Brisbane. They attracted cyclists from Sydney, Melbourne, Brisbane, Goulburn and from English clubs and it was also common for New Zealand cyclists to compete in Intercolonial Championships.

1885. In Coventry, England, John Kemp Starley introduced the Rover Safety Bicycle with an improved drive-chain system.

1887. Joseph Pearson imported a chain driven safety bicycle into New South Wales. The first safety bicycles in Australia were geared at around 57 inches and weighed 27 pounds and now featured solid rubber tyres and could travel 100 miles in six hours, 20 minutes compared with eight hours on an ordinary.

The introduction of the chain driven safety bicycle with its diamond frame design would eventually make the ordinary or high-wheeler obsolete. The rider was now positioned in a lower, much safer position as the safety's front wheel was much smaller than the ordinary. While the front wheel remained larger than the rear wheel, after 1890, wheel sizes settled at around 28 inches diameter.

1886-87. Professional track cycling began to catch the imagination of sports followers from the late 1880s. Cyclists competed for rich prizes on oval shaped bicycle tracks in Australia's major cities and towns. Handicap racing, where the top cyclists gave seemingly impossible starts to the front markers, thrilled the crowds and Melbourne soon became the mecca of Australian professional track cycling. The first official Austral Wheel began in 1887 at the Melbourne Cricket Ground.

1888-90. Scottish born John Boyd Dunlop invented the inflatable rubber tube in 1888 and patented the pneumatic tyre. Cycle dealer Mr Malcomsen imported the first pneumatic tyres into Victoria from the UK in 1889. E.W. Rudd was appointed the agent in Australia for the Dunlop Pneumatic Tyre Company of Coventry, England.

When Dunlop's pneumatic tyre patent was declared invalid in 1890 due to the earlier patent of Robert William Thompson, Dunlop bought the Welch detachable wire bead tyre patent. In October 1899, the Dunlop Pneumatic Tyre Company of Australasia floated on the Melbourne, Sydney, and Adelaide stock exchanges.

1888-91. While Australia was still a colony, the first national amateur track championships were held under an agreement between NSW, Victoria, and South Australia.

1889. Bicycle racing became more popular and the Sydney Bicycle Club held races at the Association Cricket Ground, Moore Park in 1889.

1890s. Large imports of safety bicycles and pneumatic tyres soon led to the demise of the ordinary. Pneumatic tyres were first used in a bicycle race when fitted to safety bicycles at the Melbourne Cricket Ground track. Safety bicycle manufacturing increased rapidly in cities and towns. Major makers included Bond, Carbine, Dux, Speedwell and Southern Cross.

1892. Track racing was about to change with the introduction of 'cash cycling' and rich track handicap races such as Melbourne's Austral Wheel Race and the Sydney Thousand attracted the world's best professional track cyclists. The Sydney Thousand, a one-mile handicap race with a world-record 750 pounds for first place was first held in 1903 at the Sydney Cricket Ground.

1893. Percy Armstrong and R. Craig completed the first overland ride, riding from the Gulf of Carpentaria Queensland to Sydney in mid-August (nearly 2,000 miles or 3,200kms) on safety bicycles. Armstrong continued, riding to Melbourne in 4 days, 3.45 minutes (931kms).

1895. Melbourne bicycle traders Scott and Morton organised Australia's first long-distance road race, the Warrnambool to Melbourne when cyclists rode high wheelers. It became Australia's premier road race classic.

1896. Bicycle prices began to fall and were down to 10-12 pounds by 1896. While the sport of bicycle racing prospered, the bicycle was gaining rapid acceptance as a vehicle for social enjoyment and mass transport in the cities and towns. It was an important form of transport for workers such as miners, shearers, and postal workers.

1897. More than 150 bicycle brands were being manufactured in Australia by 1897. While road and touring bicycles sold for 25 to 40 pounds, they were often out of the reach of the Australian worker. In 1901, average weekly male earnings were about one pound and six shillings for unskilled workers.

1900. About 200,000 Australians had purchased safety bicycles by 1900. It now had all the essential features of the modern bicycle such as pneumatic tyres, seamless tubing, free wheel hubs, and front and rear brakes.

1903. The first Tour de France, also the first road stage race, was started in July 1903 by the publisher of the L'Auto (now L'Equipe) newspaper Henri Desgrange to increase circulation of the newspaper. The Tour had six stages over 2428km and was won by Maurice Garin.

Percy Beauchamp winning the 1899 Austral Wheelrace at the
MCG riding off 150 yards. Photo courtesy the AusCycling Victoria
History Archive, Carmellotti/Holgate collection.

Winners of the Austral Wheel, 1891: Rear, J Mullins, A. Turner,
H.H. Lambton. Front, T.W. Busst and R. Davis.
Photo courtesy the State Library Victoria.

The Austral Wheel Race is Australia's most famous track cycling race and for a time was its most controversial cycling race due to gambling scams, rider collusion and poor handicapping. In 1886 the first 'Austral' race was started by the Melbourne Bicycle Club and was raced over three miles (4800m), a handicap race with a first prize of 200 pounds, the Drummond Trophy.

However, the first official Austral Wheel began in 1887 at the Melbourne Cricket Ground when cyclists rode the ordinary or high-wheeler bicycle. The distance raced in the Austral Wheel was over two miles (3128.7 metres), and the Austral Wheel became the oldest, continuous track cycling wheel race in the world.

Called the "Melbourne Cup on wheels" by the newspapers of the day, it was held on the MCG turf under a handicap system, with the best performed cyclists starting from scratch, often giving 200-300 yards start to lesser performed cyclists.

The first official Austral Wheel Race of 1887 over two miles was won by H.H. Lambton of Sydney riding off the 210-yard mark. The final was contested by 35 riders and Lambton won in a time of 5 minutes and 43 and a half seconds.

The Austral attracted a crowd of 20,000 to the Melbourne Cricket Ground, while torrential rain fell during the race programme. As the official Austral Wheel Race at its beginnings was an amateur event, there were no cash prizes, and the winner received a prize of a grand piano valued at 200 pounds.

Lambton had won the big Sydney Wheel Race in 1887 but was disqualified by the NSW Cycling Union for two years for an alleged, unaccountable "fluctuation of form".

The Austral gained newspaper and journal coverage across Australia and New Zealand. The Press newspaper, Christchurch said that the winner of the first Austral race was an Englishman W. Brown, who won in a rather clever manner. In a field of 28 riders, Brown started on 230 yards and won in 10 minutes, 52 and fourth fifths of a second.

"The track was like a ploughed field, for rain had been falling in torrents and in those days, the small hard tyres of the ordinaries cut deeply into the ground," The Press newspaper said. "While the other competitors ploughed through the slush, Brown rode very wide where the grass had not been cut."

Richard (Dick) Davis

Richard (Dick) Davis won the Austral Wheel in 1888 from scratch with a time of 5 minutes, 38 and three-fifths seconds, reportedly a world record for two miles. The race final was conducted on a grass track at the Melbourne Cricket Ground. Competing against 40 riders, Davis and the great English rider E. Fenton were the only scratch or back markers, giving the front markers 400 yards start.

He was the first Australian amateur track cycling champion in 1888 winning the one-mile at Adelaide and the five-mile title at Melbourne. A very popular cyclist of the high-wheeler era, Dick Davis was a member of the Norwood Cycling Club, had an unassuming nature and his "magnificent pacing, brilliant finishes and straight-out riding ability" was reported to have attracted thousands to the scene of competition.

West Australian newspaper The Carnarvon Times reported at the time that: "Davis, who was thirty years of age when at the height of his powers, did not give the impression that he was an athlete of the first order, or that he possessed staying ability rarely excelled."

Davis weighed eleven stone (70 kilograms) when in racing condition and was 5 feet 8 inches in height.

At the Norwood Sports in 1886, Dick Davis defeated the one-mile champion of South Australia Walter Tregonning and won the five-mile championship.

Competing in Melbourne, Davis broke the one-mile (2min, 37secs) and two-mile (5min, 38secs) grass track records and held world records on grass tracks for the half-mile and one mile on the high wheelers.

T.W. (Tom) Busst vs Dick Davis

The only high wheeler champion at that time that lowered Davis's colours was the Victorian champion T.W. (Tom) Busst. He won the first 10-mile Australian amateur cycling championship at Sydney in 1888 and the one-mile championship at Sydney in 1889. Busst later made a successful transition to the safety bicycle.

The Austral Wheel Race was to be held in Melbourne on November 23, 1889, with a prize to the value of 200 pounds sterling to the winner. Victorian brothers and scratch men Tom and J.W. Busst were the only riders who were allotted the back mark. But tragedy struck when J.W. Busst's arm was injured by a cold chisel in a work accident and his arm had to be amputated.

A field of 36 made it through the heats to the final of the 1889 Austral Wheel Race. The Sydney Mail said that J.J. Mullins of South Australia riding off 140 yards won the final, which included E. Mayes of England riding off 50 yards.

"One of the great champions of the era, Tom Busst, gave the front markers 350-400 yards start in the two-mile race. But he faded after reaching sixth place with around half a mile to go," the newspaper said.

There was strong competition between Dick Davis, J. E. Fenton and T. W. Busst. Both Davis and Busst won Austral Wheels from scratch on the high wheelers, while Fenton often won scratch events.

In 1890, T. W. (Tom) Busst achieved what he had tried to do for years, winning the Austral Wheel Race from behind the rest of the field as Dick Davis had done.

Tom Busst was paced up to the race leaders by his brother J.W. Busst, who started on the back mark with him, J. J. Mullins, and Frank Mills. In a field of 36 riders with a 390-yard limit mark, Tom Busst crossed the finish first in 5 minutes, 40 seconds, followed by C. N. Hall and Ken Lewis. At another meet, J. W. Busst was said to have set a mile world record of 2 minutes, 30 and two fifths seconds on the high wheeler.

Dick Davis and Tom Busst met fifteen times, Busst winning eight times and Davis six times. The remaining race was disputed after it went over the time limit. In September 1890, Davis was defeated by the New South Wales champion, W. L. Kerr, in the 5-mile Australian amateur championship held in Sydney.

During the 1989-90 season, the controlling body for professional cyclists in Victoria, the League of Victorian Wheelmen, had 1,268 cyclists registered and its ANA cycle meeting attracted 1,134 entries, believed to be the biggest number of entries for a cycle meeting worldwide.

Resistance to the safety bicycle

The new safety bicycle made its first appearance during the 1889-90 season and the early winners were often experienced ordinary riders with well-honed racing skills.

However, the safety bicycles had solid rubber tyres and low gears, while the older ordinaries or 'penny farthings' with their high front wheels were still too fast for them. As well, the followers of the ordinary did not want to see the high wheelers replaced and put up stiff resistance to the introduction of the safety bicycle.

In 1889 the NSW Cyclist's Union, which was opposed to the safety bicycle, passed the extraordinary resolution that safety bicycles be not allowed to compete against ordinary bicycles in open races.

One of the main objectives of the motion was to guard against accidents on the track as the safety riders caused collisions and spills by weaving around the towering ordinaries during races.

Eventually, race programs had races for both safety and

ordinary bicycles. The champion of the ordinary, Walter Kerr, set a mile record on an ordinary (recording 2min:49secs), while the safety's best time was 2 minutes, 57 seconds.

However, the ordinary would soon be outdated when pneumatic tyres and improved gears were used on the safety bicycle during the 1891-92 season. From 1886 to 1891-92, the Austral Wheel cyclists pedalled the high wheelers, but opposition to the safety bicycle was overcome during the 1892-93 season.

The big divide, amateur versus professional

The divide between amateur and professional almost tore the sport of cycling apart at its beginnings. Bicycle racing was not a cheap sport and the lure of 'cash cycling' proved too strong at a time when wages were low.

Organised professional cycling started in 1890 when the Melbourne Bicycle Club broke away from a group of sports carnival promoters. The club conducted the Austral Wheel Race as a separate event on a cash payment basis to the finalists. Apart from the Austral Wheel, state track cycling organisations ran cycling strictly as an amateur code until 1892.

But when the fledgling sport was further rocked by the introduction of 'cash cycling', this led to the colonies of Victoria and South Australia withdrawing from the amateur championship agreement in 1892. Cycling was no longer a gentlemen's sport.

New South Wales remained amateur and the New South

Wales' Cyclist's Union threatened NSW riders with life disqualification if they competed against professionals.

After former Austral Wheel Race winner H.H. Lambton won as a professional in Melbourne during 1892, he returned to Sydney to stage a professional meeting as a private promoter. Lambton's actions resulted in the formation of Sydney's first professional club, the Austral, and the established Speedwell club soon joined the professional ranks.

By 1893 the Melbourne Bicycle Club had outgrown its charter. A group of racing members, dissatisfied with the club's control over racing, forced a conference to be held, resulting in the formation of the League of Victorian Wheelmen in 1893.

The League of Victorian Wheelmen became the acknowledged controlling organisation for professional cycling. More attention was being directed at road racing and there was a dramatic change in the people involved in controlling cycling like the League of Victorian Wheelmen.

In the 1890s, cycling sport in Victoria was administered by city councillors, a cabinet minister, members of Parliament, leaders of the legal profession and business, doctors, and a newspaper editor.

However, cyclists and cycle traders began to take control of the sport and in 1893, a milestone agreement was made for the running of a professional Australian cycling championships.

This led to the formation of the Cycling Championships

of Australia in 1896 and cemented divisions between amateur and professional, divisions that were to last for decades. The professional Cycling Championships were formed by the League of Victorian Wheelmen, the Cyclist's Association of South Australia and the League of New South Wales Wheelmen.

It was decided to hold, "Australian Championship distances of one, five and 10 miles, held annually in the colony together with a gold medal, value five pounds, to be given to the winner of each Australian Championship."

During the 1890s, the bicycle tracks were mostly made of grass, dirt, and cinders, while many were eventually resurfaced with asphalt.

These descriptions of two Sydney tracks show, while the tracks were not considered to be up to the standard of banked tracks in Britain, they were of a high standard.

The Sydney Cricket Ground: "Runs three laps and 236 yards to the mile. The banking ranges from 3ft 9in, to 4ft 6in, and the width is about 22ft. The foundation is of sand, consolidated layers of metal and tarred metal screenings - said to be the equal of the best European tracks."

The Agricultural Ground: "A fast banked track of 554 yards to the lap, three laps and 98 yards to the mile. The surface is asphalted and there is a magnificent finishing straight."

At around this time, electric lights were beginning to replace the old gas or acetylene lamps as this report on the Adelaide Oval track in 1899 suggests. "A beautiful evening favoured the electric light fixture of the Adelaide League of Wheelmen. There was a large attendance, the racing was excellent and fast times were done."

Walter (Wally) Kerr

Walter 'Wally' Kerr was a champion of the ordinary bicycle and started his brilliant racing career in 1890. Kerr won the five-mile championship of Australia in 1890, defeating South Australia's Dick Davis and Victoria's W.H. Lewis.

"Kerr carried off all the ordinary championships contested in the colony. Then followed the blow to amateurism dealt by the 'cash' system, which practically crushed out of existence the Unions of Victoria and South Australia and the Australian championships were allowed to lapse," The NSW Cyclist said.

When the safety bicycle finally took over from the ordinary in 1892-83, Walter Kerr became the fastest rider on the safety, while Kerr and Rockhampton's Ben Goodson were among the colonies' best amateur cyclists.

At the Union's Sydney carnival in September 1893, A.C. Wilmot, a Maorilander, won the five-mile Australian championship, but the one mile and 10-mile championships of NSW were annexed by Mr 'Wally' Kerr, The NSW Cyclist said.

Kerr set his first Australasian one-mile record of 2 mins, 18&1-5thseconds at the North Sydney Reserve track on October 2, 1894. Kerr also bettered the Australasian record for the one mile in 1896 riding at the Sydney Agricultural Ground (1mins, 57secs), set against all the top cyclists of the day. His time also clipped 51 and 2-5th seconds off the record set four years earlier on a high wheeler - such was the advantage gained by the safety bicycle.

Ben Goodson

Ben Goodson hailed from Rockhampton. Considered the top amateur rider of the mid-late 1890s, he was selected by the Australian League of Wheelmen to represent Australia in England and America. In a series of five elimination races between NSW and Queensland's top amateurs at the Sydney Cricket Ground in October 1896, Goodson defeated J.A. Smyth of Brisbane and Wally Kerr of Sydney, winning three races.

In August 1897 in the Worlds Cycling Championship at Glasgow, Scotland, Ben Goodson was beaten by inches in an elimination heat to decide the track world's championship, losing to eventual winner Denmark's E. Schraeder. Goodson had an impressive record, some of which is found in the NSW Motorists and Cyclists Annual.

Goodson's titles included: amateur champion of Queensland (seven years); amateur champion of Australia several times from 1896; amateur champion of NSW and Victoria; second in the one-mile and 5-mile N.C.U. championship of England (1897); winner of international scratch races at Glasgow (1897) defeating the cream of world cycling.

In 1899, Goodson was selected to represent Australia in the world championship at Montreal, Canada and finished second in the world 100-kilometre track championship.

He led the race during the first hour, breaking world amateur records for all distances covered up to the hour, covering 32 and a half miles for the first hour.

Goodson continued his brilliant form at the national championships of America in Boston during August 1899. He won the USA track titles for the quarter mile, one-third mile and half-mile championships and came second in the 5-mile and third in the one-mile titles.

Returning to Australia, Goodson won the Australian championship but turned professional soon after. He won several big handicap races and defeated the famed American rider, 'Plugger' Bill Martin, several times. He was also successful in the burgeoning sport of road racing, winning the NSW individual road championship in 1905. Goodson suffered a bad fall on a Sydney track in 1904 that may have affected his form from 1904-05.

Professional champions target the Austral

Every year until 1903, the Austral Wheel was contested on the flat grass track of the Melbourne Cricket Ground as the annual spring meeting of the Melbourne Bicycle Club.

It became one of the social events of the year and regularly attracted crowds of 20,000 to 30,000. Two days and in some years three days racing was necessary to determine the finalists, so large were the entries for the Austral. The annual profit over a two-day annual spring meeting was usually over 1,000 pounds. It was reported that between 1886 and 1901, the Melbourne Bicycle Club paid out 11,582 pounds in prizemoney for 225 events, while the MBC made a profit that exceeded 7,000 pounds.

The Austral Wheel attracted the cream of Australia's professional cyclists and interest in the Austral race was reaching fever pitch in November 1899 when handicaps for the December meet were released.

Sol Green, a licensed bookmaker, ran advertisements in The Argus newspaper stating that S.P. betting was available on the Austral Wheel - between 11am to 6pm at the Victoria Club in Melbourne.

On the scratch mark for the Austral were: 'Plugger' Bill Martin (USA), R.H. (Bob) Walne (Australian and Queensland track champion), W. McDonald (NSW), W.C. Jackson, Forbes, and Frank S. Beauchamp (Tasmania). On 20 yards were R.W. Lewis, R. Mutton, and G. Sutherland (all NSW); Jones, Gordon, Barker, A.J. Body and Kellow. Other top track riders in the event were Don Walker and Jackie Parsons, both of Melbourne.

The first weekend of the 1899 Austral Wheel meet held at the Melbourne Cricket Ground, featured the Commonwealth Stakes and the M.B. Plate. These races were warm-up events a week before the Austral, and the Melbourne Bicycle Club wanted to show off the best cycling talent in Australia.

The Commonwealth Stakes was a series of four scratch races for 20 of Australia's best professionals with invitations issued to: Walker, Kellow, Body, Carpenter, Parsons, Jackson, Gordon, McDonald, Forbes, Walne, Barker, Lewis, F. Beauchamp, Boidi, Jones, Mutton, Wilksch, Symonds, Sutherland, and Martin.

Three races were held of one, two and three miles each, offering a prize of 20 pounds to the winner of each distance. Placed riders were asked to compete in a final over 5 miles. Most interest centred on the clash between Queensland's Australian champion Bob Walne and USA champion 'Plugger' Bill Martin.

The meeting was held on the first Saturday in December. Conditions were mostly unfavourable and rain squalls were blown across the MCG. In the final of the one-mile event, Bob Walne defeated Don Walker and Frank Beauchamp after going to the front on the bell lap to win easily.

But in the final of the 2-mile event, Martin, after being previously outfoxed by Walne, won the race easily from Forbes and Jackson. In the 3-mile final, Walne, recorded a stunning victory by passing Martin on the home turn to win by three lengths from the American with Lewis third. Seven riders qualified for the deciding event of the Commonwealth Stakes over five miles. Walne, Martin, Lewis, Forbes, W.C. Jackson, Don Walker and Frank Beauchamp were the best professional track cycling stars of the era.

Walne started favourite and gained the lead over Martin at the bell lap. But Martin was riding a big gear and swept past Walne on the back straight. Walne fought back and the two champions rode neck and neck in the finishing straight while Jackson edged closer.

At the finish of the Commonwealth Stakes it was almost a three-way tie. The judges awarded the race to Martin, with Jackson second and Walne third.

The Tasmanian Frank (F.S.) Beauchamp, showed his class in winning the final of the M.B. Plate. He rode off scratch and pegged back the middle and front markers to win easily by nearly 40 yards.

Betting on the 1899 Austral Wheel intensified as punters looked at the form recorded during the first Saturday meet. Betting was the heaviest known and it was reported that W. Martin, C. Boidi and Melbourne track ace Jack (Jackie) Parsons were backed to win between 3,000 and 4,000 pounds. Big money was also wagered on Sutherland, McCombe, Sandberg, F. Beauchamp, Brooker, and Morgan.

The Austral Wheel Race final of December 17 was held in sunny conditions at the M.C.G. with between 25-30,000 spectators in attendance.

The Austral Wheel was worth 400 pounds alone and while the Melbourne Bicycle Club had to cover the cost of other race prizemoney, gate receipts were sufficiently good to allow the Club to record a profit of around 900 pounds for the meeting.

However, the handicaps (starts) given to the front and middle markers were too much.

In the race they were too well organised so that neither Parsons nor Martin could make it through to the final. Frank Beauchamp, Lewis, and Mutton were the only backmarkers to make the final of the Austral. The race report said it was won in dashing style by Tasmanian rider P.R. Beauchamp (brother of Frank Beauchamp), riding off 150 yards, who went to the front in the last lap and won comfortably from W. Matthews on 170 yards and H. Thorn on 200 yards, Frank Beauchamp was fourth, Lewis fifth and Mutton sixth. The time for the two miles was four minutes, 28 and four-fifths seconds.

Don Walker showed glimpses of the form that was to bring him many track records when he finished third, riding from scratch in the final of the half-mile Flying Handicap.

In the 5-mile International Race, W.C. Jackson won from a crack field of 25 riders. Gordon was second and Frank Beauchamp third.

Joe Megson vs Ben Goodson

A great champion at the turn of the century was Sydney professional Joe Megson. He won seven national and nine state championships between 1894 and 1900 and held the 1900 Australasian one-mile and 5-mile championships.

Some cycling experts thought that Ben Goodson, the amateur one-mile champion of Australasia, would prove to be the fastest. Goodson, a Queenslander, had competed in the USA amateur track championships in 1899 winning three championship titles. In 1900 a one-mile match race series was arranged between Goodson and Megson. But Megson won the series easily, convincing many people that professionals were generally superior to amateurs in track racing.

George Horder

George Horder came from Dubbo was one of the greatest all-round cyclists ever to come out of New South Wales.

He was a true all-rounder able to win at any distance on the track. Horder first rode as an amateur and was a top road cyclist and became the patriarch of an amazing cycling family, with sons Horace and Harris becoming track cycling champions.

1905 was one of George's best years and he won the 10 miles track championship of Australia defeating Megson and Goodson in the final at the Sydney Cricket Ground. Horder also broke the world half-mile track record which was later equalled by Australia's Alf Grenda in the USA.

On the road, Horder also gained fastest time in the inaugural 1905 Bathurst to Sydney road race beating crack cyclists such as T. Larcombe, who gained fastest time in the 1904 Warrnambool road race. Horder won 10 pounds, 10 shillings and a bicycle for his efforts. He also amassed many road race championships and road time records.

F.S. (Frank) Beauchamp

Frank Beauchamp hailed from Launceston, Tasmania and was a champion school athlete. He gained first and fastest time in the inaugural Launceston to Hobart road race. He later went to Melbourne and had his first big win in the Bendigo Cup.

Beauchamp remained in Melbourne and was soon riding off the scratch mark. He was scoring wins in professional races from 1894 and was the Australian professional 5-mile track champion in 1901. Frank Beauchamp also broke the records for 50 and 100 miles paced on the track and he gained notoriety for pacing the American ace 'Plugger'

Bill Martin in the 1901 Austral Wheel when Martin won, and Beauchamp finished second in a controversial race. He defeated Germany's two champion riders, Robel and Dickerman in a series of match races. Dickerman, after his return from Australia, succeeded in winning the world's professional championship.

Beauchamp went abroad in 1901-02 and rode professionally in America, Canada, and Europe. He won many important track races off the scratch mark in America and Canada, beating Frank Kramer, Iver Lawson, and Major Taylor (all world or USA champions).

He rated USA sprint cycling champion Frank Kramer as the best track cyclist he had competed against. In the 1904-1905 track season, Frank Beauchamp's name was entrenched in the Australian record books, holding paced records for the flying start distances of 3/4 mile, 2, 3, 4, 20, 50 and 100 miles.

The American conquest

At the turn of the century, the Australian track aces had more competition when the cream of American track professionals toured the Australian cycling circuit, lured by good reports about the rich cash prizes and the hospitality of the people.

Among the American champions to tour Australia and meet with much success were the first official world track champion Arthur Zimmerman (1896), the endurance track champion 'Plugger' Bill Martin (1896 and 1901), Floyd McFarland, Iver Lawson, and the highly popular, official

1899 world sprint champion Marshall (Major) Taylor, the first ever black American cycling champion.

Major Taylor did two tours of Australia (1903-04) and won many big races in 1903, including an invitation scratch race worth 100 pounds for first place, the world's test mile race, a rich half-mile handicap race in Sydney, and earned a 1,200 pounds appearance fee. For his 1904 tour he was reported to have won US$35,000 including a 2,000 pounds appearance fee.

When Major Taylor defeated fellow American track cycling aces McFarland and Lawson in Sydney scratch races in 1903-04, he was reported to have suffered from unfair riding tactics and racism from his compatriots. Taylor was also known for his refusal to ride on Sundays and was the first cyclist to compete using adjustable handlebars in Australia.

In 1901, Plugger Martin pulled off a remarkable feat of cycling by winning the Austral Wheel race from scratch at 42 years of age. Martin was backed to win 7,000 pounds by young Melbourne promoter John Wren and despite claims of bribery, race fixing and collusion among the fellow contestants, only one rider was suspended for pace making during the 1901 Austral Wheel.

D.J. (Don) Walker

Don Walker was an ex-Canadian who grew up in Melbourne. He was one of Australia's fastest track sprinters who performed well against the visiting American champions such as Major Taylor, Iver Lawson, and Floyd

McFarland in the early 1900s. Between 1902-1904, Don Walker competed in the rich Sydney professional wheel and scratch races and his tally of wins and places was: first, the Orient Plate 1902; second, the one-mile Kent Plate to Major Taylor 1903; third to Floyd McFarland and Major Taylor, the Kent Plate 1904; third, the Sydney Wheel Race 1902; and second, the Sydney Thousand 1903.

Don Walker captured several Australian professional paced records from a standing start, all set on Sydney tracks pre-1905 for the quarter-mile, half-mile, and three-quarter mile and the records still stood in 1937.

Walker went to the USA with noted Australian six-day track rider Ernie Pye in 1906 and was based in Salt Lake City, which at the time was the citadel of USA track racing. He retired in Melbourne where he worked for the Dunlop company as a dispatch rider and later as a salesman of Dunlop golf balls.

The times recorded by Australian cyclists from 1899-1905 often better than those in Europe and the UK. Arthur Smyth set many Australian paced and unpaced records at the Sydney Cricket Ground and set a world amateur record there in 1905 for the 30 miles motor-paced. At this time, most track cycling was held at the Sydney Showground, while the international races were held at the Sydney Cricket Ground.

Jackie Parsons

Jackie Parsons was one of the best track sprinters and handicap riders to ride on the Melbourne tracks during the

1890s. Cycling ace George Broadbent, writing in the letters of the Australian CYCLING and MOTOR CYCLING, July 14, 1932, said Jackie Parsons was not only a good sprinter, but had above average staying powers.

"He was equally adept in following pace, accomplishing many meritorious rides behind multi-cycles, tandems, triplets and quads," Broadbent said. "He achieved many brilliant victories in scratch events, beating at times overseas riders of note in Zimmerman, Martin (USA), Porta (Italy), and Harris (England) and established many short and middle-distance records. He also was particularly good at winning handicap events.

"It was on the Exhibition Oval at one of the big meetings that Jack and I, on the back marks, had big fields to overhaul, and we agreed that without mutual assistance we would never catch the leaders. We then arranged to pace lap and lap about until we caught the field, the best man then to win if he could. That was the introduction of the system of 'taking a lap' and unselfishly sharing the pace. In races under notice we scored a first and a second in the two handicaps contested."

Jackie Parsons, who grew up in Melbourne, owed much of his success to his trainer and mentor, former velocipede champion Joe Royal. Parsons created Australian and world records, especially on the grass tracks on which the Austral Wheel Race was decided and won championships at all distances from half a mile to 10 miles.

He visited America and raced there successfully in 1896, and was credited with: an indoor record of one minute,

54 seconds for a mile; 30 minutes, 25 seconds for a quarter of a mile; 51 minutes and one-fifths seconds for half a mile; one minute, 51 and four-fifths seconds for a mile on an open-air track; and 58 and fourth-fifths seconds for half a mile on grass.

On his return to Australia in 1898 he was reported to have covered a paced half-mile in 47 seconds. Parsons also won the 50-miles road championship of Victoria and retired in 1900.

End of the boom days of track cycling

Melbourne became a mecca for professional track cycling and the Austral Wheel Race was its showpiece cycling race. Sydney answered with the Sydney Thousand in 1903, also a handicap race with a world-record 750 pounds to the first-place winner and overall prizemoney of 1,000 pounds.

The Austral Wheel Race, with prizemoney of 1,000 pounds, was for a while the world's richest track cycling race. Prizemoney for the Austral Wheel varied, from a grand piano to monetary prizes of 240 pounds in 1898 and 1,050 pounds in 1902. Basic wages for factory workers from 1900 to 1904-08 were around one pound 10 shillings to one pound 16 shillings a week.

Because immense cash prizes were available in major Australian handicap races, top class professionals were known to not ride up to their true ability all season to get an easy mark in a rich handicap race.

Collusion between riders, race fixing, and gambling

scams started to have a detrimental effect on the sport around 1904-05. Betting was allowed at some bike tracks as on-course gambling was still legal in some states. Even after on-course gambling was declared illegal, bookmakers worked the track racing calendar without fear of arrest and were often seen at the rear of the grandstand taking bets.

In the Sydney Thousand track race of March 1904, Laurence Corbett riding off 120 yards finished first with A. O'Brien (off 180 yards) second, while D.J. Plunkett (off 120 yards) was third. O'Brien protested against Corbett, Plunkett and others for collusion and Corbett and Plunkett were disqualified from the race over evidence that they had colluded to pace and help each other in the race.

The first prize of 750 pounds was awarded to O'Brien and the American Major Taylor, who finished fourth, was awarded the second prize. The ongoing controversy over the 1904 Sydney Thousand and the bad press it generated helped to erode public confidence in the sport.

H. 'Curly' Grivell, in his small book on professional track cycling, Australian Cycling in the Golden Days, said track cycle racing declined after 1906. He cited reasons such as too much prizemoney in handicap wheel races, handicaps not developing champions, incapable controlling bodies, unrestricted betting, and Australia's focus on handicap racing not producing good sprinters until around 1910.

"In 1906-07, the boom days were over as overseas drawcards did not appear and the public did not attend meetings," Grivell said.

Competitors at the Warrnambool to Melbourne road race c.1910.
Photo courtesy Museums Victoria collections.

Harold K. Smith and R.W. Lamb, professional and amateur fastest
time winners of the 1926 Warrnambool road race, with
Bruce Small (centre). Photo courtesy Harold K. Smith.

I. R. MUNRO put up a

——WORLD'S RECORD——

Covering the distance, 165 miles, in 7 hours 12 minutes, winning the Australian Championship, and beating the Warrnambool Express by 5 minutes.

A Barnet-Glass Rubber Co. advertisement promoting Glass's Flite Tyres used by I.R. 'Snowy' Munro in his world record breaking, winning ride in the 1909 Warrnambool to Melbourne road race.

Australia's classic road cycling races developed from the late 1890s and illustrated the great talents of our early road racing champions. Public interest in road racing grew rapidly and the introduction of the safety bicycle led to longer road events. Important state-based road races became classics of the sport and Australian-Australasian championships, among them the Warrnambool-Melbourne (1895), the Beverly to Perth (1897), and the Goulburn to Sydney (1902).

The Warrnambool was conducted in early October each year. It is Australia's oldest road cycling handicap or massed start race and the world's second oldest one day race after the Liege-Bastogne-Liege classic, while the Tour De France didn't start until 1903.

Up until the first year of the Warrnambool-Melbourne road race in 1895, most road events were ridden against the clock or were solo long-distance rides. But in the 1896 Warrnambool race, cyclists were allowed to provide human pacemakers.

The event began in 1895 when Melbourne bicycle traders Thomas Scott and Robert Morton organised Australia's first long-distance bicycle road race as an annual trial of speed and endurance. Scott and Morton undertook all arrangements and donated the principal prizes, The Age newspaper said in 1897.

Scott and Morton also aimed to promote more sales of the newly arrived safety bicycle and were agents for English Raleigh and American Yellow Fellow bicycles. Scott and Morton selected the Warrnambool-Melbourne race route as being the best and as they had bicycle agencies along the route at Geelong, Colac, Terang and at Warrnambool.

The announcement of the Scott and Morton race caused a great stir in cycling circles, the Sporting Globe newspaper said. The race winner was decided on a handicap basis with first prize of a Raleigh bicycle and there was an award for fastest time. Third grade riders received two hours start, second grade riders a one-hour start, while first class riders started from scratch.

In 1895, riding high wheelers, 24 cyclists started the first Warrnambool, heading off before dawn with lamps on their machines. Only seven riders finished the race in near dark and established Australia's most famous road classic.

The race attracted much publicity and a good crowd along the route, finishing at the Melbourne Haymarket at North Melbourne. The winner was New Zealand's Andy Calder off the two-hour mark in a time of 11 hours, 44 minutes and 30 seconds, while J. Carpenter of Victoria was the fastest rider (10hrs:52mins) off the scratch mark.

To promote the new safety bicycle, another Warrnambool to Melbourne road race was organised in 1895 in the reverse direction. The winner was W. (Bill) Nicol, who rode an English Raleigh machine off a mark of 90 minutes (time 13hrs:34mins).

J. Carpenter established a unique record by being the fastest rider twice in the same year. Riding of the scratch mark in 1896, he won his third Blue Riband for the fastest time winner and was also first over the finish line.

Since that first race in 1895, 126 editions of the Warrnambool were held in both directions to 2019, the deficit mostly due to the disruption caused by the two World Wars. The race direction settled on the Melbourne to Warrnambool direction from 1939, while 32 of the races have been held from Warrnambool to Melbourne.

Drastic changes were made for the 1896 race. While it remained a handicap, individual riders were classified according to riding ability and not put into graded groups and cyclists could also provide their own pacemakers.

The Sporting Globe newspaper called the Warrnambool "the Melbourne Cup of road racing" that drew the best cyclists from all parts of Australia and New Zealand. From 1901 to 1939 the title of long-distance road champion of Australia was awarded to the fastest time in the Warrnambool to Melbourne road race over 165 miles (266km), but the long-distance or national road championship was subject to more changes.

In 1927, the Warrnambool to Melbourne was replaced by the Dunlop Grand Prix, a road race over 690.5 miles (1,11.3km) held over four stages. The race was again replaced in 1934 by the Centenary 1000, a road race held over seven stages and 1,102 miles (1,773km).

From 1947 to 1949 the title of long-distance road champion of Australia was awarded at a sprint point, 150 miles (240 km) into the Warrnambool to Melbourne.

Among the cream of Australasian cyclists to ride in the Warrnambool were champions such as Hubert Opperman. Opperman was the 1924, 1926-27 and 1929 winner and the three-time Blue Riband winner for the fastest time.

Other fastest time winners were New Zealand road champion Phil O'Shea who claimed three fastest times in 1911, 1922 and 1923; R.W. 'Fatty' Lamb with his record 1932 ride of six hours, 21 minutes and 18 seconds, and twice fastest man; I.R. 'Snowy' Munro known for his record ride in 1909, "the rider who beat the train"; Australian road and track champion, Harold K. Smith, the Blue Riband winner for fastest time in 1925; and South Australian road ace Dean Toseland's two Blue Riband fastest times in 1938 and 1939.

The Warrnambool, a great tradition is born

All one-day road cycling classics are spectacles of strength and endurance, but the Warrnambool to Melbourne developed a tradition, toughness and fame and glory no other Australian road classic could match.

The Warrnambool also won its glory and traditions as Australia's premier professional road race not because of the wealth of its prizes, but because it became the pinnacle of road cycling achievement where the best road racing men from all parts of Australia and New Zealand came to prove themselves.

Frank Roche joined Scott and Morton and took over the running of the 1897 race. Roche approached the Dunlop rubber company who agreed to supply refreshments at various points along the course. Previously, contestants had to make their own arrangements for refreshments during the race.

Dunlop's energies at that time were directed towards cycling and Dunlop manager Harry James was a competitive cyclist of some note and became the organiser of the race for Dunlop.

The Warrnambool became, under Dunlop's control and promotion, the world's greatest handicap road cycling race. During the race, Warrnambool cyclists were not permitted to accept food and drink other than from officials at feeding stations provided by Dunlop, according to Melbourne's The Argus newspaper in 1927.

Harry James decided to supply each rider with suitable food packed in a calico satchel, hung by a tape over the rider's shoulders. The calico satchel or food bag was later used for feeding cyclists in long distance road races and was only superseded by the bidon in the mid-1930s.

Dunlop decided that along with food, riders would be supplied with milk in tins with a small spout and hot bread at the 43 miles and 125-mile marks from Warrnambool. The race started at 4.30am in the pitch black of a September morning and riders needed sustenance on the long journey to Melbourne. The Dunlop company did its task so well during the 1897 race that a high standard of feeding was expected at all Dunlop road events.

There were no cars in the early days of the Warrnambool and race officials would rush to the railway stations at points along the route to catch the Melbourne train, which left Warrnambool shortly after the scratch riders started. With the railway track running parallel at many points with the Warrnambool to Melbourne highway in those days, the race officials and train passengers could watch the progress of riders along the route.

At railway crossings and other points, the engine driver would slow the train to a crawl so that the riders could be observed and cheered on their way. At North Melbourne, race officials would rush to hansom-cabs and be driven at high speed to the finish line.

The 1898 Warrnambool was run as the 'Humber Road Race' when the Humber Co. donated a bicycle as the first prize. The race was not run in 1899. In 1901, the race was promoted as the Dunlop Road Race when the company undertook the promotion of the race and inaugurated the series of annual events that quickly became world famous.

Prior to 1901 it was the practice of the big trade houses, with their powerful stables of 'salaried' cyclists, to give assistance to the riders during the race.

They would station cyclists with spare machines along the route in case their sponsored riders had machine problems. The cyclists, in turn, followed the competitors as best they could so that in the event of a puncture etc., they would hand over their machine, thereby enabling the contestant to continue without loss of time.

Dunlop introduces 'one man - one machine'

The management of Dunlop was persuaded by Harry James to introduce a new rule in Dunlop-promoted road races, the 'one man - one machine' principle. This stopped the practice of allowing helpers to follow the racers and hand over their bicycles if trouble struck and the new rule introduced a new principle into road racing in the region.

Dunlop management had some misgivings that trouble would follow its introduction as the leaders of the bicycle industry were Dunlop's best customers for their tyre and rubber products.

Executives of the big bicycle companies responded and lobbied Dunlop to try and stop the new ruling. Some threatened reprisals and cessation of orders for tyres.

Charlie Neunhoffen of the Massey-Harris Co. threatened to stop business dealings with Dunlop and declare that all Dunlop races were 'black' for Massey-Harris riders.

However, most agreed to the 'one man - one machine' proposal put forward by James.

The new rule was printed in the 1901 Warrnambool record. Cycling clubs and supporters of the sport gave total support to the 'one man - one machine' proposal and for the first time, 100 entries were received, a record at that time for a long- distance road event in Australia.

A Victorian farmer from Nullawil, Albert Nioa, rode some 200 miles to get to the start of the 1901 Warrnambool race. Nioa won the 1901 race riding from the 40-minute mark in atrocious conditions in a time of 9 hrs:20mins:40secs, according to the Melbourne to Warrnambool website.

Nioa won a gold stopwatch and chain but was reported to have ridden off before the prize could be presented.

Fastest time went to scratch rider A. Ralston, a New Zealander. Ralston finished fifth in 9hrs, 30mins & 5secs, winning the 1901 Australasian Road Championship and the Blue Riband, awarded by Dunlop to the fastest time winner. The 1901 Warrnambool race conducted under the new rules was an unqualified success and Dunlop's initiative became a fundamental rule of road racing in Australia and New Zealand.

The race attracted its largest number of entries in 1910 when 355 riders lined up at the start. But the number of entrants for the Warrnambool became so great that a limit of 500 was imposed to prevent the field of starters becoming unwieldy, before the growth of amateur road cycling, which eventually grew larger so that entries had to be split into two groups.

Dunlop's influence and prestige in road racing increased and the company dominated the sport. The Warrnambool and its amateur section, the Colac to Melbourne road race were attracting big crowds and nominations for Dunlop long-distance races reached 1,500.

While each race would involve an outlay of 1,000 pounds by Dunlop, the expenditure was an investment that brought dividends and expanded the business due to the increasing use and popularity of the bicycle.

In the early days of the Warrnambool, an artistic, printed certificate was awarded to contestants who covered the 165 miles within 11 hours. Later in 1907, the awards of bronze and enamel medallions proved treasured possessions to some competitors up to the 1930s.

Over its 100-year history, the Warrnambool-Melbourne attracted the cream of Australia and New Zealand road cycling champions. It was the scene of many remarkable performances and record-breaking rides, but it is only possible to highlight some of the more remarkable and dramatic performances up until the World War II.

In 1909, two records were established that were to last for 22 years. W. (Bill) Knaggs gained the fastest winners time (7hrs, 32mins, 19secs), whilst I.R. 'Snowy' Munro, the little giant of Victorian road racing, set a record fastest time of 7 hours, 12 minutes and 51 seconds, helped by a strong tail wind.

George Lessing from the Brighton Cycling Club was 52 when he rode off 63 minutes in the 1931 Warrnambool, cutting the winners time to 7hrs, 13mins, 18secs. Mat Lynch of the Hawthorne Club, riding off a handicap of 8 minutes, gained fastest time (6hrs, 31mins, 28secs) and Lynch's bunch (3hrs, 56min, 10secs) knocked over 22 minutes off Jack Beasley's best time for the 100 miles.

Of the 238 starters, 165 rode the distance in under the time limit of 10 and a half hours. Although the road was much improved since Snowy Munro's record, the new record was established in rain and strong cross winds. The strong scratch bunch were gradually reduced by punctures and other mishaps, and the 8-minute men never conceded time, covering the 118 and a half miles to Geelong in 4 hours, 35 minutes and 30 seconds, an average speed of nearly 26 miles per hour. The Camperdown Chronicle newspaper said in 1931: "It was a remarkable feat of speed and stamina in adverse conditions by George Lessing first, Peter Halsell second, Charlie Pearson third, and by the fastest overall rider, Mat Lynch."

Two years later in 1933 the race was won by Les Willoughby, one of the oldest winners at 41, while the fastest time was made by W.F. (Hefty) Stuart, the youngest rider to achieve the feat at 20 years of age.

Before and after Federation, the competition from the New Zealand (Kiwi) professional cyclists was strong, especially in the road racing classics such as the Warrnambool-Melbourne and Goulburn-Sydney, when the Warrnambool was also the Australasian road championships.

New Zealand challenge to Australian dominance

Phil O'Shea and Jack Arnst were two of many great Kiwi road cyclists to ride successfully in Australia and O'Shea gained fastest time for the 1904 Goulburn-Sydney road race over 131 and a half miles.

In the 1903 Warrnambool-Melbourne race, Jack Arnst finished first and he also took fastest time from the scratch mark. His time of 7 hours and 43 minutes was a world record, and he won the Australasian road title. Jack Arnst also finished with the second fastest-time in the 1904 Warrnambool road race.

Arnst's time and that of Tommy Larcombe (fastest time) were considered superior to times being recorded in the big European road races.

Phil O'Shea was a top New Zealand road cyclist known as "The Champion" in his country, who figured prominently on the Australian professional road racing circuit. The Kiwi road ace had a terrific cycling brain and knew the capabilities of his Australian opponents. He recorded fastest time in the 1911 Warrnambool road race over 165 miles, also winning the Australasian Road Championship. O'Shea returned to the Warrnambool classic to again take fastest times in 1922 and 1923.

The Warrnambool-Melbourne road race closed between 1912 and 1921 after Dunlop decided to suspend the 1912 race until better arrangements could be made to handle the crowds and due to the First World War.

Top races preceding it in other states were tests from which cyclists were selected as state representatives to ride in the prestigious Warrnambool road race.

Pressure was mounting to allow amateur cyclists to ride in the Warrnambool and on August 1, 1922 a motion was passed by the Victorian Amateur Cyclist's Union meeting, urging other state amateur bodies to allow amateurs in the race. When the proposal was rejected by New South Wales and Queensland, many amateur cyclists turned professional to ride a Warrnambool.

J.J. (Jack) Beasley

In the early days of bicycle racing, it was not uncommon for father and sons to win the same cycling classics of the road and track. One such family was the Beasley's of Victoria: J.J., Clinton, Vin and Vin junior, and John.

J.J. (Jack) Beasley was a champion of the 1908-26 period who defeated international cyclists in big races. Jack Beasley broke the world's record for the 100 miles riding in the Warrnambool-Melbourne road race in October 1923, over a measured 100 miles (4hrs, 37mins, 57secs), breaking Snowy Munro's record by 23 minutes.

The Sporting Globe said the race was remarkable up to Geelong (121 miles) when the long markers maintained a pace of 26 miles an hour and a slight tail wind assisted the riders, but the wind veered to the north-west and slowed the riders. P. Wells (Victoria) won the race off 56 minutes and Beasley finished second by a length to New Zealand champion Phil O'Shea for the Blue Riband fastest time.

Jack Beasley's son Vin Beasley won the Warrnambool in 1952. Clinton and John, like their father, rode from scratch in the Warrnambool. In 1935 Clinton gained fastest time. In 1951 John Beasley won the Victorian 150-mile championship and rode in the road world championships in 1952 and Tour de France in 1955.

Harold K. Smith

Harold K. Smith came from Western Australia. He won four West Australian road championships and three Australasian Road Championship in the 1920s. When he won the 33-mile Australasian Road Championship in 1926 at Melbourne his time was over four minutes faster than Fatty Lamb's amateur championship time on the same course. Smith set many road race records and was Australian all-round track champion in 1929-30.

Riding for Malvern Star Cycles he won the 1925 Warrnambool to Melbourne classic and gained fastest time (7hrs, 24min, 1sec) and his second Australasian Road Championship. The Sporting Globe reported that Smith and Jack Beasley "engaged in the most thrilling finish seen in the history of the race, in which the West Australian just secured the verdict by a tyre." In 1926 Harold was second to Hubert Opperman in the Warrnambool, despite riding with a knee injury.

Harold K. Smith competed against and knew all the best road cyclists in the 1920s and said that the amateur champion Fatty Lamb was a brilliant rider up to the 75-100-mile mark, while Hubert Opperman was the best rider for over 100 miles. Harold Smith said: "Oppy took on the stuff that would frighten everyone else and he trained harder than anyone I knew. Jack Beasley was a tough opponent on the road and was the top professional road rider in the Twenties."

Opperman won the Blue Riband in 1924, 1926, 1927 and 1929 and his fastest time for the Warrnambool-Melbourne distance of 165 miles was made in 1924 when he defeated Ern Bainbridge (7hrs, 15mins, 37 secs). Another close finish was in 1938 when South Australian ace Dean Toseland beat fellow South Australian Keith Thurgood by half a wheel and won the Blue Riband.

R.W. (Fatty) Lamb

Richard 'Fatty' Lamb won the Blue Riband for fastest time and the Australasian road championship at the Warrnambool in 1930 and 1932. An all-round road and track cyclist, he broke 10-mile motor-paced track records, won the Austral Wheel and rode in the USA and was also one of Australia's best amateur road cyclists of the 1920s.

When 18 years old in 1925 he broke E. Pederson's 1913 race record at the Goulburn to Sydney road classic riding from scratch and won the race again in 1926. When he was not selected to ride in the road events at the 1928 Olympic Games despite winning two trial races, he turned professional and rode for Malvern Star Cycles.

Lamb won the Tour of Tasmania stage race in 1933 and in 1934 when it was called the Batman 1000, beating Ern Milliken and Hubert Opperman, while he placed third in the Centenary 1000 road race in 1934.

Warrnambool prizemoney in 1936 was 276 pounds. J. McEvoy (43 minutes) won 50 pounds and a Dunlop Cup (value 10 pounds, 10 shillings), while A. Angus (scratch) won 25 pounds for fastest time. In 1936 The Sporting Globe called for the Warrnambool to be restored to its former value or 100 pounds cash to the winner, when the minimum wage was three pounds, nine shillings.

I.R. (Snowy) Munro, the rider who beat the train

Iddo (I.R.) Snowy Munro was considered one of the greatest cyclists who won the Warrnambool Melbourne and the toughest and best performed Australian road cyclist overseas until 1920. The diminutive champion stood about 5ft 2ins, weighed eight stone and was the lightest A Grade rider competing at professional road cycling championship level at that time.

Don Kirkham had won the Goulburn to Sydney in 1910, made a record fastest time in 1911 and rode with Munro in the 1914 Tour De France. Munro and Kirkham were back markers and were noted for their outstanding rides in the Warrnambool-Melbourne road race.

In the 1909 Warrnambool, 312 cyclists competed in the race, a world record for a road race. Snowy Munro shattered the Warrnambool race record in the 1909 race while riding off the three-minute mark, beating the record of T. Larcombe (7hrs, 40mins, 10secs) and winning the Australasian Road Championship. Munro's time for the 165-mile journey was 7 hours, 12 minutes and 5l seconds. The record was to remain unbroken for the next 22 years.

Cycling experts considered Munro's performance in the 1909 classic the best-ever and better than the time recorded by ex-amateur champ R.W. (Fatty) Lamb in 1932 (6hrs, 21mins) made on a better road surface.

Munro was a rider who didn't fully believe in his ability and in the 1909 race he thought he may have met his match in top European cyclist, Tommy Gascoyne. Snowy Munro was just outside of Geelong and travelling well.

Munro was thinking he had let the great Gascoyne slip away when former road champion and Argus newspaper cycling writer George Broadbent drew alongside in a car.

Broadbent held most Victorian and Australian road records and two made on solid tyres: 203 miles (327 km) in 24 hours on a high wheeler and 100 miles (161 km) in 6 hours, 20 minutes on a safety bicycle were never bettered. Broadbent yelled at Munro to keep going and that he had record by half an hour. But Munro believed that the European stars were miles in front of him.

When Dunlop's Harry James told Munro that Pianta fell

at Geelong and Gascoyne punctured nearby, Munro decided to get moving, knowing how good Gascoyne was. Between Geelong and the finish, he overhauled 101 riders and over the last few miles from Coburg to the Melbourne Haymarket, he overtook 40 weary road cyclists.

Snowy Munro, just 21-years-old and described in one race report as "a mere boy to look at" had clipped impossible figures off the Warrnambool to Melbourne road race record and received a thunderous applause at the finish and became known as the 'rider who beat the train'.

Snowy reached the Haymarket five minutes before the Warrnambool steam train pulled into stop at Spencer Street Station. Snowy Munro's feat was widely publicised and appeared on posters, and Victorian railways were shamed into changing their train schedules to avoid the feat being repeated.

Munro rode a fixed wheel with an 88-inch gear, which made him really pedal every inch of the journey to Melbourne. His bike weighed in at around 25 pounds, considered light for his day and was shod with heavy detachable (pneumatic) tyres as the lighter singles or tubular tyres were banned, reportedly as the less fortunate competitors couldn't afford them. The only solution for riders like Munro if they punctured was to stop and repair the tube, which could take around five minutes.

In the 1909 Warrnambool race, Munro rode on 26-inch wheels while most other riders used 28-inch wheels. He believed rightly that the weight reduction saved him priceless energy but in bad and muddy road conditions he was at a disadvantage, as the smaller wheels risked getting sucked into potholes.

In 1911, Munro travelled to Europe to explore the continental cycling scene and discovered that 26-inch wheels were almost exclusively used in road racing. Back in Australia Munro recruited a team of top-line Australian professional road cyclists, with the objective to compete in the major 'tours' in Europe in 1914. They were all scratch riders and included Don Kirkham, Geo Bell, Fred Keefe, Charlie Snell and Charlie Piercy.

Kirkham & Munro, our first Tour De France riders

When the team left for France, they agreed that Munro would lead the team, with winnings to be shared equally. On their arrival, the Aussie team were contracted to ride for four pounds per week for three months, which was much more than they had ever earned in Australia.

By the time the 1914 Tour De France came around, only Munro and Kirkham remained in France and they earned their places in the Tour De France on merit. Of the 200 riders who started the 1914 Tour, Kirkham finished 17th and Munro finished 21st in the GC, while Munro was a best-placed sixth in the last stage to Paris.

Snowy said on his return that he thought he knew what hills were until he saw the Alpine stages of the Tour. "I'd been on climbs of 20 and 25 miles in heartbreaking conditions. But when you've battled up a few 50 and 60-mile climbs you realise what bike racing is," he said.

"Anyone who knows the Tour De France will realise

just how much bike riders are prepared to sacrifice to win the final stage. More than 100,000 people pack the Parc des Princes and they go crazy with excitement when the winner comes in."

The Warrnambool reversed direction from Melbourne to Warrnambool in 1939 and 1947-54. The classic settled on the Melbourne to Warrnambool direction in 1959 and in 1996 it was held as a massed start event for the first time.

The Warrnambool and the Melbourne to Colac road races were held on the same day each year and the Colac race, the amateur version of the Warrnambool race, was highly regarded on the national road racing circuit.

Ern Milliken, the 'Eagle of the road'

Among the early amateur champions to have won the Melbourne to Colac are R.W. 'Fatty' Lamb and Victoria's Ern Milliken. Milliken won the 100-mile Colac race three times recording the fastest times in 1931-32-33. Riding in the Colac race he broke the world record for 100 miles in two consecutive years, in October 1931, and October 1932 (3hrs, 35mins, 15secs.).

The Argus Newspaper, Melbourne said on October 5, 1931 that Ern Milliken (Coburg), riding from scratch made the fastest time for the Melbourne to Colac amateur road race, averaging 26.5 miles an hour and breaking a course record established in 1925.

He was the Australian 100-mile amateur road champion in 1933 and held many Victorian and Australian road race records. Milliken set 13 new race records in 1933 and set a world 25-mile amateur road race record in 1935 when he won the Campbellfield Open road race.

Milliken later turned professional to ride with Hubert Opperman in the prestigious Malvern Star road racing team. In 1935 he was part of Bruce Small's team that travelled to England. It included Hefty Stuart, Joe Walsh, brothers Harold K. Smith and Eddie Smith, and New Zealand's Hubert Turtill.

The Australians competed at the ninth road world championships held at Florette, Belgium when Opperman finished eighth, while Milliken punctured, fell and had to retire. While in England, Milliken broke the road record for the London-Brighton-London distance and combined with Stuart to break several tandem road records.

Jack Centre worked for Dunlop for 51 years and recalled competing in the Colac to Melbourne race in 1927 when he experienced very rough, bad roads and said that the amateur rider had to contend with race regulations that did nothing to enhance performance.

"Cycles were not the sophisticated machines we know today, and amateurs were not permitted to use the single tube tyre but were forced to use a tyre and tube assembly with a loss of racing time due to frequent punctures. Amateurs were not permitted to use 3-speed gears, brakes or a clutch - none of these restrictions applied to the professional," he said. Centre said that the clothing worn by the riders consisted of light woolen knicks and a jersey of some sort, usually the club jersey. "Helmets were not compulsory, although riders did wear them in track work.

The helmet of that time consisted of one-inch wide strips of felt covered with thin leather crisscrossing the head."

The Goulburn to Sydney, another classic is born

The Goulburn to Sydney professional road race was inspired by the success of the Warrnambool race after the Dunlop Rubber Co decided it was time to build a similar handicap classic in New South Wales. The course covered a distance of 132 miles, from Goulburn Post Office to the finish line at the Ashfield Post Office, when all road events were conducted from post office to post office.

New South Wales had established an amateur cycling administration. In Victoria, amateur riders rode in open competition with professionals under the control of promoters. It was decided that the Goulburn to Sydney race would be a professional event and it became well established before an amateur version started in 1913.

Great riders of the calibre of Don Kirkham, Tommy Larcombe, George Horder, and Jack Arnst (New Zealand) gave the race a high profile before 1913.

They were followed by R.W. 'Fatty' Lamb, Hubert Opperman, Ken Ross, Norm Gilroy, Harry Cruise, Joe Buckley, Bill Moritz, Ern Milliken, Charlie Winterbottom, and Alf Strom until the outbreak of the Second World War in 1939, increasing the Goulburn to Sydney's status as a classic road race.

The Goulburn race of August 9, 1902 saw 67 starters in front of the Goulburn Post Office. When the 30-minute bunch was flagged away, a relatively unknown Monaro cyclist L. Littlechilds made an almost immediate attack. Half an hour later when the scratch riders were flagged off, there was a great charge from the spectators to catch the special train to Ashfield, where a large indicator board displayed telegrams advising the state of the race as the riders passed through the towns.

Many spectators had backed Littlechilds to win and cheered when race officials posted up his progress. Don Harvison, considered to be the best of the scratch markers, was catching up on the field, despite puncturing twice.

The inaugural race resolved itself into a battle of tactics and endurance between E.S. Harris off 35 minutes and Littlechilds off 30 minutes for mile after mile, with J. Brennan off the 45-minute mark, 100 yards in arrears. A treacherous stretch of loose gravel into Mittagong took its toll on the bunch chasing the three leaders with panic and much skidding and a fall. Meanwhile, the two leaders, refreshed with food at the Picton control, walked up the Razorback 'mountain' and still led the race.

Littlechilds and Harris came into sight at Ashfield and sprinted wheel for wheel. But with less than 60 yards to the line, a sheep dog rushed in front of Littlechilds and Harris.

When they swerved to miss the dog, Littlechilds recovered the best and crossed the finish line one length ahead of Harris to win the first ever Goulburn to Sydney bicycle race, with A. Allsop off 30 minutes third and J. Brennan off 45 minutes fourth, while Littlechilds also made the fastest time (7hrs, 52mins, 49secs).

The win by Littlechilds had pulled off one of the most

sensational betting coups seen in Australian road racing.

The amateur version of the Goulburn to Sydney race started in 1913. It was won by E.W. Pederson off scratch in a time of 6 hours, 24 minutes and 30 seconds.

Australian amateur riders of international class competed in Goulburn to Sydney races and up until the commencement of the Second World War, cycling fans witnessed great stars such as Richard (R.W.) 'Fatty' Lamb.

Edgar Johns, the Newcastle star, gained fastest time in 1927 was also three times second fastest and placed twice three times. He finished third fastest in his final Goulburn after six appearances.

Ernie Milliken won in 1932 after pushing his co-scratch rider Edgar Johns up Razorback mountain while riding with broken handlebars and gained fastest time in 1933.

Alfred Strom was another to distinguish himself in the Goulburn, winning the fastest time in 1937-38 before joining Roger Arnold in Europe to form one of the best six-day teams of all time on the European 6-day track circuit.

In 1931, The Sydney Morning Herald reported on September 23, that there was a dead heat in the Goulburn to Sydney on the same day, Hubert Opperman's record for the 128-mile course was broken:

"On Saturday, for the first time in the history of the professional race, there was a dead-heat for the fastest riding time between two riders, J. Buckley and the Victorian, H. Veitch, who made the quickest time ever recorded, 5hrs, 2mins, 31secs, reducing Opperman's record by almost 20 minutes," the newspaper said.

Riding in favourable weather conditions, several riders not only beat the record time for the 128 miles course established a few years ago by Hubert Opperman (5hrs, 22min, 30secs) but averaged more than 25 miles an hour for the whole distance, the newspaper said.

Charlie Winterbottom was the greatest amateur cyclist to ride the Goulburn and the fastest three years in succession (1934-35-36), John Drummond said in National Cycling.

Winterbottom's 1935 performance was considered the best ride in the 90-year-old history of the classic when he covered the 132-mile course in 5 hours, 5 minutes and 23 seconds, six minutes faster that the fastest professional on the same day. Winterbottom's win was accomplished as the sole scratch marker conceding three and a half minutes to his closest rivals.

The Warrnambool-Melbourne and the Goulburn-Sydney (amateur and professional) road race classics had a long and celebrated history and stood out as true classics of Australian road cycling. Australia's best amateur and professional road cyclists are found on the honour rolls of these classic road races.

The success of the Warrnambool-Melbourne and the Goulburn-Sydney road races was due to the foresight of the Dunlop tyre company management and bicycle traders such as Scott and Morton, as well as the incredible talents and performances of the cream of Australian and New Zealand professional and amateur road cyclists.

Malvern Star trade card for Hubert Opperman, courtesy AusCycling Victoria History Archive.

Below: Opperman's 1932 1,000-mile motor-pace world record, The Sun News-Pictorial May 25,1932.

Cadel Evans leads the chase group, stage 14, 2011 Tour de France.
Graham Watson photo.

Left: Sarah Carrigan holds the gold medal at the Olympic Games road
race, Athens, 2004.
Right: Kathy Watt wins the Olympic Games road race at Barcelona
in 1992. Graham Watson photos.

Left: Oneone Wood riding for the Equipe Nurnberger team in 2005-06.
Graham Watson photo.
Right: Amanda Spratt on her solo attack at the 2019 La Course by the
Tour de France at Pau, on the last steep climb before she was caught by
the chasing bunch. W. Beaumont photo.

Richie Porte (on right) on the podium at Paris holding the trophy
for his GC third place in the 2020 Tour de France. Photo SWpix.com

Above: Phil Anderson leads Bernard Hinault on stage 6 at his first Tour de France in 1981 when he finished third ahead of Hinault. Graham Watson photo.

Centre: Grace Brown, the 2019 national road time trial champion, capped 2020 with a win and third in the European road classics and fifth at the world individual time trial championships in Italy. Sara Cavallini photo.

Right: Robbie McEwen wins stage 5 at the Tour de France in 2005, one of three stage wins at the 2005 Tour. Graham Watson photo.

Left: World road individual time trial champion Michael Rogers in the 2006 Giro d'Italia time trial.
Graham Watson photo.

Below left: John Trevorrow, a three-time winner of Australia's greatest stage race the Sun Tour, pictured at the 1978 Victorian road championships at Sandown.
Ray Bowles photo.

Below right: Andrew Logan, one of only four Australians who won the Commonwealth Bank Classic up against the world's best amateur road cyclists.
Ray Bowles photo.

Cadel Evans acknowledges the crowd on the Champs-Elysees at Paris after winning the 2011 Tour de France. Graham Watson photo.

Michael Matthews, one of our top one-day road cyclists wins stage 5 at the 2013 Vuelta a Espana grand tour. Graham Watson photo.

Caleb Ewan gets the wheel of Dylan Groenewegan at the 2019 Tour de France at Toulouse, where he won the stage in a brilliant sprint performance. W. Beaumont photo.

Kaarle McCulloch and Stephanie Morton win gold medals in the team
sprint at the 2019 track world championships, Pruszkow, Poland.
AFLO/Alamy Live News Photo.

Left: Anna Meares celebrates her sprint final win against Victoria
Pendelton at the 2012 Olympic Games, London.
PA Images/Alamy Stock Photo.

Right: Annette Edmondson on a victory lap after winning the
omnium race at the 2015 track world championships, Yvelines,
France. ABAC APRESS/Alamy Stock Photo.

Top: Danny Clark and Don Allan in the Rotterdam Six-Days race, late 1970s/early 1980s. Graham Watson photo.

Centre: Scott McGrory and Brett Aitken do a victory lap after winning gold medals in the madison race at the 2000 Sydney Olympic Games. Graham Watson photo.

Below: Rochelle Gilmore (on left) won the silver medal in the scratch race at the 2002 track world championships, Denmark. Graham Watson photo.

The Australian men's team pursuit team of Sam Welsford,
Michael Hepburn, Miles Scotson, Callum Scotson,
Luke Davison and Alex Porter won gold at the
track world championships, London, 2016.
PA Images/Alamy Stock Photo.

Left: Among track champion Gary Sutton's many gold medal wins were
the Australian amateur road championships in 1977 and the point score
at the 1980 amateur track world championships in France.
Ray Bowles photo.

Right: Ryan Bayley catches Theo Bos to win gold in the track sprint at
the 2004 Olympic Games, Athens.
Alamy Stock Photo/dpa picture alliance.

Hubert Opperman was Australia's greatest ever road cyclist and long-distance champion whose amazing rides and record setting exploits raised the profile of road cycling in Australia and Australian cycling internationally. Born in 1904 in the Victorian country town of Rochester, he grew up in Melbourne where he rode his road cycling father's Turner 19 racing bicycle. Opperman, known as 'Oppy' during his cycling career, started working at 15 in a newspaper office as a copy boy, and delivered mail by bicycle for the post office while studying to be a clerk.

Oppy joined the Oakleigh West Cycling Club at the age of 16. He was about 5 foot 7 inches tall and weighed around 65 kilograms. He never represented Australia at Olympic or Commonwealth Games due to his professional road cycling career.

When 17 in 1921 he won his first championship and a cash prize of fifteen shillings for winning the 10 miles senior cadet championship of Victoria, not enough to pay for two new bicycle tyres.

His third placing in an 80 miles event early the following season, sponsored by the Cycle Traders of Victoria, was to be one the most important of his career.

The prize included a Malvern Star bicycle, John Drummond said, writing in National Cycling magazine.

"For it was in that small Malvern Star shop that Oppy was persuaded, when he offered to sell the machine back to its donor (Malvern Star's) Bruce Small, that he would be better off on a Malvern Star." From this meeting began a partnership between Hubert Opperman, now 19 years old and a salesman for Malvern Star Cycles and professional racing cyclist, and Malvern Star proprietors Bruce, Frank and Ralph Small.

It was under the mentorship and exacting training schedules designed by Bruce Small that began to pay off for Opperman and Malvern Star when Oppy won the Barnet-Glass Launceston to Hobart road classic in late 1922. When Opperman made his first attempt at winning the prestigious 261-kilometre, Warrnambool to Melbourne road race in 1922 he could only finish fourth.

However, in 1924, Opperman really hit the big time as a professional cyclist when he set a record fastest time in the Warrnambool to Melbourne, Australia's most famous, classic. The Warrnambool win also gave Opperman his first official Australasian (including New Zealand) road racing championship, sponsored by Dunlop.

Oppy continued his great form by winning the Blue Riband for fastest times in the 1926, 1927 and 1929 Warrnambool road classic; two first and fastest times in the Goulburn to Sydney (Enfield) road classic in 1924 and 1929; and fastest time in the 1930 Goulburn to Sydney. Opperman was the Australian Road Champion four times, in 1924, 1926-27, and in 1929.

The Dunlop Grand Prix

In 1927, Dunlop organised the Dunlop Grand Prix stage road race that ran over four stages and 690.4 miles across country Victoria, finishing in Melbourne, the first time in Australia that a 'continental style' road stage race was held in Australia and the first time that riders left in a massed start, Hubert Opperman said in his autobiography, Pedals, Politics and People. Contestants from each state and New Zealand were put through a selection process of events to contest the race.

The Farmers and Settler Newspaper, Sydney reported on November 25, 1927 that Hubert Opperman won the 690-mile Dunlop Grand Prix road cycle race that finished in Melbourne the previous Saturday, the longest and most richly endowed road cycle race held in the British Empire. The first prize of a cup, a blue ribbon given by the Dunlop Rubber Co and 250 pounds in cash was presented by Mr C.B. Kellow, and Opperman won 400 pounds for his race performances.

About 1,000 pounds in prizes was given out overall. Sixty riders started and 29 completed the grueling road race. And 24,000 people turned out to witness Opperman's record-breaking win at the Melbourne Showgrounds at Flemington, which also gave Opperman the road championship of Australia.

"Almost from the start Hubert Opperman, the Victorian crack rider, had things his own way. He won almost every special prize offered for special hill climbs, fast finishes at controls, sprints and handicaps, and was mobbed at his arrival at the Melbourne Showground," The Farmers and Settler said. "Opperman's aggregate time for the journey was 40-hours, 41-min, and 34 seconds. Second was H.G. 'Harry' Watson of New Zealand in 41 hours, 52 minutes and 25 and one-fifths seconds and he received 134 pounds in cash, a cup and a blue ribbon. Third was Ern Bainbridge of Victoria, in 42 hours, seven minutes and 21 seconds, winning 84 pounds.

"There were many falls, but wonderful sportsmanship was exhibited by all competitors and not a man withdrew without justifiable cause. The team championship went to Victorians Watson and Rennie."

The Melbourne Sun newspaper ran a story and photo on its front page on the finish of the race: "Opperman sets world's record in Grand Prix". Arthur Drakeford, then an MLA for Victoria and later the Minister for Air in the Federal Parliament said: "Opperman has been one of the most outstanding advertisements Australia has produced."

The race was witnessed by huge crowds at every centre and was a great success. Opperman won 12 of the 16 stages during the race and finished strongly riding at 30 miles an hour. Over the last 10 miles, he was followed by a three-mile-long procession of cars and cyclists.

The challenge of the Tour De France

Opperman competed in the 22-day, 3,000 kilometre Tour De France in 1928 at age 24. He was the captain of a team of four Australian and New Zealand professional road cyclists, believed to be the first English-speaking team to compete in the Tour de France.

It came about after the Melbourne Herald and Sporting Globe in Australia and The Sun in New Zealand started a fund in 1927 to send an Australasian team to the Tour.

The four cyclists were members of the Ravat-Wonder-

Dunlop team, selected from the best performed cyclists of the Dunlop Grand Prix cycling stage race held in Victoria in 1927 that included Ern Bainbridge, Percy Osborn and New Zealand cyclist H.G. 'Harry' Watson.

Hubert 'Oppy' Opperman arrived in Europe with Harry Watson and two other Australians, Ernie Bainbridge and Percy Osborn. When the four-man team started in the 1928 Tour de France they had a huge disadvantage riding against European teams that had up to 10-12 cyclists in their team and the French newspapers said the Australians would only last three stages.

Opperman finished 18th, one of the 39 riders to complete the Tour out of 169 starters. "The team stayed competitive for the first 1,000 Miles before disintegrating in the Cols of the Pyrenees and it was a symbol of their tenaciousness that three of the team finished the tour," said John Drummond, writing in National Cycling.

Opperman returned to ride the Tour De France in 1931 with a stronger team that included R.W. 'Fatty' Lamb, Frank Thomas and Ossie Nicholson, all road aces and well performed professionals.

But Thomas retired ill after the third stage, Nicholson was eliminated at the end of the fourth stage, and Oppy and 'Fatty' Lamb did well to finish the race with Opperman officially 12th.

Opperman's 12th placing in the 1931 Tour De France was an incredible achievement. This wasn't bettered by an Australian until Phil Anderson set a new standard by finishing fifth in 1982.

Opperman conquers Paris-Brest-Paris

Opperman was considered Australia's best endurance and long-distance road cyclist and one of his biggest achievements was seen in the world's longest single stage bike race, the famous Paris-Brest-Paris road race that was held every 10 years. But in 1931, Opperman was ready having trained for the two days and nights event for years. Paris-Brest-Paris was a 'non-stop' race for 726 miles (or nearly 1170 kilometres) and Opperman was up against well-performed classic and Tour De France cyclists such as Bidot, Pancera, Louyet and Decroix, and two Tour winners in Franz and De Waele.

One hundred kilometres out of Paris, Opperman led the peloton but had learnt that two of the big teams had combined to try and beat him. Soon Oppy had a big bunch of cyclists closing in on him, the combined power of Louyet, Bidot, Frantz, Pancera, De Waele and Decroix was organised and was in pursuit. At fifteen miles to go the bunch was one minute behind and at twelve miles to go four of the group were about 30 seconds behind.

"Opperman was riding like a demon but soon he heard the familiar noise of car horns and voices. He was caught. In that moment he was overwhelmed with bitterness. Then his feeling turned to one of rage and he tried to break away again, just three miles from the finish, but the four riders clung to his wheel like glue," John Drummond said in National Cycling.

At Montrouge, Paris, the five cyclists sped into the Le Stade Buffalo Velodrome with Decroix leading from

Louyet followed by Bidot on his wheel and then the Italian Pancera, who decided to make his move. Oppy had taken last position at the bell lap and said he knew every angle and slope of the track where he had won the Bol d'Or 24-hour race in 1928.

Opperman stuck to the wheel of Pancera high on the track and just before the last bank moved around Pancera and went past all his competitors to beat Louyet on the finish line and win Paris-Brest-Paris, beating the big teams of European long-distance racing.

The next day he was the hero of the French press. Cables were pouring in from all over Europe, Brussels, Amsterdam, Paris, Milan and London and the world. Opperman's winning time of 49 hours, 23 minutes, and 30 seconds broke all previous records for the distance.

Oppy was popular with the French and in 1928 was voted 'sportsman of the year' in a French sporting newspaper L'Auto. In 1991, Opperman and his wife returned to France for the centenary celebrations of the first Paris-Brest-Paris race.

Another record achieved by Opperman was in 1928 at Paris, the Bol d'Or (Bowl of Gold) 24-hour, track classic held on the 500-metre Buffalo Velodrome at Montrouge. The Bol d'Or was a paced bicycle race and Opperman won covering 950.06 kilometres in the allotted time, despite being out of the race for over an hour after his two bicycle chains appeared to have been tampered with. He rode an old, borrowed bicycle for some time until manager Bruce Small could fix one of the Malvern Star bicycles.

Opperman still won the Bol d'Or race 30 minutes ahead of his nearest rival in a time of 52 hours.

Land's End to John o' Groats, Oppy's greatest test

In Great Britain in 1934, Opperman set five British records over five weeks, including the London-Bath-London record. Then 29, he attempted another amazing endurance road record when he set out in July 1934 to better the Land's End in Cornwall to John o' Groats in Scotland record, set by J. W. (Jack) Rossiter (2 days, 13 hours and 22 minutes) over 866 miles.

It was reported that Opperman had covered 431 miles when he reached the village of Shap in Cumbria and had bettered the world's 24 hours record and should comfortably establish a new record.

The Argus newspaper, Melbourne, said on July 18, 1934 that Opperman was in top form and had set a new 750 miles record nearing John o' Groats. "At 12.16 p.m. yesterday Opperman passed through Crawford (520 miles) at 1.15. He was then 3 hours, 56 minutes ahead of Rossitter's time. He pressed on through Robberton to Lanark (541 miles) which he reached at 2.30 pm.

"At Carluhe, which he passed at 2.56pm he was still riding strongly gaining time with every mile. Leaving behind Newmains, Chappelhall and Cumbernauld, he reached Stirling at 4.49 pm, and Bridge of Allen at 5.01pm. Opperman was now riding sluggishly. The glare of the sun was affecting his eyes and he was fighting against sleep. Several times he almost fell on his bicycle.

"At Abington he had a puncture and lost four minutes and a little later Opperman took a wrong turn."

On the run into Dunblane (581 miles), Opperman lost four minutes. The road was under repair and he had to make a detour through Crieff and was suffering a slight cramp in the stomach. But he made up time on the next section, through Perth and passed through Dunkeld (622 miles) at 7.51pm.

After 48 hours of riding, he had increased his lead to five hours and nine minutes. He had been riding for 37 and a half hours without sleep but became sick and tired.

He reached Tomatin at 2.40am and had covered 700 miles in 43 hours and was four hours and 48 minutes ahead of the record. Opperman reached Inverness (723 miles) at four in the morning and the Inverness Cycling Club was waiting to give him a hearty welcome.

After Inverness, Opperman faced rugged and difficult country and the strain of the ride was plainly visible on the Australian champion as he fought against fatigue and stomach cramps.

Three hours before he reached Dingwell, 18 miles further on, he was forced to rest an hour by the wayside, and the officials were doubtful whether he would be able to continue. His pace had decreased greatly, and very cold conditions lay ahead.

However, Opperman continued and at Alness (750 miles), broke his own record for the distance by 56 and a half minutes, while the worst hills of the ride were ahead. But Oppy rode doggedly on through Evanton and reached

Bonar Bridge (773 miles), having increased his lead by a further eight minutes. The section from Beauly had been the hardest of the ride and it started to rain and was very cold and Opperman battled with stomach trouble.

Oppy made it to John o' Groats on July 18 and smashed the 866-mile record. The Sydney Morning Herald on Friday July 20, 1934 said that "Opperman Breaks Six Records, One Thousand Miles Ride.

"Hubert Opperman, the Australian cyclist, has broken still another record. After his record-making ride to John o' Groats, he went on to make a new world's record for 1,000 miles, breaking that established by England's J. W. (Jack) Rossiter in 1930 by 9 hours 43 minutes. This is the fourth record Opperman has broken since he set out from Land's End last Monday morning, and the sixth record he has broken in the past fortnight."

Opperman had broken the London to York record; the world 12-hour record; world 24-hour record; 750 miles unpaced record, breaking (his own record by 33 minutes); the Land's End to John o' Groats (866 miles) record, breaking Jack Rossiter's record by 4 hours 21 minutes; and the world 1,000-mile record on July 19, breaking Rossiter's record by 43 minutes.

"After completing his ride from Land's End in Cornwall, Opperman arrived at John o' Groats (Caithness, Scotland), 866 miles away, at 4.01 p.m. He slept for six hours, and then went on to break Rossiter's 1000-mile record," the newspaper said.

While this meant he had to ride another 134 miles, he

rode further as he had to make several detours, anxious that there should be no mistake about his total mileage. Opperman chose a less hilly route along the coast than the road he covered during the last stages of his ride to John o' Groats.

The elapsed time during the 1000 miles ride was 74 hours 15 minutes, while Opperman lost 11 hours 49 minutes due to sleeping or eating, or through punctures.

During his incredible endurance ride, Opperman lost three pounds in weight.

The Referee newspaper, Sydney on 26 July 1934 called it: "World's greatest ride by world's wonder cyclist. Hubert Opperman, the 29 years old Australian cyclist, has added lustre to a brilliant career, and further established the fact that he is without an equal in the world at long-distance riding, either paced or on the track, or unpaced on the road," the newspaper said.

Mr. W. Maddock, president of the Australian Federal Cycling Council, the national professional controlling body, said that the ride was the greatest in Opperman's amazing list of performances, and for stamina and lion-hearted courage was unparalleled in cycling history.

Mr. Maddock sent a cable telegraph message to Opperman: "Federal council's congratulations on your success. Well done."

In Australia Opperman set many world unpaced road records including the 1,000 miles record of 63hrs, 37 mins, 30 seconds in 1938; the 12-hours record of 264 miles in 1939; and the 24-hours record of 506 miles, 396 yards in

1939 and Opperman was credited with 58 world records during the 1920s and 1930s.

At the Melbourne Motordrome on May 23, 1932 in winter conditions, with his manager Bruce Small and a team riding motor paced machines, Opperman smashed international paced track cycling records set by cycling idols, Englishman A.E. Walters, and French rider Emile Bouhours' 24-hour record set on the Velodrome d'Hiver in Paris. Oppy's time for the 24 hours was 859 miles, an Australian record that also broke Bouhours record by 44 miles. He continued riding to break the Australian 1,000-mile paced record in 28 hours, 55 minutes and 39 seconds.

Opperman also set many capital-to-capital or trans-continental road records, including in Australia, the time records for Sydney to Melbourne (1929); Perth to Adelaide, Perth to Melbourne, and Perth (Fremantle) to Sydney (1937); Melbourne to Sydney and Adelaide to Melbourne (1938); and Brisbane to Sydney in 1939.

In 1937, his endurance ride from Fremantle to Sydney over 2875 miles cut an incredible five days off the previous record. In 1940, Oppy set over 100 new track cycling distance records in 24-hours of continuous, paced riding at the old Sydney Sports Ground velodrome.

Opperman retired from professional cycle racing in 1940 after joining the Royal Australian Air Force during World War II, achieving the rank of Flight Lieutenant.

In 1949, he entered national politics and was elected to the Victorian seat of Corio for the Liberal Party and held the seat for 17 years until 1966. Opperman became the

Minister for Shipping and Transport in 1961 and championed the use of seatbelts in cars, while insisting that bicycles should not require a licence.

In 1964, he was appointed the Minister for Immigration in the Liberal Government and was credited with taking the first steps to dismantle the White Australia policy.

Opperman was knighted in 1968. Opperman was the High Commissioner to Malta and moved overseas to fulfill the role from 1969 to 1972. In 1977 he published his own biography, Pedals, Politics and People. He suffered a cardiac arrest and retired from public life in 1982, settling in Melbourne.

In 1991, Opperman was invited to the centenary of the Paris-Brest-Paris 1200 kilometre road race, 60 years after he had won the event, where he was presented with the gold Grand Vermeil Medal by the Mayor of Paris, the highest honour of the City of Paris.

Two months short of reaching 92, Hubert Opperman died from a heart attack after riding his bicycle trainer at his retirement village.

Opperman was held in high esteem by his cycling peers of the 1920s and 1930s.

Dunc Gray described Oppy as "a real gentleman and a dam good sport". Harold K. Smith said that Oppy was "Australia's best ever road cyclist in races of over 100 miles". Oppy's mentor Bruce Small described Oppy as never losing his "unassuming personality and his unfailing sense of humour".

Newark scratch race 1913-1916 era. L-R: Bob Spears 1st, Arthur Spencer 3rd, Alf Goullet 4th, USA sprint champion Frank Kramer 2nd. Photo courtesy The Gallery of Sport, MCG.

Left: Australian track stars Harris Horder (on bike) and Alec McBeath at Newark, New Jersey, 1927. Right: Australia's USA all-round track champion Cecil Walker at Newark, 1927. Photos courtesy of Harold K. Smith.

From 1906 to 1936, Australian cyclists travelled by steam ship from Sydney to San Francisco then by overland train to ride on the cycling arenas of Salt Lake City, New Jersey and New York.

The emigration of Australia's best professional track cyclists to the USA became one of the greatest migrations in the history of sport and they proved themselves to be the best track cyclists in the world. The first wave of Australians arrived in the USA in 1906, led by Jackie Clarke and Ernie Pye. They battled incredible odds but were soon breaking USA and world track cycling records and paved the way for other Australian champions who followed.

Around 30 Australian professional track cyclists were based in New Jersey during the 1906 to 1936 era and some of them became American citizens.

According to famed Newark sportswriter Willie Ratner, writing in the Newark Sunday News on January 29, 1968, the bike stars of Europe and Australia sought eagerly to be invited to race at Newark's South Orange Velodrome. He said that to perform at the Newark arena meant a great deal in prestige, as only the best were asked to ride the summer season against the cream of American cyclists.

"Australians especially settled at Newark. Among them being Reggie McNamara, Alf Goullet, Alex McBeath, A.J. (Jackie) Clarke, Bob Spears, Gordon Walker, Cecil Walker, Charlie Piercy, Harris Horder, Mory Gordon, Alf Grenda, Ernie Pye, George Dempsey, Jumbo Wells, Frank Corry and Paddy Hehir," Ratner said.

Australians at Newark for a season were West Australian track aces Harold K Smith (1927) and brother Les Smith (1924). Harold was the all-round track champion of Australia in 1929-30 and held many track records.

Newark, New Jersey was the epicentre of the professional track cycling boom and the scene of one of the most amazing challenges in the history of sport, a veritable bicycle racing war between the cream of Australian track cycling, pitted against the best trace cycling aces the Americans could offer.

The Newark Velodrome board track was built in 1907 and was six laps to the mile and a little over 300 yards. It had steep 52-degree banking at the top of the turns, 25-degree straights and a dangerous one-foot drop on the inside. Cycling fans flocked to the Newark saucer from its opening in 1905 and up to 20,000 spectators watched its programs. The fans wanted action, spills and thrills, and genuine heroes.

Salt Lake City was the track racing capital at this time, while other top tracks were found in New York, Philadelphia, Hartford, Boston, and New Haven. After America's bike racing citadel, the Salt Palace track at Salt Lake City burned down in 1910, Newark became the undisputed centre of American professional cycling.

When the Salt Palace's track manager and promoter John Chapman moved to Newark to run the Newark Velodrome in 1910, he formed a partnership with the Velodrome's owner Frank Mihlon. Chapman was also instrumental in bringing Australia's A.J. (Jackie) Clarke to the USA for a series of match races against the American track champion Frank L. Kramer.

John Chapman gave the American cycling crowds all they wanted and more. They warmed to the Australians, who soon had mastery over the Americans, Canadians, Italians and the other Europeans drawn to New Jersey by the rich prize-money and positive conditions for professional cycling.

The Australian cyclists excelled in major races on the USA cycling calendar, from gruelling 6-day races to two-mile scratch races and match sprints, won all the USA championships and held many USA cycling records for nearly 30 years.

From 1910, the USA all-round track championship was almost monopolised by Australians such as A.J. Clarke and A. T. Goullet (Victoria), A. F. Grenda (Tasmania), R. J. McNamara (NSW) and Cecil Walker (NSW).

It was only through the genius of American sprint champion Frank Kramer, who held the USA sprint (one mile) title 18 times, that the Americans could keep the sprint title from the Australians and the Canadians.

A.J. (Jackie) Clarke 'The Kangaroo Rocket'

Track sprinter A.J. 'Jackie' Clarke came from Shepparton in Victoria and was one of the first Australian track cyclists to taste success on the board tracks of New Jersey, New York and Salt Lake City, after arriving in the USA with Victorian track ace Ernie Pye in 1906.

Known as the 'Kangaroo Rocket', Jackie Clarke enjoyed

a sterling career in Australia, America and Europe between 1905 and 1920, broke USA and world records at the Salt Lake City and Newark tracks, defeated USA and Australian champions, and paved the way for other Australian professional cyclists in America.

America's National Sprint Champion Frank Kramer held many battles with Jackie Clarke on the Newark velodrome. On September 19, 1910, The New York Times said: "FRANK KRAMER WINNER. Champion Cyclist Defeats Clarke, the Australian, In Straight Heats. NEWARK, N.J. September 18. One of the largest crowds that has attended the bicycle races at the Velodrome track this season saw Frank L. Kramer, the champion, defeat Jackie Clarke, the speedy Australian, in a match race here to-day the best two in three one-mile heats. Kramer captured the affair in straight heats."

On October 24, 1910, The New York Times reported on special match races between Jackie Clarke and the top long-distance track champions of the USA.

"CLARKE DEFEATS KRAMER. Australian Cyclist Beats Our Champion in Exciting Five-Mile Race. NEWARK, N.J., Oct. 23. Jackie Clarke, the Australian cyclist, captured the special five-mile and the five-mile open races here today at the Velodrome track, which now places him for honors for the world's long distance with Frank L. Kramer, the National cycle champion. In the special three-cornered match race between Kramer, Clarke, and Iver Lawson of Salt Lake City, Clarke rode a remarkable race.

"The pace was so swift for Lawson that he dropped out after riding a mile and three laps. This left the fight between Clarke and Kramer. Clarke took the pace and Kramer followed his opponent's rear wheel for about a mile and a half. The wind was blowing so hard across the track and was so fast for the champion that he dropped back, and Clarke managed to gain two yards.

"At the beginning of the home stretch Kramer pulled up within a few feet of Clarke's rear wheel, but the latter, with a sudden burst of speed, shot out and beat Kramer to the tape by three yards. Clarke was as fresh as a lilly at the finish, while Kramer showed evidence of the hard grind."

In the five-mile open event, The New York Times said that Clarke won the race by only a few inches from Joe Fogler, the top USA long-distance track and six-day rider.

Alf Goullet, track & six-day champion

Because Alfred. T. (Alf) Goullet rode for most of his professional career in the USA and became a naturalised American, his deeds were somewhat obscured from the Australian cycling public, but Goullet was unrivalled in all-round track cycling ability.

Alf Grenda and Goullet rode what was described as the greatest six-day race in history in 1914 at New York's Madison Square Garden. Alf Goullet became known as a six-day track racing 'iron man' in America for over two decades from 1910 and was considered by cyclists and cycling writers alike as Australia's greatest ever all-round track cyclist up until the Second World War and also the best six-day cyclist in the history of cycling. He came from Gippsland, Victoria and was born in the town of Darnum on April 5, 1891. Australian sprint champion Bob Spears thought Goullet was a Tasmanian like Alf Grenda, who was Goullet's best pal. The Americans came to think of the Australian as their own and after he took out USA citizenship, called Goullet 'Our champion'.

Journalists and cycling experts in Australia and the USA agreed that Goullet was the best all-round track cyclist of his era, 1920-1925, including cycling champions Hubert Opperman and Harold K. Smith.

American sportswriter John R. Crawford named Alf Goullet as "the greatest all-round cyclist seen in the USA up till 1950". This was an amazing tribute as Crawford had known all the great champions who raced in the USA. Crawford says Goullet was better than Germany's world champion Walter Rutt and American champions like Marshall Taylor, Floyd McFarland and Frank Kramer.

Alf Goullet took up competitive cycling in 1907 at age 16. He quickly established himself as a class professional rider and during the 1908-09 season was winning races at Bendigo, Ballarat and at Melbourne's Exhibition track. He quickly became a track cycling ace and was put on the back or scratch mark in handicap races.

In 1910, Goullet was recruited by Victorian cycling ace and record-holder Ernie Pye, who saw the potential in young Goullet, who was then 19. Pye convinced Goullet that his future was assured on the board tracks of Newark and New York.

Pye and Goullet arrived in the USA in 1910 and took up residence with the Australian contingent of professional track aces at Newark that included Jackie Clarke and Paddy Hehir. Ernie Pye later made bicycle tyres in Newark and his family continued in the tyre business.

Not long after arriving at Newark, Goullet competed in his first six-day track race at Madison Square Garden, teaming up with Paddy Hehir. The Australians were placed fourth behind Americans Eddie Root and Jimmy Morgan. However, the race taught Goullet a lot about six-day tactics and he proved to be a quick learner.

Goullet soon hit top form and during his first season was winning all types of races over all distances. He earned the title 'Pursuit King' after defeating all the established stars like Frank Kramer, Eddie Root, Joe Fogler and Peter Drobach in pursuit match racing, and also was defeating them in sprints, handicaps and scratch races.

In 1911, Alf won his first six-day race when teamed with Paddy Hehir in the New York 'six'. He was narrowly defeated by Australian ace Jackie Clarke for the USA 5-mile championship and recorded 20 wins for the season.

When Goullet returned to Australia in 1912 with expatriates Jackie Clarke, Paddy Hehir and Alf Grenda, he teamed with Paddy Hehir to win both Melbourne and Sydney six-day races. On the Sydney Cricket Ground one-third of a mile dirt track, 57,000 spectators saw Goullet and Hehir win their first six-day race in Australia. In Melbourne, 40,000 people turned out to see the pair repeat their Sydney victory.

Back in the USA Goullet was in devastating form, capturing world and USA records. He travelled to Salt Lake City, Utah and on June 17, 1912, broke Jackie Clarke's record for 2/3-mile unpaced against-time, recording 1min, 11&1-5seconds for the journey. On July 1, 1912 at Salt Lake City he broke two USA records for unpaced against time. He also took the 3/4-mile record in 1min, 24&3-5secs and the one-mile record in 1min, 51secs, with the latter a world record.

Later when riding at Newark in a one-mile handicap in 1912, he broke the world record for unpaced competition by recording 1min, 47&3secs. Then in a human-pace handicap riding from scratch, Goullet broke the one-mile world track record in 1min, 39&2-5secs.

At this time, the Newark track drew around 17,000 fans twice a week and often pulled in more fans than the baseball stadium where the Newark Bears played.

Goullet continued his incredible form in 1912 and won the Western quarter mile and USA one-mile (sprint) championships. With 22 wins for the season he took out the USA all-round track championship for the first time.

When Goullet raced at Salt Lake City in 1912, he was signed up by a new manager, former USA all-round champion Floyd McFarland. McFarland could see the enormous potential in Goullet and teamed him with the toughest six-day racer around, American Joe Fogler.

McFarland took Goullet and Fogler to France to ride in the first Paris six-day race at the Velodrome d'Hiver. The Australian-American team won the Paris 'six' in January

1913 against strong opposition from Europe's finest. While in Europe, Goullet was tested when he was pitted against ex-world sprint champion Victor Dupre. In a best of three series of match sprints, Goullet won two out of three sprints to defeat Dupre.

Back in the USA in 1913, Goullet was in devastating form. In the point score for the USA sprint title he lost to the legendary Frank Kramer by just several points. Then he teamed with Joe Fogler to win the Madison Square Garden six-day race covering 2,751 miles.

At this time, Goullet had no peer in six-day racing and more amazing race victories followed. Partnered by Alf Grenda, he set a world record for a six-day race, under the old 'Berlin system' rules, where one rider in the team had to stay on the track the whole time.

The Australians set the record in 1914 at New York's Madison Square Garden, after covering 2,759 miles and two laps over the six days.

Teamed with America's Freddie Hill in 2014, Goullet won the New York six-day race after Hill had retired injured on the last day and showed his incredible stamina and speed by winning all but two of the last days sprints to snatch victory.

During the 1914 track season, Goullet continued his brilliant form and defeated Frank Kramer and former world champion, Germany's Walter Rutt to win the USA half-mile championship. He won the USA all-round track championship and 10-mile titles and finished second to Frank Kramer in the USA sprint championship.

Alfred Goullet dominated USA professional track cycling and won the point score for the USA all-round track cycling championship 10 times. Goullet set many USA track records, four world track records, and won 15 six-day races during his amazing career. If not for the brilliance of USA sprint legend Frank Kramer, he may have held many USA sprint titles as well.

In 1918, Goullet didn't compete due to his service in the USA Naval Reserve at the Naval Air Station, New Jersey.

In 1937, 12 years after he retired, Goullet still held four USA professional competition unpaced track records (one mile, three miles, two-thirds of a mile, and three-quarters of a mile). His 1912, one-mile world record for the professional against time unpaced (1min, 51secs) in Salt Lake City still stood in 1937. During his 16-year career as a professional cyclist in America, Goullet won more than 300 races. The 3,000 dollars in prizemoney he won in his best year, 1915, was almost a fortune.

Of Goullet's 15 six-day race victories, 12 of these wins in the grueling sixes were in the USA, including eight at Madison Square Garden. He also enjoyed riding at the Newark Velodrome, where the conditions suited him and where many of his USA and World records were set.

Famed USA sportswriter and newspaperman Damon Runynon described Goullet as "the Babe Ruth of six-day bicycle racing". And sportswriter Willie Ratner of the Newark Evening News and Sunday News, said Goullet had speed, strength and endurance and was one of the most versatile cyclists the game ever had.

"Goullet stood head and shoulders above all other cyclists because of his approach to the sport - he trained hard and entered every race determined to win," Ratner said. When 35, Goullet stopped riding at the end of 1925 on medical advice. He remained in the cycling game as a manager and promoter of velodromes and entertainment venues until 1937 and was the only Australian to be admitted to the USA Cycling Hall of Fame.

In December 1986, Alf Goullet, then 95 and an American citizen, arrived in Melbourne with his daughter Susan and was inducted into the Sport Australia Hall of Fame at the Melbourne Cricket Ground. Goullet had a reunion in Sydney with Australian road and track champion of the 1920's, Harold K. Smith, then 83, who met Goullet during the 1927 USA season when Smith was a successful track pursuit ace at Newark. The two former champions discovered that they were the last of the 31 Australian professional cyclists based in New Jersey in the 1920's that were still living.

Alf Goullet, at the age of 103, passed away in New Jersey in March 1995.

Alf Grenda, USA and world champion

They called Alfred T. (Alf) Grenda a giant of a man, but he was certainly a 'giant-killer' who lowered the colours of many champions and established plenty of cycling records during his amazing career. Alf Grenda set many precedents as the first Tasmanian to win Australian, USA, and World Cycling Championships.

It was at the Sydney Sports Ground on October 25, 1911, that Grenda recorded his most important win in Australia by winning the final of the One Mile Professional Cycling Championship of Australia. A large crowd of 25,000 watched the programme of cycling and motorcycling events. In the final, Grenda lined up on the scratch mark with Gordon Walker; local champ Perc Mutton was on 25 yards; and George Horder was the front marker on 45 yards. Grenda proved too strong and after holding the other riders in check, took the lead at the bell and won easily by two lengths in the time of 2mins,12secs.

Alf Goullet returned to Australia from the USA where Colonel John Chapman, the manager of the Newark velodrome had asked him to recruit Australian riders with potential. The Sydney six-day race was held at the Sydney Sports Ground from January 1st to 6th, 1912. An enthusiastic crowd of 60,000 on the final night watched Goullet cross the line first, just ahead of Grenda. The team of Goullet-Paddy Hehir took out 500 pounds for winning, while Grenda and Gordon Walker claimed 200 pounds for second place.

Alf Grenda was the only rider to be offered the chance to ride in the USA by Goullet, and Grenda had no hesitation in accepting. Launceston cycling club Ramblers held a dinner for Grenda at the Central Hotel and raised 50 gold sovereigns for his USA campaign.

Grenda firmly imprinted his name into the minds of American cycling fans with a stunning victory over USA pro champion Frank Kramer soon after his arrival in New

Jersey in 1912. Kramer was considered unbeatable and had held the USA Sprint Championship since 1901.

The Newark Star newspaper of May 28, 1912 said: "A.F. Grenda, the Australian Champion, gave a good exhibition yesterday. He rode four miles and three laps before he caught Peter Drobach in a pursuit race, and to follow this with a victory over champion Kramer after such a gruelling race, stamps Grenda as a rider of marvellous all-round ability, and he received a heroic ovation after the race.

"Grenda won the scratch race by a foot in the fast time of 10mins, 49&25secs; and is now racing twice a week - Wednesdays and Sundays and will be the first Tasmanian cyclist to compete in the world's cycle championship to be run this year at Newark on August 25 and 28."

On the opening day of the world titles. Alf Grenda etched his name into world cycling history when with Walter De Mara (USA), he won the World Tandem Championship in 2mins, 27&1.5secs.

On the second day, August 28, Grenda won his heat of the World One Mile Championship. He came out after this race and won the three-mile open handicap from scratch.

Alf Grenda had defied expectations by winning through to the final of the World One Mile sprint championship with Frank Kramer and French cycling stars Andre Perchicot and Emil Friol.

The Newark Evening Star said that Kramer won the world sprint tile by two feet, but that Grenda flashed over the line to claim second place three feet ahead of Perchicot. Grenda quickly became a track cycling star on the Newark and New York board tracks and he also became established as a six-day track cycling champion.

Of all the Australian contingent stationed at Newark and New York, Goullet rated Alf Grenda, Reg McNamara and Bob Spears (who became the 1920 world sprint champion) of equal ability and the best. He named America's Frank Kramer as the best American and greatest sprinter he competed against.

Grenda was unlucky to meet Cecil Walker at his peak and in 1924 and 1925, finished second to Walker in the USA all-round track championships. After 1926, Alf Grenda scaled down his career and retired to California in 1930, after marrying Isabel Crawford in Harrison, New Jersey.

Reg McNamara, 'iron man' of 6-day cycling

R.J. (Reg) McNamara came from Dubbo New South Wales. He was known as the 'iron man' of six-day track cycling due to his refusal to quit when injured during his long career competing in Australia and the USA between 1910 and 1930.

He fractured his skull twice, broke his jaw three times and broke his collarbone six times.

Riding with his Italian partner Linari, Reg won a six-day day event in New York in 1926, while competing with three broken ribs.

In 1913, Reg McNamara won the Sydney six-day race on Monday, January 6 with Frank Corry as his partner, covering 1833 miles, beating the combination of Bob Spears and Don Kirkham in front of 40,000 excited cycling fans, Sydney's Evening News said. McNamara put on a blistering turn of pace to beat Spears by half a length, with a time of 29 & 4-5 seconds for the last lap.

This performance was noticed by Alf Goullet, who was asked to take back two top cyclists to Newark with him. But he only signed McNamara to race in the USA.

While Reg McNamara was better known as a six-day specialist in the USA, he rode just about every race on the program from sprints and five-mile races up to longer endurance races. He rode 3,000 races on three continents over 30 years and won more than 700 races.

McNamara won 19 six-day races between 1913 and 1933 with 17 different partners and incredibly, had his last race at the age of 54.

Cecil Walker, our greatest track cyclist?

Cecil Walker was the New South Wales amateur track champion in 1918-19 for the five and ten miles. He had many close tussles with the reigning NSW sprint champion Jerry Halpin, who finished a close third in the World Amateur Sprint Championships. After turning professional in 1919, Walker finished fourth in a Sydney six-day race with Cliff Papworth and was advised by Bob Spears in 1920 to try his luck in America.

Writing the story of Cecil Walker in National Cycling magazine, John Drummond said that while Alf Goullet of Victoria was the hero of the first wave of Australian cyclists in America at the turn of the century, it was Cecil Walker of Marrickville, New South Wales who was the star of the second wave from the 1920s and into the 1930s.

"Cecil Walker won the American professional all-round track championship nine times, took the American sprint championship three times and became the first cyclist ever to hold these two championships at the one time," Drummond said.

"Fifty miles in one hour, 42 minutes, seven seconds, with a sub 12 secs the last 200 metres of a sprint; 2 miles handicap win from scratch in 3 minutes, 37.8 secs; 5 mile scratch race win in 9 minutes, 29 secs; and a one mile standing start in one minute, 27.8secs, add to this impressive list the all-round championship of America for nine years - we get a picture of his greatness."

John Drummond said that by equating times set in America by Cecil Walker with those set in Australia by Sid Patterson, some 20 years later, it is possible to rate Walker equal to the Victorian (and world champion), and the greatest track cyclist in the world. However, Walker also rode on the smaller and faster USA tracks.

During the 1921 season, Cecil Walker was reported to have won six races in America and claimed many places.

Sydney newspaper The Arrow interviewed Cecil Walker for a story published on December 2, 1921: "Cecil Walker, the Sydney cyclist, just back from two seasons' racing in America, states that the bunch of Australians have made the sport there. The popular Sydney rider who left these shores a year and seven months ago, returned by the Ventura on Tuesday.

"The racing is exciting in America. It would take just as

well in Sydney if we had six or seven-lap board tracks. It is a pity to see a city like Sydney, where track racing could boom, without an up-to-date track," Walker said. "Grenda is the best pursuit rider, and the best in the world. At long distance racing Goullet stands alone. He always races on his own and never teams with others."

Walker's best win in 1921 was the 100 kilos team's race with Alex McBeath as a partner, one of the principal track cycling events of the year. Walker was only just beaten by Grenda in the 25 miles single-paced, scratch race, when a world's record of 51min, 18 & 2-5secs was established.

The Sydney Morning Herald reported (Thursday 16 October 1930) on "CECIL WALKER. UNIQUE CYCLING SUCCESS. According to a cable message received by his parents yesterday, Cecil Walker the brilliant Marrickville professional cyclist, has capped all his former performances by winning both the sprint and the all-round championships of America."

Walker had previously won the USA all-round championship six years in succession, with points awarded for wins and places in all races run during the season, handicap, scratch and match events included, the newspaper said. But this was his first win in the USA sprint or one-mile championship with points awarded over a series of 24 track races.

Cecil Walker joined Harris Horder, both Sydney track cyclists, as the only two cyclists not native born or naturalised citizens of the United States to have won the prestigious USA sprint championship.

Bob Spears, 1920 world professional sprint champion,
shown winning the Grand Prix de Paris in 1922.
Photo courtesy of AusCycling Victoria History Archive.

Rough Race Staged at Newark Velodrome

Reggie McNamara and Bob Spears Show to Front in Team Race—Ride Fined for Violation of Rules—Grenda and Goullet Second

Reggie McNamara (on left) and Bob Spears, Australians, winners of Newark team race, who ride Boston six-day race together

Newark, New Jersey, newspaper photo, 1915 era.
Courtesy The Gallery of Sport, MCG.

Robert (Bob) Spears was Australia's first world sprint champion and our most famous track cyclist pre-1940 after he won the world professional one-mile (or sprint) championship in 1920 and he became very popular in Europe. Spears was known for his amazing kick, an explosive finishing burst that often took him from a seemingly hopeless position 100 yards from home to victory on the finish line.

Spears competed mostly in sprints, match races and handicaps, preferring shorter races, although he excelled in the arduous grind of six-day track racing. Around six feet tall with a strong physique, he also became known for his unique sprinting style and his unorthodox straight arm style paid dividends.

USA sports writers called Spears, "the master of the delayed sprint." He sat rigidly in the saddle with his arms straight. The faster he went, the tighter he sat in the saddle.

Born on August 8, 1893, Bob Spears came from a small property near Dubbo, New South Wales. He learnt his craft competing on country dirt tracks and travelled to the surrounding towns to the weekend cycling races that attracted cyclists from hundreds of miles away.

While still a raw bush kid, Bob won his first bicycle race at Dubbo in 1907 when 14 years of age and raced on an old bicycle put together using second-hand and discarded parts. In 1910, he started serious racing, attracted by the large prizemoney offered in professional cycling. Bob entered the Rockhampton Wheel race in 1910 but could not afford the rail fare. However, Bob decided to ride his bicycle about 1600 kilometres to the Queensland town.

Spears was a total unknown and the handicapper gave the Dubbo lad a generous mark, in front of a professional cyclist from Tasmania riding as a 'ring in' under a false name, who was backed before the race by supporters to win big money. But in the race, Spears flew to the line to win his first major race by half a wheel.

Riding at the Eight Hours Day carnival in Sydney the same year, Spears won the one and two-mile handicap races. He was now billed as the 'Boy Champion' of New South Wales. He visited Kadina in South Australia with another rising young star in Frank Corry where he won several handicap races. Corry later teamed up with Spears in the USA, where they became a noted team in six-day and long-distance track cycling events.

Bob Spears won his first New South Wales professional title in 1911 in the one and a half miles. In 1912, he won the Australian 5-mile Championship and found himself on the scratch mark. He was now an Australian back marker or 'ace' and would have to give away big starts to front markers in the rich handicap races.

Spears never tried to win races by large margins, preferring to win by the least possible effort - even if that meant a dash to the line to win by a few inches. He was accused by many writers of not training but by his own admission, he was well prepared and fit.

In a self-penned story in Australia's Sports Novels magazines, Bob Spears said: "They say I never trained. I did enough to keep in good shape to hold my own, but I could never have been accused of leaving my form on the training track.

"I'll never forget a cartoon in the Paris Soir, the famous French paper, on the eve of an important race. The sketch showed my trainer riding along the road up hill and down dale while I rested at home.

"Translated from the French, the caption stated: 'Spears must be in good condition. Look how hard his masseur is training'.

"I looked after myself well enough and never raced unless I was in really good nick. What they missed was the fact that I was riding regularly, and my physique stood me up against smaller opponents."

In 1913, Spears was lured into six-day racing by the big prizemoney offered in the marathon track races and decided to team up with Melbourne cycling ace Don Kirkham. Kirkham was a champion road rider and a noted six-day cyclist.

He contested the Sydney six-day race of 1913 with Don Kirkham and the new team finished second. But when they raced in the Melbourne six-day race Spears and Kirkham took the honours from Reg McNamara and Frank Corry.

Encouraged by his six-day success, Spears decided he was ready to try his luck in America against the established stars who rode the New Jersey and New York tracks, where he would join the contingent of Australian professional track cycling champions based in Newark, New Jersey.

Spears said in Sports Novels: "My lucky star must have been shining brightly when I decided to make my first trip to America in 1913. Over in the States things broke my way immediately and a series of wins culminating in the conquering of the great Frank L. Kramer.

"I settled down quickly and the tracks, smaller than here and accordingly faster, suited my style of riding. The money was good, the races frequent, and the promoters were always anxious to see new faces, especially if they could spin the pedals around fast enough to keep the other track idols busy.

"I went over with Frank Corry and Reggie McNamara and by showing good form we were able to boost Australia and Australians as bike riders, and thus mutually assisting ourselves. Already doing well when I arrived were Jackie Clarke, famous sprint rider whose name still stands in the record books, Alf Grenda and Alf Goullet."

When promoter and local cyclist Jay Eaton engaged Spears and Corry to ride at the rebuilt Newark Motordrome, that soon rivalled the famed Newark Velodrome, Spears struck form instantly and was beating Eaton and local hero Eddie Root at the Motordrome.

An incident Spears recalled involved the local star Eddie Root. In the Sunday night races at the Motordrome, both Corry and Spears had defeated Root and then Spears lined up against Root in a 10-mile race. Root fell while riding alongside Spears and after the race he accused Spears of crowding him up the track.

Root took his frustrations out on his bike, smashing the front wheel. He waited until Spears came around the track and hurled the wrecked bicycle at Spears, who darted up the track to avoid being hit and officials had to quieten Root down. Local riders like Root and Eaton found it hard to cope with the thrashings handed out by the likes of Spears, Clarke, McNamara, and Corry and this led to a lot of clashes with the American riders.

A dispute between Velodrome promoter Chapman and the rival Motordrome riders was resolved and Spears was allowed back into registered ranks. The quick-thinking Chapman arranged for a 'revenge' match between Spears and fellow Australian ace Alf Grenda. One sportswriter said the so-called hostility that was showing between Grenda and Spears was because of a feud with their families back in Tasmania. Writers sometimes got confused, believing that because Grenda, Goullet and Spears were good pals, they all originated from Tasmania.

The match race took place at Newark with Spears winning in two straight heats.

The cyclists who had been at the Motordrome were scorned to some extent by Kramer and his fellow Velodrome riders and were always called 'outlaws' by them. Frank L. Kramer, an outstanding professional cyclist, was recognised as the world's best sprint cyclist and made cycling his religion.

Bob Spears first clashed with Kramer in 1913 in a two-thirds of a mile handicap on the Newark Velodrome. Kramer followed Grenda out and on the bell lap they had a good lead on Spears. With less than 150 yards to go, Spears flew from fourth place to pass Kramer and Grenda on the finish line. A newspaper report said: "Spears went past

Kramer like an ocean liner passing a fishing smack."
Kramer immediately challenged Spears to a match race but
later said he was too ill to ride, and Jackie Clarke was
substituted. Sports writers commented that Spears was
only a boy of 19 and was being rushed into matches with
the top riders too soon. One newspaper said it might be
going too far to give Spears any chance of beating Clarke.

Spears recalled that: "One critic said I made Kramer look
like 30 cents at Monte Carlo. But I knew how good Kramer
was and that I was just a 'bugs bunny' from Dubbo and that
any time I licked Kramer I would know I had been in a bike
race. The match ended with Jackie Clarke giving me a
lesson and putting me out of the running for a shot at
Kramer for a time. I came again with a win over Kramer
and Clarke in a team's race and had to be given another
match with Kramer."

From 1914 Bob Spears was winning important races. The
New York Times said in August 1914 Spears set a new
track record at the Newark Motordrome winning the one-
mile professional handicap and in 1914 took out the USA
three-mile professional championship. He was beating
Kramer, the top Italian sprinter Moretti and Goullet in
match races and pushed Kramer hard to finish second in
the USA sprint (one-mile) championship.

Spears had one of his best years in the 1916 season at
Newark and recorded nine straight wins over Frank Kramer
in match races and had burst the king's aura of
invincibility. USA sports writers praised Spears and he was
called "one of America's cycling idols."

The 1918 season was another big year for Spears in the USA, and he won the USA all-round professional cycling championships with 27 wins in important track races.

At the end of the 1918 American season, Spears made his first trip to Europe, arriving just after the war had ended. During the 1919 season Spears won 19 major track races, became recognised as the fastest sprinter in the world and showed the Europeans his incredible all-round ability by winning the Brussels six-day race.

When Spears returned to Sydney at the end of the European season, he won several big handicaps including the Golden Wheelrace and the six scratch races he rode in. Australian cycling newspaper The Wheeler said in 1920: "Bob Spears may fairly claim to be the world's best cyclist having defeated most of the champions of America and Europe."

Spears was primed for a big season in Europe when he returned there in 1920, winning the 2000-metre Grand Prix of Paris, regarded as a prelude to the world sprint title. He entered for the 1920 world sprint championship at Antwerp in Belgium, giving Australia its first world championship in the sprint. In the final he lined up against Bailey of England and Kaufmann of Switzerland. Spears won the final ride-off with his trade-mark finish, the paralysing burst to the line, which saw him defeat Kaufmann by a mere 30 centimetres.

Spears said: "Better than all the cash reward was the pride I had in winning the 1920 professional sprint championship of the world at Antwerp for Australia on

August 8, 1920. The date was my birthday and what sportsmen could give himself a better celebration than by collecting a world's championship."

Controversy continued for many years as to whether Bob Spears rode to his true ability in the 1921-22 world sprint championships when he finished second to the Dutch sprinter Piet Moeskops. Spears was considered the better sprinter and if he had used all his brilliance, he may have been world champion two to three years in a row. Questions were asked whether Moeskop's connections offered Spears large sums of money to throw the 1921 race. We will never know.

However, Spears proved he was the best cyclist riding in Europe during the 1920-22 era. He became the idol of the press after he stamped his supremacy in the cycling record books with a record that included: 23 Grand Prix races and European Championship events; teaming with Frank Corry to win two 100km teams events; and wins in two big six-day races. He was clearly the best all-round professional track cyclist in Europe of the early 1920s and won the Grand Prix of Paris three times.

The European press was fascinated with the cycling wonder from Australia. Photographic reports were often published with Spears presented as the perfect example of physical development and celebrities clamoured to be photographed with the Australian cycling champion.

Bob raced in Australia between 1922 and 1927. After reducing weight to get back his old form, he competed at Melbourne's Exhibition track in 1924. Almost back to his best, he was beating cyclists of the highest calibre in the USA's Willie Spencer and Australia's Harris Horder and Jack Fitzgerald.

By 1927 he was still able to draw large crowds but was having trouble keeping his weight down. However, when he was pitted against Australian cycling idol and USA all-round champion Cecil Walker in March 1927, he surprised commentators who thought he was not at top class by defeating Walker in a thrilling match race series.

He was still winning against the top liners in scratch races. In a five-mile scratch race at the Sydney Sports Ground, he claimed victories over the two current stars of Australian track racing, Jack Fitzgerald and Harold K. Smith. While Spears still had the sprinting ability that took him to World success, track ace Harold K. Smith inflicted many defeats on Spears during the 1927 track season. The former world champion could not recoup his brilliant form of the 1920-22 era.

Spears spoke of his great love for cycling and said: "Most of my experiences in the bike game were pleasant, and if I had my time all over again, I'd be in there. Cycling is a great sport and while there is not so much in the way of overseas opportunities for our boys today, the dollars, guilders and francs were there for the catching in the time when I was at my best."

He estimated his earnings at around 30,000-40,000 pounds for riding professionally and believed that Jackie Clarke, Frank Corry and Alf Grenda earned about the same. "Alf Goullet raked in about 80,000 pounds and the famous 'iron man' Reggie McNamara, the king of the six-day riders, pulled in the same. Six-day races paid off well. Whenever I went through one, I took punishment but always came out on top financially, at the same time swearing never again."

Spears was a great fan of boxing and an avid supporter of USA heavyweight boxing legend Jack Dempsey, the 'Manassa Mauler'. He was also friendly with Australian heavyweight boxing champion of the 1920s, George Cook, and was a great admirer of the aviator Smithy, Sir Charles Kingsford-Smith.

Bob Spears couldn't understand why the public would want to follow horse racing when they had the option of watching men do battle in what he believed were the truly fine sports of cycling, cricket and boxing.

It wasn't too easy for Spears later in his career. Harold K. Smith competed against Bob Spears and remembers that in 1927, some of the up and coming professional cyclists used "rough house" tactics to unsettle the ex-champion. Spears became worried about having bad falls on the track and Harold Smith believed this is the reason that Spears was semi-retired after 1927. He finally retired in 1932.

Harold Smith knew Bob Spears well and recalled: "Bob was a big strong sprinter with physical ability. He was easy going but very shrewd for a country boy. Spears was top of the world after he won the world sprint title in 1920. He was immensely popular in Europe. The French people were great followers of cycling and would say Bob Spears was the best in the world."

Harold Smith said that Spears met his wife Marguerite, a figure skater, at the Newark, New Jersey track. "She was born in Italy and her family moved to Newark. She would watch the bicycle races and that's how Bob met her."

Around 1950, Bob and Marguerite (Marg) went on a long holiday and to live in Paris. They could speak fluent French and wanted to spend the rest of their days in Paris.

"They got off the ship in Italy and went to Milano," Harold recalled. "Bob was about 59 at the time. They went to the local bicycle track and Bob didn't think he would be known. But when the cycling people found out who he was the races almost stopped and they put on a fantastic reception and it was reported in the local press."

However, after reaching Paris, Spears' health suffered, and he had to be nursed constantly by Marg. After an operation for cancer, Bob Spears died in Paris in 1950. His small legion of French fans erected a monument to their Australian hero.

Harold Smith visited the old cemetery at Clemart in Paris. He can recall the inscription on the memorial of Bob Spears which read: 'Mr Robert Spears of Australia.' Harold and his brothers, Eddie and Les, who were also professional track cyclists, were friends with Bob Spears and his family.

On December 10, 1985, Robert (Bob) Spears was inducted into the Sport Australia Hall of Fame at the Melbourne Cricket Ground, along with Sir Hubert Opperman, E.L. 'Dunc' Gray, Russell Mockridge and Sid Patterson.

Left: Dunc Gray, our first Olympic gold medallist in the
1000m time trial, Los Angeles, 1932.
Right: Russell Mockridge the 1000m time trial gold medallist
at the 1952 Helsinki Olympics.
Photos courtesy Auscycling Victoria History Archive.

Gordon Johnson,
the 1970 world
professional sprint
track champion,
pictured winning the
1973 Austral Wheel
Race.
Ray Bowles photo.

From the late 1920s to the 1990s, Australia continued to produce world-class sprinters, one kilo time triallists, pursuit and endurance track cyclists who won medals at the Olympics, British Empire (Commonwealth) Games, amateur and professional track world championships. The Australians were able to beat higher rated opponents in the match sprint, time trial, pursuit and other track events helped by tough competition and qualities of strength, track cycling skill and tactical ability.

Curly Grivell, writing about professional track racing in Australian Cycling in the Golden Days, said it is not the number of races one wins, but the class of the rider defeated: "Champions are not made in one season, it takes years of perseverance and sacrifice to make the grade." The top amateur and professional track champions of the 1920s to 1970s era were often multiple winners of Australian track championships and all-rounders, capable of winning any event on the track, from the sprint to the 10-mile and also six-day races.

Among those who performed well on the world stage in the 1920s to 1940s were Gerald Halpin, who won a bronze medal in the 1920 world amateur sprint championships in Belgium. Jack Standen, a national amateur track champion (1925-29) won bronze in the 1928 world amateur sprint championships held in Hungary.

At this time and up to the 1950s the top amateur and professional track champions included Edgar 'Dunc' Gray, George Dempsey, Russell Mockridge, Dick Ploog, Harold Smith, Billy Guyatt, Mac Sloane, Keith Reynolds, Horrie

Pethybridge (sprint silver medallist at the 1934 Commonwealth Games), Len Rogers, Charlie Bazzano, Sid Patterson, Jack Fitzgerald, Dean Whitehorn, Jimmy Beer, Bill Moritz, Laurie Venn, and Jack Walsh.

Copenhagen held the first world amateur track championships in 1921. The Australian Amateur Track Cycling Championships were conducted from 1927 under the Amateur Cyclist's Union of Australia rules and only stopped in 1941-45. Each state Amateur Cycling Union took their turn to hold the titles in March each year.

According to Grivell, Australia's professional track racing championships started in 1921 when Harris Horder won the one-mile professional track championship. The championships ran from November to March and were Australasian Championships until 1927.

The Australian amateur and professional track cycling championships were run by separate bodies, the Amateur Cyclist's Union of Australia and later the Australian Amateur Cycling Association or Federation and their state equivalents, while professional track cycling was run by the League of Wheelmen in each state. A breakthrough came in 1993 when Australian amateur and professional cycling re-unified and races were declared open, while state and national amalgamations were finalised by 1995.

Edgar (Dunc) Gray, first Olympic gold medallist

From 1928 to the end of the 1930s, one amateur track champion, Edgar 'Dunc' Gray, was to make national and international history for Australia as one of our best ever and fastest track cyclists in the 1,000 metres time trial.

In 1932 at the Los Angeles Olympic Games, E.L. 'Dunc' Gray won Australia's first Olympic Games gold medal in the 1,000 metres time trial on the track (from a standing start) in a world record time of 1 minute, 13 seconds, despite contracting influenza during the Games.

Controversially beaten by French cyclist Chaillott in the sprint semi-final, Dunc, on the advice of the team manager, decided not to ride in the race for the sprint bronze medal, but concentrate on the time trial on the same night. Racing against the clock in the 1,000 metres time trial, Gray set a new Olympic record and won Australia's first cycling gold medal.

Regarded by his amateur and professional cycling peers and commentators as Australia's greatest ever amateur track cyclist, he refused lucrative contracts to turn professional. Gray grew up near Goulburn, New South Wales (born 17 July 1906) and competed for the Goulburn Cycling Club from 1923.

He won his first national track title in 1928, the one-mile championship at the Sydney Sports Ground and between 1925 and 1943, Gray won 20 national track titles from 1,000 metres to 10 miles, 25 NSW track titles and 36 club championships. He also held NSW time trial and sprint titles in the same year eight times.

The Sport Australia Hall of Fame said that despite not having a coach and limited international time trial experience, Gray won Australia's first ever Olympic cycling medal at the 1928 Amsterdam Olympic Games, winning the bronze medal in the 1,000m time trial. In 1929 Gray won the one-mile and 5-mile track championships at the Brisbane Exhibition grass track. In 1930 at the Melbourne Motordrome concrete track, he repeated the Brisbane wins in the one-mile and 5-mile. Dunc won the same two events for a third time in 1931 at the Canterbury Velodrome board track in Sydney. He won the first national time trial championship 'test race' and half-mile track championship competing at the Brisbane board track in 1932 and won sprint titles in 1936-37 and 1939.

Dunc Gray became Australia's first British Empire 'Commonwealth' Games track champion in 1934 when the won the 1,000 metre time trial in Manchester.

Two years later at the 1936 Berlin Olympic Games, Gray reached the quarter finals of his only event, the sprint and had the honour of carrying the Australian flag in Berlin. Gray again carried the Australian flag at the 1938 Empire Games in Sydney, where he won the track cycling gold medal in the sprint.

Gray, who told reporters that Bob Spears was Australia's greatest track sprinter of his era, was a teammate of Spears in the track events at the 1928 Budapest track world championships.

Edgar Dunc Gray died in 1996. The Dunc Gray Olympic Velodrome at Bass Hill near the Sydney suburb of Bankstown was named in Gray's honour. It was the track cycling venue for the 2000 Sydney Olympic Games. He was inducted into the Sport Australia Hall of Fame in 1985 and the Cycling Australia Hall of Fame in 2015.

Billy Guyatt

In 1935 Billy Guyatt (born 1921) won the Victorian junior road championship at the Albert Park Lake track and in 1937 he won his first Australian amateur junior track championships as a 16-year-old, winning the one-mile and 5-mile titles at Brisbane's Lang Park dirt track.

A top sprinter and all-rounder, Guyatt missed selection for the 1936 Empire Games in Sydney after losing to Dunc Gray in the national sprint championships. When 17 he turned professional and at the 1939 Australian professional track cycling championships, won four track titles from the quarter mile to the one mile.

"Billy Guyatt most successful rider", The Argus newspaper said on 4 May 1939. "Billy Guyatt, the former amateur champion, was the most successful rider in professional cycling events during the track season just ended, winning 13 races, finishing second in three, and third in two." Guyatt had won one more race than South Australia's top track cyclist Keith Thurgood, who was the Australian professional track champion in 1935-36.   At the Sydney Sports Arena in April 1941 and December 1941-January 1942, Guyatt won two six-day track races with partners Ray Brooking and Jack Walsh.

Guyatt's career was put on hold during the Second World War. In 1948 he won the Australian professional track sprint title and 12 national track titles to 1951. When 34 years old in October 1954 he won the Melbourne to Warrnambool road classic off 27 minutes outsprinting Don Williams (fastest time) and Ken Stewart.

Ploog, Tressider, Baensch, Browne & Marchant

Richard 'Dick' Ploog came from Ballarat, Victoria (born 1936) and was a seven-time national track champion competing in the time trial and sprint. He became one of our most successful track champions of the 1950s and represented Australia at the 1956 Olympic Games in Melbourne, winning a bronze medal in the track sprint. He placed second in the amateur Grand Prix of Paris in 1957 and in 1958 at Paris, won a bronze medal in the track sprint at the world amateur track championships.

Ploog also won two gold medals on the track at the Commonwealth Games. In 1954 at Vancouver, he won the gold medal in the one kilo time trial and in 1958 at Cardiff, UK, he won gold in the match sprint.

From the 1950s, Australia produced more amateur and professional track champions who won multiple national championships and medals at world track championships, Olympic and Commonwealth Games. John Tressider won the silver medal in the 1954 world amateur sprint championships and in 1955 won the bronze medal.

Ron Baensch won bronze at the 1961 world amateur sprint titles, and at the world professional sprint titles, won silver medals in 1964 and 1966, and bronze in 1965.

Competing at the 1956 Olympic Games in Melbourne, national track champions Ian Browne and Tony Marchant won the Australian tandem championship. Browne and Marchant were not considered medal chances at the Olympics and only made the final after the Russian team crashed out. But mentored by former champ Billy Guyatt,

Browne and Marchant outfoxed the Czechoslovaks in the tandem final winding up a long sprint before the last lap to win Olympic gold medals. At the Commonwealth Games, Browne won track gold medals in 1958 and in 1962.

Mockridge, track cycling superstar

Edward (Russell) Mockridge (born 18 July 1928) was one of Australia's greatest track cycling champions and all-round track and road champion cyclists from 1947 to his untimely death in 1958.

When 18 in 1946, he won his first race at Geelong riding a roadster and won eight of his first 11 starts. Mockridge was the Australian amateur road champion in 1947, set a race and world record in the 1956 Melbourne to Warrnambool road race, won the Sun Tour in 1957, and three national elite road race titles (1956-58). On the track he won five national championships in 1950 and in 1952.

At the Empire Games held in Auckland in 1950, Mockridge, then called 'Rocket Man', won gold medals in the 1000-metre time trial and the 1000m sprint, where he defeated fellow Australian Sid Patterson in straight heats. He also claimed silver in the 4,000m pursuit. When he returned to Australia, Mockridge decided to quit cycling and become an Anglican minister. However, he returned to the world of cycling within 14 months.

Russell Mockridge became better known for his Olympic Games performances and wizardry on the track. In 1952 he became Australia's most successful Olympian when competing at the Helsinki Olympic Games, winning two gold medals in three races contested on the track, only equaled in 2004. Mockridge won gold in the 1,000m time trial and teamed with Lionel Cox to win gold in the 2,000m tandem sprint. He stood aside to allow Cox to ride in the Olympic sprint, after he refused to sign a bond to remain an amateur cyclist when cycling experts believed Mockridge was a certainty to win a third gold medal.

The Australian Olympic Committee's historian Harry Gordon said what separated Mockridge from other cyclists was his mastery of all disciplines of the sport.

When Mockridge competed in the world amateur sprint championships final in Milan, Italy in 1951, the other finalists Sacchi and Morenttini rode him off the track. But Mockridge won the silver medal, according to the UCI records. A week later, Mockridge easily defeated amateur world champion Enzo Sacchi in a match race.

In 1952, Mockridge won the amateur Grand Prix of Paris track sprint championship beating Sacchi and was invited to compete against the world's best professional sprinters in the professional Grand Prix of Paris. Mockridge defeated world professional champion Reg Harris of Great Britain and French champion Bellinger and his humiliation of the top professionals led to amateur riders being barred for many years.

He won 10 Australian amateur track titles and three Australian professional track titles during his remarkable career on the track and in 1955, Mockridge teamed up with fellow Australians Roger Arnold and Sid Patterson to win the Paris six-day race.

Lionel Cox

Lionel Cox was born in Brisbane (5 December 1930) but was based in Sydney from the age of 15. He was a top junior cyclist and worked at the Sydney fruit market to build up his strength. Cox won the New South Wales 1000 metres amateur sprint title in 1948 and in 1951 won the amateur one-mile championship.

He faced strong competition from Dick Ploog and Russell Mockridge in the time trial and sprint up to 1954, when Cox beat Ploog in the 1000m sprint and was second to Ploog in the 1000m time trial. Cox also won 12 titles at the New South Wales and Victorian amateur track championships from 1948 to 1955. In 1956 Cox turned professional but was reinstated as an amateur in 1958.

In March 1952 a fund was opened at the City Markets to raise several hundred pounds towards sending Lionel Cox to the Olympic Games when the 22-year-old Cox was the next cyclist waiting for endorsement for the Olympic team, but had to raise 750 pounds before April 15.

Victoria's Russell Mockridge was selected in the track team but had to equal the 1948 Olympic Games winning time to beat Cox in the Australian 1,000m championship. When Cox and Mockridge travelled to the Helsinki Olympics in 1952, they were given a discarded, unassembled tandem bike by a British competitor. They decided to give the tandem event a go and assembled the bike at Helsinki, despite never riding in a tandem race.

Cox and Mockridge won the Olympic gold medal in the tandem sprint, then decided that Mockridge would ride in the time trial and Cox in the sprint. Cox posted the fastest time of the series at 11.3 in the sprint semi-final and won the silver medal in the 1000m sprint final after a great tussle with the winner, Italian world champion Sacchi, losing by a wheel. Then Mockridge won the gold medal for Australia in the time trial.

Competing in Europe, Cox was fourth in the Grand Prix of Paris in 1952, won Denmark's all-round point score championship in 1952-53, was fourth in the world amateur championships in Switzerland and finished third in the Grand Prix of Paris in 1953. Cox coached at Sydney's Camperdown and Tempe tracks, helping to guide young cyclists to state, national and international success. He was admitted to the Sport Australia Hall of Fame. He died in March 2010.

Sydney (Sid) Patterson

Sid Patterson was 5 feet 11 inches tall and powerfully built and looked every inch a world champion from the moment he sat on his bike. Patterson won more track titles than any other cyclist in a 25-plus year career and was the first cyclist to win the Austral Wheel twice off scratch.

"Unquestionably, Patterson is the greatest track cyclist ever to turn a pedal in Australia. He had a tremendous amount of energy and was noted throughout Europe for his long sprint," National Cycling's John Drummond said in late 1977. Born 14 August 1927, Sid, when 14 years of age, won his first event, a 25-mile road race and had his first win on the track, taking out an open handicap race.

While still a teenager, Patterson won Victorian and Australian titles from distances of 1,000 metres to ten miles. Between 1946 and 1949 he won 10 titles over four years at the Australian amateur track cycling championships, including 4 titles in 1949 in the 1,000m sprint, 1,000m time trial, the one mile and 5-mile. He represented Australia at the 1948 Olympic Games in London, finishing sixth in the 1,000m time trial.

Patterson won the 1949 world amateur sprint championship at Copenhagen, Denmark, defeating all the top champions in two straight heats to progress to the final, where he conquered the French champion Bellinger.

He followed this up by winning the 1950 world amateur pursuit title at Leige, Belgium and at the 1950 Empire Games in Auckland, he claimed the silver medals in the 1,000m sprint and the 1,000m time trial.

He was sent to the 1950 world amateur titles not by the national amateur body, but with funds raised by a group of supporters led by Leo Keating, Nick Grey and Hubert Opperman, including funds raised at a track meet at the Melbourne board track and a 25 pounds gift from the Victorian Amateur Cycling Union. A return flight to London around this time was about 600 pounds.

When Patterson turned professional in 1951, he secured sponsorship from Malvern Star bicycles. He won the world professional pursuit championship held in Paris in 1951 and again in 1952 at Zurich, his fourth world track championship title. He teamed with Russell Mockridge and Reg Arnold to win the Paris six-day race in 1955.

Between 1962-67 Patterson won 13 professional track championships and 22 national track titles. At Tasmania's Christmas cycling carnivals, he was a crowd favourite. Riding off scratch between 1951-63, he resembled a freight train winning two Devonport and Latrobe wheel races and a Burnie wheel race.

Patterson set an Australian 1000m time trial record of 1mins, 13.4secs in 1949. In March 1954 at Bundaberg he was reported to have broken British sprint champion Reg Harris's 1000m world record of 1mins, 12.2secs.

When he won Melbourne's famous Austral Wheelrace in 1962 from scratch, the first back marker to win in 40 years since Jack Fitzgerald took it out in 1922, he said he'd been trying to win the race for 10 years and had finally done it. He won the Austral Wheel again in 1964.

At age of 40 in 1967, he contested three six-day races in Europe, finishing third in Madrid. Patterson won 16 six-day races on the track and equalled the world six-day record holder at the time, Australia's Roger Arnold.

Patterson retired in 1968 when 40 and opened a cycling shop at East Bentleigh in Melbourne. He was estimated to have won half a million dollars in prizemoney. Sid Patterson died aged 72 years. He was inducted into the inaugural Cycling Australia Hall of Fame in 2015.

Graeme French

Tasmanian track cyclist Graeme French (born 1926) competed in his first race at the Burnie Club in 1942 when 15 and won the Burnie Wheel race when 16. In 1950-51,

French won the 5-mile and 10-mile Victorian track championships and Commonwealth Jubilee 10-mile title.

The Sport Australia Hall of Fame said French arrived in Antwerp, Belgium, inexperienced in riding against the giants of the motor pacing world. But Grolimond, a famous Swiss star of motor-pacing - the one who rides the derny (a small motorcycle), came out of retirement to help French in the 1956 world motor-paced championship. French received a boost prior to the race, when pacing behind a derny, he broke the world record for one hour.

In the 100-kilometre championship, French made it through to the final held in front of 50,000 people and led from start to finish. After covering 24km of the scheduled 100km of the final, he began to suffer from the continual strain imposed by the 60 mile an hour average speed. But on the final lap, he won by 22 yards. His winning time on the difficult Copenhagen track was a world record. French was inducted into the Tasmanian Sporting Hall of Fame.

Danny Clark, all-round track champion

Cycling experts compared Danny Clark to Australia's greatest all-round track cycling champions Sid Patterson, Cecil Walker and Alf Goullet, while he was recognised by his peers as Australia's best six-day track cyclist of the modern era.

Daniel (Danny) Clark was born in August 1951 in Launceston. After finishing third in the junior time trial at the 1968 Australian amateur track championships, he then won three national junior amateur track titles in 1969.

When 18, Clark won the silver medal in the 4000m individual pursuit at the 1970 Edinburgh Commonwealth Games. In 1971 at Perth, he claimed three senior Australian amateur track championship titles. Clark won two national amateur track titles in 1972 and four in 1973 at distances of 1,000m to 16 kilometres, showing his impressive all-round track cycling ability.

At the Munich Olympics in 1972, Clark won the silver medal in the 1000m time trial, despite fracturing a finger when training. He lost by just 0.43 seconds to win Tasmania's first individual Olympic medal.

He turned professional in 1974 and won the 10,000m and 15,000m Australian professional track titles in 1975. Clark rode on the six-day cycling circuit from 1975 and was based in Ghent with his Belgian wife. After Clark posted 42 European six-day wins in 1987, he and Patrick Sercu, the greatest modern day six-day cyclist with 88 six-day race wins, were voted the best all-round track cyclists to race in Europe.

At the world professional track championships, Clark won three titles in the keirin sprint (1980-81, 1986) and two in the motor-paced (1988, 1991), his last claimed in Stuttgart when 39 years old. He also won five silver medals: two in the keirin, two in the motor-paced and one in the point score, and two bronze medals. But he told National Cycling in December 1981 that it cost him $4,000 to win the keirin title in Czechoslovakia "and the Australian Federation didn't shell out a cent."

At the Tasmanian Christmas Carnivals from 1973-1981,

Clark won three Latrobe and three Burnie 2-mile wheel races off the scratch mark, giving huge starts to the front markers. Riding off scratch, he won three Austral Wheel races in Melbourne in 1977, 1986, and 1990.

Back home in Launceston, Clark used an unorthodox training method for motor-paced track titles by riding a track bike for 50 kilometres, behind large logging trucks from George Town to Launceston.

In Europe, Danny Clark won the omnium championship held over 4-5 different events six times (1978-79, 1984-86 & 1988), the derny and motor-paced titles (1983, 1985-86, 1988 & 1990), and the madison title in 1979 with Don Allan and with Tony Doyle in 1988. He won the USA omnium title in 1987. Clark also won a record 74 six-day races for an Australian during his brilliant career.

He excelled in master's road cycling, winning: Cyclist Master of the Year awards in 1999 and 2001 (25 masters wins), masters world road champion 2003-04, and World Cup, Italian and Grand Fondo championships in 2003. When 49 in 2000 he won a stage at the Tour of Tasmania.

Danny Clark's awards include a Medal of the Order of Australia in 1986, induction into the Sport Australia Hall of Fame in 1987, the Cycling Australia Hall of Fame in 2018, and the Tasmanian Sporting Hall of Fame.

Talking in July 2020 about his best three to four performances, wins and medals in international track cycling and those that stand out as being special, Clark said these were: "My 1977 Burnie Wheel victory, when the response from the 18,000 patrons was quite special; the two professional world keirin titles using outdated equipment and no training riding at 80kph behind motor-pace; my ride in the point score to win the silver medal the day after my 1981 keirin win; and my silver medal for Australia in the 1972 Olympics one kilometre time trial.

"I'm proud of my versatility during my cycling career. I admired Russell Mockridge. He could ride in the Tour de France and also beat the world's best sprinters in the Grand Prix de Paris."

Gordon Johnson

Gordon Johnson (born 1946) was from Victoria and grew up in a cycling family. He became a multiple track world sprint medallist for Australia. A top junior in the amateurs in 1962-63, he won five out of six national titles, including the 1000 metre sprint twice and rode for the Brunswick cycling club in Melbourne.

Johnson was the son of Tas Johnson, the time trial silver medallist at the 1938 British Empire Games who competed at the 1936 Berlin Olympics. Johnson went on to win 15 elite national track titles in amateur and professional branches of cycling between 1964 and 1973.

He faced stiff competition from John Nicholson and Danny Clark at the track nationals until 1972. Representing Australia on the track at the 1964 Olympic Games in Tokyo when 18, he crashed while training and went out in a repechage heat. He competed at the 1968 Olympics at Mexico City in the early rounds of the sprint.

At the 1970 Commonwealth Games in Edinburgh, he

won the silver medal in the track sprint, beaten in two races by Nicholson for gold by the narrowest of margins, one by one-one-hundredth of a second. Johnson also won a gold medal in the tandem track sprint with Ron Jonker.

Johnson travelled to the 1970 world professional sprint track championships in Leicester UK. He had prepared well with three or four weeks of structured training and was in good shape. He stunned the Europeans, defeating Dutch favourite Loevesijn then Italy's Gaiardoni in the final, Australia's first world professional sprint champion since Bob Spears in 1920.

Johnson was approached by Gaiardoni's coach Guido Costa before the final. Costa asked him how much money he would need to throw the race. Johnson told Costa: "Not for a Mercedes Benz with the trunk full of gold bars!"

At the 1971 world professional track championships, Johnson was set to win the sprint bronze from Italy's Turrini, but Turrini went under Johnson on the edge of the track and Johnson was disqualified for alleged rough riding. However, in 1972 he returned to the professional track world championships held in Marseille and claimed the silver medal in the sprint.

Johnson won big professional track races in Amsterdam, Milan, the 1971 Copenhagen Grand Prix and the 1971 British national sprint championship and was sponsored by the UK's Carlton-Raleigh cycles. Johnson rode professionally on the track in the UK and Europe including in six-day and madison races until 1974. He was inducted into the Sport Australia Hall of Fame in 1989.

John Nicholson

John Nicholson (born 1949) grew up in Melbourne and when 14, won his first race at the East Burwood cycling track and went on to become our most successful track sprinter since the late 1940s. A top junior track cyclist, he won the Australian amateur time trial title in 1966-67 and competing at elite level in 1968, placed second to Gordon Johnson at the 1968-69 Australian 1000m sprint titles.

In 1970 Nicholson won his first Australian amateur 1000m sprint championship defeating Johnson at the Brunswick velodrome in Melbourne and in 1971 finished second in the sprint to Danny Clark. But he turned the tables on Clark winning the 1972 sprint title at Adelaide.

Nicholson was the youngest cyclist to compete at the Mexico Olympic Games in 1968 and in 1970 at the Edinburgh Commonwealth Games, he won gold in the match sprint defeating teammate Gordon Johnson.

When the Olympic Games came to Munich in 1972, Nicholson won the silver medal in the 1000m sprint behind France's defending Olympic and five-time world champion, Daniel Morelon. He successfully defended his Commonwealth Games sprint title at Christchurch in 1974 where he also won silver in the 1000m time trial. Nicholson turned professional and won the 1975 and 1976 Australian professional sprint championships titles.

At the UCI track world championships, he won silver in the men's sprint at Montreal in 1974. In 1975, Nicholson became only the third Australian to win the world professional track sprint title claiming gold at Rocourt in

Belgium. National Cycling magazine said Nicholson won his second world professional track sprint title at Monteroni di Lecce, Italy in 1976 in two straight heats defeating Giordano Turrini of Italy. Nicholson's record at track world championships puts him ahead of Bob Spears and Gordon Johnson as Australia's best track sprinter up until the 1970s. In his final track worlds appearance, Nicholson won the bronze medal in 1977 at Venezuela. Later that year he broke a hip at Coburg, which appears to have affected his form. He was inducted into the Sport Australia Hall Fame in 1986.

Nicholson, who is on the Cycling Victoria Board, said he was inspired by sprinters of the early years like Major Taylor and Reg Harris.

Kenrick Tucker

Kenrick Tucker (born 1959) came from Rockhampton. Coached by his father Ken Tucker, a coaching legend, he won the Australian amateur junior sprint title in 1977.

Dubbed the 'Rockhampton Rocket', Tucker became one of Australia's best track sprinters of the 1970-80s era. Tucker won 10 Australian amateur track championship titles between 1979-1984, including four in the time trial and five in the sprint.

In April 1979 National Cycling said that Kenrick Tucker, "a brilliant sprinter at 19 years of age, completely dominated the sprint and time trial championships" held in Tasmania. Selected to ride at the 1978 Commonwealth Games in Edmonton, Canada, he won the gold medal in the sprint and the silver medal in the one kilo time trial, one of his greatest achievements on the track. In 1981 at the world amateur track championship in the Czech Republic, he finished fourth in the one kilo time trial.

At the 1982 Commonwealth Games held in Brisbane, Tucker claimed the gold medal in the sprint. He competed in the 1980 Moscow Olympic Games and the 1984 Olympics in Los Angeles, where he made the quarter finals. Tucker was second in the national sprint title in 1985-86.

Steele Bishop

West Australian Steele Bishop (born in 1953) took up track cycling at age 13 and won the state championship at age 15. In 1972, Steele won the 4000 metres team pursuit riding for the Victorian team and when 19 was selected to represent Australia in the 4000m team pursuit at the 1972 Munich Olympics. Better known for his stellar career in the track pursuit, Bishop won the Westral Wheelrace six times between 1975-1984 and won the first two Griffin 1000 five-day road races in 1982-83.

Bishop won 20 West Australian road and track titles between 1968-1974. In 1973 he represented Australia in the individual pursuit at the world track championships at San Sebastian. He turned professional and between 1976 and 1984, won 13 Australian professional track titles, including eight in the 5000m individual pursuit.

After his 1982 Australian championship win in the 5000m individual pursuit, he became the first Australian cyclist to break six minutes for 5,000 metres. He was awarded the Oppy Medal with a return airfare to the 1983 world championships in Switzerland. He won the gold medal in the 5000m individual pursuit at the Zurich world track championships, catching Switzerland's Olympic champion Robert Dill Bundi well before the finish line.

In 1983 Bishop won the Bendigo Madison and the Shepparton Madison. He was a winner of major Australian wheel races riding off scratch and won the Latrobe Wheel (1979), Melbourne's Austral Wheel (1982), the Burnie Wheel and Sydney Thousand (1983), and the 1984 Westral Wheel Race, the last of his career.

Steele took up Masters track cycling in late 2017, 34 years after he retired. He set a Masters world record in the individual pursuit in 2018. Bishop was awarded the Order of Australia Medal.

Gary Sutton

Gary Sutton (born 1955) came from Moree in New South Wales and when 15, joined Sydney's top cycling club St George CC. He became one of Australia's best all-round track cyclists, posting an incredible record during the 1970s and 1980s. In 1974 Sutton won his first elite Australian amateur track title at Sydney's Wiley Park track in the 4000m individual pursuit and the 20km title.

Between 1975-78 he won another five Australian amateur track titles. John Drummond said in National Cycling, March 1978, that Sutton "was easily the best Australian cyclist amateur or professional in 1977 and was the best all-round cycling star since Russell Mockridge".

In 1979 at Devonport he won three titles including the new 50km point score title and the 'Champion of Champions Award', equalling Gordon Johnson's 17 national track championships. In 1980-81, Sutton won another five titles including the 50km points score and equalled Dunc Gray's 20 national track titles in 1981.

In 1974 in the Commonwealth Games at Auckland, he claimed bronze in the 4000m individual pursuit and a silver medal in the team pursuit. Returning to the Commonwealth Games in Edmonton in 1978, Sutton won bronze in the 10-mile scratch race and gold in the 4000m team pursuit with brother Shane Sutton, Kevin Nichols, and Colin Fitzgerald. In 1976 he represented Australia in the individual pursuit at the Montreal Olympics.

Sutton focused on road racing in 1977, winning the Australian amateur road cycling championships in Sydney, the Sanyo Tour of the North in Tasmania, fastest time in the Grafton to Inverell and first and fastest time in the Goulburn to Sydney road classics. In 1984 he claimed the GC at the Sun Tour and two stages of the Yorkshire Classic in the UK. In 1982 teaming with brother Shane Sutton, he won the first Bendigo international madison.

His greatest achievement came in 1980 when he won the track world amateur point score title. "Gary Sutton wins Points Score Championship at Bescanon in eastern France. Sutton with 49 points, defeated Russia's Victor Manakov on 45 points with West Germany's Joseph Kristen in third place on 42 points," National Cycling reported.

Sutton won other world amateur championships medals: a silver medal in the keirin at Leicester, UK in 1982; bronze in the points race at Zurich in 1983; silver in the points race at Barcelona in 1984; and in 1989, silver in the points race at Lyon in France.

St George Cycling Club president, former cyclist and race promoter Phill Bates said Sutton became Australia's most decorated cyclist: "Gary Sutton won 45 national titles, an all-time record and went on to represent Australia at two Olympic Games and won countless medals including gold at Commonwealth Games. His victory in the 1980 World Points race is legendary, as is his four placings in world amateur titles."

From 1992 Sutton became a coach at the NSW Institute of Sport, was the national coach of Australian juniors from 1997-2008 and the national women's track endurance coach from 2010, becoming one of the world's most successful coaches.

In late 2017 Sutton joined the USA elite athletics department as the new head endurance track coach.

Kevin Nichols

Kevin Nichols came from Grafton in New South Wales (born 1955) and was an outstanding juvenile and junior track cyclist. He won four Australian amateur track cycling titles between 1971 and 1973 and developed into one of Australia's best cyclists in the team pursuit.

He rode for the Bankstown Sports Amateur Cycling Club in the 1970s and later rode for St George Cycling Club.

Competing at senior level in 1975 and 1976, Nichols won the 20 kilometre Australian amateur track title both years, and in 1981, the 50km point score title. He also won six team pursuit titles between 1974-1981 as part of a star New South Wales team that included Gary Sutton, Shane Sutton, Geoff Skaines and others. Nichols was Australia's most selected cyclist during this era.

From 1974 he competed at the Commonwealth Games on the track winning silver in the 4000m team pursuit at Christchurch in 1974; gold in the team pursuit at Edmonton in 1978; and two gold medals at Brisbane in 1982 in the team pursuit and the 10-mile scratch.

He represented Australia at the 1976, 1980 and 1984 Olympic Games. The Australian Olympic Committee said that Kevin Nichols won gold alongside Michael Grenda, Michael Turtur and Dean Woods in the men's 4000m team pursuit at the 1984 Olympic Games in Los Angeles. "His experience and finishing burst proved invaluable to the pursuit team. The foursome, dubbed 'Charlie's Angels' because they were coached by Charlie Walsh, were the first Aussie cyclists to win Olympic gold since 1956," the Australian Olympic Committee said.

Mike Turtur

From Adelaide (born 1958), Michael (Mike) Turtur rode for the Norwood Cycling Club. He represented South Australia as a juvenile and junior cyclist at the Australian amateur track cycling championships. Turtur won the junior 10 kilometre track championship in 1976 and in

1982 he won the national track points score championship.

Riding with the South Australian team in the national track championships in 1979 he won gold in the 4000m team pursuit with brother Chris Turtur, Gary West and Peter Kesting, winning the Southcott Cup and breaking a 17-year grip NSW and Victoria had on the team pursuit.

At the 1982 Commonwealth Games in Brisbane, Turtur won gold medals in the 4000m team pursuit and individual pursuit, and a bronze medal in the 10-mile scratch. He won a second gold medal in the team pursuit at the 1986 Commonwealth Games in Edinburgh.

Part of the iconic 'Charlie's Angels' team pursuit, Turtur delivered one of the gutsiest performances of the Los Angeles 1984 Olympics. After breaking his wrist earlier in the competition, Turtur, Grenda, Nichols and Woods won gold against a well-prepared USA team.

Turtur became a cycling coach at the South Australian Institute of Sport. His other accomplishments off the bike include establishing Australia's first World Tour event, the Tour Down Under, where he held the role of race director since its inception in 1999 to 2019.

Turtur received the Medal of the Order of Australia in 1985. He was appointed an Officer of the Order of Australia in 2018 and was inducted into the Cycling Australia Hall of Fame.

Michael Grenda

Michael Grenda (born 1962) was one of Tasmania's best track cyclists who came from a celebrated cycling family.

Great uncle Alf Grenda was a six-day race record holder and world tandem sprint champion, while his father Ron Grenda was a national sprint champion in the 1980s.

Michael Grenda broke through at elite level in 1982 when he won the senior national amateur 20 kilometre track title. He won the national 50km points race title in 1983 and in 1984, the team pursuit title. At the national professional track titles in 1986, Grenda won the 10km title and the 1000m sprint title and was named the Champion of Champions. In 1988 he won the elimination race title.

When he was selected for the Brisbane Commonwealth Games in 1982. Grenda and teammates Gary West, Mike Turtur and Kevin Nichols set themselves up as one of the world's best 4000 metres pursuit teams by winning the gold medals. Grenda placed in three six-day races and won the Launceston six-day race in 1987.

Grenda became Tasmania's first Olympic champion when he teamed with Nichols, Turtur and Dean Woods to win the gold medal in the 4000m team pursuit at the 1984 Los Angeles Olympics. "Grenda's powerful finish was a feature of Australia's remarkable run in Los Angeles. He also raced in the 4000m individual pursuit at the Games, being unlucky to be eliminated by the eventual gold medallist, American Steve Hegg, in the quarter-finals," the Australian Olympic Committee said.

After a successful year on the Japanese professional track and keirin circuit, Grenda retired in 1991. Grenda was awarded the Order of Australia Medal in 1994 and was inducted into the Tasmanian Sporting Hall of Fame.

Stephen Pate

Stephen Pate (born 1964) from Melbourne, Victoria, was one of the best track sprinters to come out of Victoria and was compared to the great Sid Patterson.

According to the Carnegie Caulfield Cycling Club's website, Stephen Pate won many national amateur track championships starting in 1984, when he won the 20 kilometre scratch race, repeating the win in 1985-87. In 1986, Pate turned professional and won the Australian track championships in the sprint, the keirin, and the 20km scratch race and in 1987, won the Australian professional track team pursuit title.

Between 1988 and 1997, Pate won around 30 titles at the Australian professional track championships in the sprint, keirin, 20km scratch race, one-mile scratch, and team pursuit, and at the national road championships he won the criterium in 1997.

Pate set world professional records for the 200m, 500m, and one kilo. At the UCI world track championships, Pate won the gold medal in the sprint in 1988 at Ghent, Belgium and in 1990 won bronze at Maebashi in Japan. In 1992, he won silver in the keirin at Valencia, Italy.

After Pate won bronze at the world professional championship at Stuttgart in 1991, he and Carey Hall tested positive for steroids and were stripped of their bronze medals.

Pate was also one of our top madison cyclists and won four Australian madison track titles: in 1995 riding with Scott McGrory; in 1997 with Brett Aitken; in 1998 with

Matthew Allan; and with Baden Cooke in 2000. In 1996, Pate and McGrory won silver medals in the madison in the UCI world track champions at Manchester, UK.

In 1993, Pate set a race record in the Austral Wheel, winning the race from an incredible back mark of 20 metres behind scratch. Pate suffered depression after he was left out of the 2000 Sydney Olympics team and stopped competing in cycling.

Dean Woods

Dean Woods (born 1966) came from Wangaratta, Victoria. After watching his older brother ride in the local track races, Dean took up the sport in July 1976 when 11 years old. In 1983, he won the senior amateur individual pursuit title and the junior world individual pursuit at the world championships in New Zealand. He won the junior individual pursuit title again in 1984 in France.

Earlier, in December 1983, Australian track coach Charlie Walsh contacted Woods, then a full-time plumber. When 17, Dean was selected for the 1984 Los Angeles Olympic Games track team and rode in the individual pursuit and in the team pursuit with Michael Grenda, Kevin Nichols and Michael Turtur.

Riding Australian-made bikes that didn't have the latest technology like the Americans such as disc wheels, Woods, Grenda, Nicholls, and Turtur pulled off a big upset by defeating the Americans to win the gold medals.

Woods later said that Charlie Walsh was the first proper track coach that he had access to.

In 1985 at the national track cycling championships at the Launceston International Velodrome, Woods broke the world record in the 4000m individual pursuit. National Cycling's John Drummond said: "Dean Woods caught Michael Grenda in 3 mins, 30.03secs then set a new Australian time of 4mins, 36.32secs, lowering Russian Vicktor Koupovets' world record of 4mins, 37.681secs. It was sheer magic, and the crowd loved it."

Competing at the 1986 Edinburgh Commonwealth Games, Woods won gold medals in the individual pursuit and 4000m team pursuit, silver in the scratch race, and bronze in the points race. He also won bronze in the individual pursuit at the 1986 track worlds in the USA.

Woods became one of our all-time greatest track pursuit cyclists. He was in top form at the 1988 Olympic Games in Seoul, winning a silver medal in the 4000m individual pursuit and bronze in the 4000m team pursuit. At Lyon in 1989 at the UCI track world championships, Woods claimed the silver medal in the individual pursuit.

Switching to the road he competed for French amateur team ASCM Toulon in 1986-87. Turning professional in 1989 he raced for German road cycling team Stuttgart in the Vuelta a Espana, the Paris-Nice race and placed second in Belgium's GP Ardennes. Woods rode for Germany's Team Telekom in in 1990-91 and was a GC fourth at the Tour of Sweden, but admitted he struggled in the first few years in the long road races. In 1990, Woods posted a new race record and fastest time (5hrs, 12mins) in the Melbourne to Warrnambool classic.

Woods won the Warrnambool road race again in 1993 when he joined new pro road team Jayco.

At the Commonwealth Games at Victoria, Canada in 1994, he won a gold medal in the team pursuit and a bronze medal in the points race. Woods claimed the Australian individual pursuit championship in a new national record in 1994, won four criteriums in in Germany and the Grenoble six-day race in France.

In 1995, he won gold in the team pursuit at the UCI track world championships in Colombia. At the 1996 Atlanta Olympic Games, Woods won bronze in the 4000m team pursuit. He claimed the 1996 Australian madison title but retired at age 30 and operated cycling shops. Woods was awarded the Medal of the Order of Australia in 1985 and in 2000 was admitted to the Sport Australia Hall of Fame.

Gary Neiwand

Gary Neiwand (born 1966) came from Melbourne and placed third in the sprint and the time trial competing in the Australian juvenile track titles in Brisbane in 1982 at age 13. In 1984-85 he won the national junior sprint title then the national senior track title in the sprint, and from 1983 to 1990 won five national sprint championships.

When he won the sprint final at the Launceston Velodrome in March 1985 against Kenrick Tucker, the Queenslander was in scintillating form and was tipped by cycling experts to take the title, but Tucker was no match for Neiwand. According to the Australian Olympic Committee: "Four-time Olympian Neiwand achieved the rare feat of winning Olympic medals 12 years apart – an accomplishment considered even more remarkable in a power endeavour such as track cycling."

Neiwand won sprint medals in three of the four Olympics he participated in: bronze in the sprint at Seoul in 1988, silver in 1992 in the sprint at Barcelona, and bronze in the team sprint and a silver in the keirin in 2000 at Sydney. At Atlanta in 1996 he narrowly missed the bronze medal.

At the Commonwealth Games he won gold medals in the sprint at Edinburgh in 1986 and at Auckland in 1990.

Competing at the UCI track world championships in 1991, he won his first track world's medal at Stuttgart, taking bronze in the sprint. In 1992 he won the silver medal in the sprint at the Olympic Games in Barcelona and won Denmark's DBC Open Grand Prix. Neiwand produced two stellar performances in 1993, winning gold medals in the sprint and keirin at the UCI track world championship in Norway.

In 1994, he won his third gold medal in the individual sprint at the Commonwealth Games at Victoria, Canada. At the 1996 track world championships at Manchester Neiwand won gold in the team sprint and silver medals in the sprint and the keirin. Niewand proved he was our best and most successful track sprinter of the 1980s-1990s era.

Neiwand's good form continued at the Sydney Olympics in 2000, when he won a silver medal in the keirin and a bronze in the team sprint. He retired from international competition in 2000 and battled depression.

Reg Arnold and Alf Strom, riding in the Wembley, London Six-Day race in 1952. Photo courtesy of Reg Arnold.

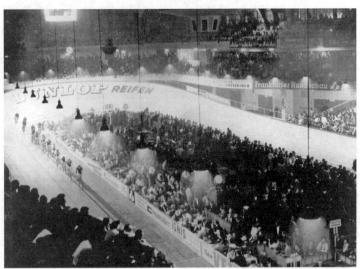

The Frankfurt Six-Day race in 1960, when Reg Arnold rode with Sid Patterson. Photo courtesy of Reg Arnold.

The Six-Day track cycling race is the iron-man event of professional track cycling, a race of extreme endurance and rivalled the fame of the tortuous Tour De France, when six-day riders could cover the same distance as that of a grand tour. The first reported six-day track race was an individual time trial held at Islington, London in 1878, when David Staunton rode a high wheeler for 18 hours a day for six days to win a 100-pound bet.

Six-day racing became popular in the USA in 1891 when the first six-day races started at what became known as the Madison Square Garden track, which opened in 1879 as an outdoor arena near Madison Square Park.

The first race was open to solo riders and held over six consecutive days, initially stopping each evening to give riders a rest. The winner was the cyclist who competed the most laps and distance at the end of the six days.

Riders would employ a soigneur or second to help the rider keep going, and it was said that the soigneurs used doping to keep their cyclists on the track. Hallucinations were common, riders collapsed and fell and were lifted on and off their bikes and carried to their rest quarters.

When Teddy Hale won the six-day race in 1896 The New York Times said: "He won like a ghost, his face as white as a corpse, his eyes no longer visible". After newspaper reports described the brutal conditions under which the six-day cyclists competed and that many were hospitalised due to exhaustion, the New York and Chicago authorities passed laws so that the cyclists could only spend 12 hours on the track each day.

The six-day promoters decided to put a team of two riders on the track who rode 12 hours each day to get around the rules and the two-man six-day race was born. The two-man six-day race also became known as the Madison format, when riders would take turns to hand-sling each other back into action.

The six-day race quickly moved to the 24-hour format. One of the two riders was always on the track (the Berlin system) and it was still a test of extreme endurance. Up until 1954, a team of two riders rode their bikes on the concrete or board tracks for up to 21 hours a day and the winners were the team that covered the most distance at the end of the six days.

Alf Goullet, six-day cycling legend

Australia's Alf Goullet was the highest paid six-day rider on the American tracks and won 15 six-day races during his amazing career. He earned US$1,000 a day plus cash prizes during the sprints.

In 1914, Goullet and Alf Grenda set a world record for the six-day race under the old 'Berlin system' rules at New York's Madison Square Garden, covering 2,759 miles and two laps over the six days.

Australian cycling greats of the 1910-1930 era – Alf Goullet, Reg McNamara, Alf Grenda and Bob Spears were also top six-day cyclists internationally. Spears excelled in six-day races in Australia and Europe and other top Australian six-day riders of this era were Don Kirkham, Paddy Hehir, Ernie Pye and Frank Corry.

The first six-day race in Australia was held at the Melbourne Exhibition track in 1881. English cyclist Jack Rolfe won five out of the first six, six-day races held in Melbourne, Adelaide, and Sydney between 1881-1883.

Jack Rolfe came out from Birmingham, England in 1879 and worked at the Sydney Bicycle Works in 1894. Newspapers at the time proclaimed him "world champion cyclist" after he challenged riders from Scotland and America. He moved to Ballarat and later Bendigo in Victoria where he started making Rolfe Cycles.

Alf Goullet and Paddy Hehir won the six-day race held in January-February 1912 at the Sydney Cricket Ground and later won the Melbourne six-day race at Melbourne's Exhibition track.

At the Sydney Cricket Ground in January 1912, 14 teams of riders competed for total prizemoney of 1,000 pounds, cheered on by around 58,000 fans. Goullet and Hehir took first place ahead of Alf Grenda and Gordon Walker, with Reg McNamara and Frank Corry third.

In 1913, the team of Reg McNamara and Frank Corry won the Sydney six, while Bob Spears and Don Kirkham won at Melbourne.

When the six-day race was introduced in Paris in January 1913 on the 250-metre track at the new glass-domed Velodrome d'Hiver, Australia's Alf Goullet and America's Joe Fogler won the first-ever Paris six-day race.

American novelist Ernest Hemingway used to bet on horseracing when living in Paris in the 1920s. When he was talked into visiting the Velodrome d'Hiver to watch a six-day race he became a big fan of six-day track racing.

Hemingway said in his novel, A Moveable Feast that he had started writing many stories about bicycle racing but had never written one as good as the bicycle races are on the indoor tracks or on the roads. He captured the extraordinary atmosphere of the 24-hour, non-stop action of man and machine on the high-banked wooden tracks at six-day races such as: "The whirring sound the tyres made on the wood as the riders passed.

"The efforts and the tactics as the riders climbed and plunged, each one a part of his machine.

"… and the duels that were more exciting than any racing, the put-putting of the motorcycles and the riders elbow to elbow and wheel to wheel up and down and around at deadly speed until one man could not hold the pace and broke away and the solid wall of air that he had been sheltered against hit him."

From the 1940s to the 1960s, Australia's world sprint and pursuit champion Sid Patterson won 16 six-day races on the track and equalled the world six-day record holder at the time, Australia's Roger (Reg) Arnold with 16 wins. Patterson and his six-day contemporaries such as Sercu and Pjinen rode under a different system when riders were on the bike for six to 10 hours a day.

Danny Clark, Australia's multiple world track champion in the keirin and motor-pace, won an Australian record 74 six-day races during his brilliant career in Europe and internationally from the 1970s to the 1990s.

Australian six-day cycling stars who were successful on

the European and international six-day circuit include Ken Ross (1920s); Graeme Gilmore (1970s); Donald Allan, who teamed with Danny Clark for 15 six-day wins before being injured; madison gold medallist in the 2000 Sydney Olympics Scott McGrory, who is credited with around 17-20 six-day wins in Europe from the late 1980s; and Belgian-Australian Matthew Gilmore with around 17 six-day wins in Europe since the 1990s.

In the 1940s to 1960s, the promoters of the main tracks at Paris, Brussels, Berlin (2 six-day tracks) Gent, Antwerp, Essen, Munich, Munster, Dortmund, Madrid, Milan, and at Aahrus and Copenhagen in Denmark introduced ladies and amateur race sessions, and off-track entertainment such as restaurants, bowling alleys, fun parlours, rock bands, film star appearances, and burlesque shows held in halls around the tracks.

At the Dortmund and Berlin tracks some nights, up to 18,000 spectators would turn up to watch the six-day racing.

Reg (Roger) Arnold and Alf Strom

It was into this electric atmosphere that Reginald Arnold thrilled his growing legion of European fans with brilliant displays of six-day racing between 1946 and 1963, teaming up with fellow Australian cycling champion Alf Strom to continue the six-day cycling tradition.

Reg Arnold (born 9 October 1924) came from Murwillumbah in New South Wales. He started riding with the Ashfield Cycling Club in Sydney at age 17 when his brothers Fred and Lindsay gave him a bicycle for his birthday. Blind in one eye from a childhood accident, he was the club's sprint champion from 1943 to 1945.

Reg and his brothers joined breakaway cycling league the Australian Cycling Association, formed by several Sydney clubs and Reg won their sprint championship. He trained every day with a 100km training run on Sundays.

The British League of Racing Cyclists issued an invitation for two cyclists to ride in the Brighton to Glasgow stage race. Reg Arnold and Alf Strom, the ACA long distance road champion and three-time Goulburn to Sydney road race fastest time (blue riband) winner from 1938 to 1940, were selected by the ACA to attend.

In an interview with this writer in Freewheeling magazine in 1987, Arnold said that the ACA were short of funds and he faced a dilemma – how to get to the UK to compete in the race. Arnold worked his passage to England on a Norwegian freighter and after seven weeks at sea he was badly out of condition.

Arnold was 21 when he arrived in England and discovered that Alf Strom had arrived two days earlier. Due to last minute donations, Strom, who was 29, flew over on a Sunderland sea plane.

Unfortunately, Arnold and Strom were not race fit and after leading the team's race during the Brighton to Glasgow race, they did not figure in the finish.

On October 11, 1946, Arnold and Strom arrived in Bruges, Belgium where they were introduced to local promoter and bike shop owner Oscar Daemers, a former professional sprint champion of Belgium who had competed in six-day races in Belgium and France.

Daemers took a gamble on the unknown Australians and entered them for a 40 kilometre amateur team's race and drilled the Australians in the techniques of continental racing. Arnold and Strom defied local pundits and won the teams race by the barest of margins – half a wheel.

Soon after in 1946, Reg Arnold (now known as Roger) and Alf Strom turned professional and riding in their second six-day race, finished second to the strongest six-day team in Europe, Schulte and Boyen.

Daemers then arranged a contract for the Australians and they received appearance money to ride the European six-day circuit. Arnold and Strom later purchased two cottages in the little Belgian town of Oost-Eeklo. In 1948, Strom brought his wife June over to Belgium. Arnold's finance Margaret joined Reg and they married in London.

Earlier in 1947, Arnold and Strom posted a second and a third in madison races in France, while Arnold was second in an elite criterium in Belgium. In 1949, Arnold and Strom came second in the first Berlin post-war six-day race, the Belgium six, and in a major madison race in France.

The Australian pair's first six-day win was in the New York City Six Days race of 1949, the first post-war race held in the USA.

The Argus newspaper reported on Tuesday 8 November 1949 that: "Strom, Arnold Won Race In Last Hour. New York. Alf Strom and Reg Arnold, Australian cyclists, who won the six-day bike race which ended here on Saturday night, covered 2,168 miles in 146 hours, and gained a total of 1,617 points, before a crowd of 12,000 people. The Italians, Severino Rigoni and Fernando Teruzzi, who were second, scored 911 points. Arnold won eight of the last 27 sprints, and Strom four. Between them they won seven of the last eight sprints."

Roger Arnold and Alf Strom made Australian cycling history and were recognised as the greatest Australian six-day track cycling team that rode under the three older more arduous six-day race rules, winning eight six-day races.

At one stage, Roger Arnold remembers having 30 to 40 fans following his progress with his name sewn on their sweaters while the fans often had detailed scrapbooks. Arnold said the Germans were the noisiest and most appreciative fans at the six-day races, while the Danish fans were not far behind.

Roger Arnold won 16 six-day races on the European circuit and was placed second or third 34 times. He won five madison races including the European madison championship in 1957 with Italy's Fernando Teruzzi and was ranked the number one rider on the European six-day circuit in 1951-52. Arnold's record was second to Australia's 'iron man' of six-day cycling Reg McNamara under the three older six-day systems. McNamara won 19 six-day races between 1913 and 1933 with 17 different partners and had his last race at the age of 54.

Newspapers reported on Arnold and Strom's Wembley, London six-day race success in May 1952: "Australians Alf Strom and Reg Arnold won the six-day cycling race at

Wembley by a lap from the Italians, Rigoni and Teruzzi. Strom and Arnold won after three hours hard riding when they took sprint honours in nine laps." Sporting Life's Jack Pollard said at the time that Strom and Arnold are among the best exponents of six-day racing in history.

When interviewed for Freewheeling magazine, Arnold was keen to clarify one aspect of six-day racing during the 1947 to 1963 era – the neutralisation period. "In Goullet and McNamara's time there was no rest or neutralization period," Arnold said. "For 24 hours per day, the race was open for teams to take laps on opponents. The 1946 to 1954 period was the six-hour neutralisation period. The riders were forced to take a three-hour break between 6am and 12." Under this system, the cyclists rode for 21 hours out of 24 and took time off for breakfast.

A 1954 a rule change introduced neutralization from 3am to 12. Cyclists could rest for four and a half hours each during the shared nine-hour break, with one rider on the track at all times. In 1958 the six-day became a 15-hour event when another rule change saw both riders forced to rest for nine hours each.

Today the six-day race runs from 1pm to 1am with cyclists on the track from 6 to 9 hours a day. The main action is from 7pm with sessions of sprints, fast chases and madisons. Arnold saw the race tempo increase, from 48kph in 1947 to 53kph in 1953, with speeds of 55kph common in the 1980s. It's now easier to win six-day races and harder to compare today's champions with Arnold and Strom. Arnold said that Danny Clark was the world's best track cyclist riding in Europe in the 1970s and 1980s.

Arnold's most memorable win was the 33rd Berlin six-day of 1950, partnered by Alf Strom. His last six-day win was at Antwerp in 1963 with the legendary Peter Post and Willy Vannitsen in a three-man team. He said his biggest assets were his stamina and recovery powers, being good enough to win sprints then perform well in a four to five-hour jam session: "I was using 70 percent head and 30 percent legs towards the end of my career," Arnold said.

Roger Arnold arrived back in Australia in 1953. He was feted in newspapers but couldn't get invites to major track events due to old animosities between cycling bodies.

He competed successfully in road racing in 1953 winning the 95-mile grand prix at Centennial Park, Sydney; claimed a GC second (riding solo) in NSW's Tour of the West; won the Sydney to Goulburn classic and fastest time; and was fourth in the GC at the Herald Sun Tour. In 1954 he won the Tour of Echuca and Tour of Tasmania.

Back in Europe in 1955, Arnold won the Paris Six Day race teaming with Russell Mockridge and Sid Patterson. When he visited the Tour de France in 1984, Arnold was paid the highest compliment by French sports newspaper L'Equip, who invited Roger to follow a 140 kilometre stage of the Tour De France in an official car and his name was announced to spectators lining the 140km course. Arnold stopped racing in 1963 and retired when 39. In 2012, Arnold was awarded the Medal of the Order of Australia for services to cycling.

Iris Bent, the three-time women's national track championships' Champion of Champions to 1951. Photo AusCycling Victoria History Archive.

Sid Patterson won four world track championships from 1949. Photo courtesy AusCycling Victoria History Archive.

John Nicholson was the world track professional sprint champion in 1975-76. Ray Bowles photo.

The Sydney Mail, Saturday September 21,1895 profiled
Mrs E.A. (Sarah) Maddock and Mr Maddock, "who have
journeyed to Melbourne and Brisbane on bicycles".
Photo courtesy of City of Sydney News.

Australia's women cyclists started riding the new safety bicycle in the 1890s and switched from wearing long dresses to the more comfortable and safer 'Rational Dress' of bloomers or knickerbockers that did not hinder movement. The 'Rational Dress' started in London in 1881 and caused a scandal in London, New York, Melbourne, Sydney and Christchurch. Newspaper articles appeared showing women wearing the new 'rational' dress and they were accused of being immoral or scandalous.

It was common for women to ride with a male 'chaperone', a cycling club, or a church or community group. For many Australian women, the safety bicycle allowed them more freedom and became a symbol of emancipation and women 'cyclistes' were not uncommon on the streets of cities and towns, while churches questioned the morality of Sunday cycling.

In the 1890s, women 'scorchers' (speeding cyclists), were being apprehended by the bicycle police for riding at 12 to 15 miles an hour.

The advent of the little 'safety' bicycle from the early 1890s with its diamond frame, chain-driven rear wheels and pneumatic tyres led to a bicycle participation boom. The recreational cycling craze took off when bicycle prices fell to 10-12 pounds by 1896 and bicycle use was taken up by women of all social classes.

As prices came down, more women took up cycling for leisure, transport and for long-distance cycling, while the bicycle rapidly gained acceptance as a vehicle for social enjoyment and for mass transport in cities and towns.

On November 1, 1868, the first recorded women's race took place in France at Parc Bordelais in Bordeaux, involving four women riding velocipedes. Le Monde Illustre ran a brief report on the race won by Mademoiselle Julie who had used "superhuman effort" to beat Mme Louise, who led from the start, with Mme Louisa finishing in third place with Mme Amélie fourth.

In Australia in 1896, the Beazley sisters of Sydney rode 180 miles (280.682 kilometres) in a day to set a new Australian record, riding in the new "rational dress" described as "natty knickers". This was acclaimed as a victory for the rational dress against riding in skirts.

The first bicycle races for women in Australia were believed to have been held over two miles in February 1888 at the former Ashfield Recreation Grounds in Sydney. Women rode the high wheelers and the two-mile champion's race was won by Dot Morrell, following three days of racing over one, two and three-mile handicaps; a half-mile handicap race; and a half-hour tournament.

Cycling for women's sport and recreation became popular in Australia from the 1890s and was at the height of popularity in the 1930s. The first women long-distance cyclists appeared and setting classic road race and long-distance records by women increased.

Women formed women's cubs within men's clubs in the 1930s and the Victorian Women's Amateur Cycling Association formed in 1936.

The long-distance women cycling pioneers captured the public's imagination. According to historical researcher

Dr Michelle Bootcov in the International Journal of the History of Sport (2019), the female endurance cyclists were instrumental in wresting control of the sport from male administrators and epitomized athletic femininity.

Among the notable early cycling pioneers, long-distance cyclists and record holders of the 1890-1940 era were Sarah Maddock, Doreen Middleton, Irene Pyle, Edna Sayers, Joyce Barry, Valda Unthank, Billie Samuel, Iris Dixon (Bent), and Margaret McLachlan.

E.A. (Sarah) Maddock

The National Pioneer Women's Hall of Fame in Alice Springs said that Sarah Maddock (nee Porter), also known as Mrs E.A. Maddock, was the first Australian woman to achieve a long-distance cycle ride from Sydney to Bega in 1893, and was the first woman to ride a safety bicycle from Sydney to Melbourne in 1894 (924km in nine days).

Sarah was born near Eden, New South Wales on October 29, 1860. Known by her married name of Mrs E.A. Maddock, Sarah Maddock was Australia's premier long-distance cycliste and in the 1890s and was also the first woman to ride a bicycle from Sydney to Brisbane (2575km), averaging 129km a day.

Mrs Maddock took up cycling in 1893, presumably after moving to Sydney. Accompanied by her husband, she achieved many cycling firsts in Australia, including rides along the NSW south coast, from Sydney to Melbourne at the age of 34, and a Sydney-Brisbane return ride.

"A LADY BICYCLIST. 600 MILES ON A SAFETY,"

The Advertiser newspaper, Adelaide said on October 3, 1894. The newspaper posted "an interesting account of the bicycle ride of Mr. and Mrs. Maddock from Sydney to Melbourne", who rode 574 miles in nine days.

The Maryborough Chronicle said on 11 October 1894: "Mr Maddock was a fresh as paint when he arrived, and his wife seemed none the worst for the fast ride. She was dressed in a neat navy serge costume, and each carried a complete change of clothing on their handlebars."

In his book, The Bicycle and the Bush, Jim Fitzpatrick said that Sarah Maddock was prominent in the Sydney social scene and in 1897 formed the Stanmore Lady Wheelers club.

"For some time, she wrote the 'Ladies' Page of the N.S.W Cycling Gazette, commenting upon the social and cycling scene. She was inclined to take a stand for 'dignified' cycling and did not encourage the use of 'rational' dress or 'bloomers', as they are now known."

In April 1898, Mrs E. A Maddock, the club captain, led the Stanmore Lady Wheelers club's new season opening ride from Stanmore to Sandringham.

Another report in the Evening News, Sydney on 25 November 1985 said that the honorary secretary and treasurer Miss Etta Todd and the captain Mrs E.A. Maddock of the Sydney Ladies Bicycle Club had organised two cycling outings a week.

"Last Saturday, sixteen members of the club escorted by about 40 gentlemen riders rode to Parramatta and were met at Ryde by a strong contingent of riders from the

Parramatta Cyclists Touring Club, who joined in and escorted the party into town. A pleasant social evening was subsequently spent at the Woolpack Hotel," the newspaper report said.

Sarah Maddock had inspired many women to cycle in Victoria and New South Wales and helped found several women's cycling clubs. After 1914, Sarah separated from her husband and concentrated on golf, embroidery, wood carving and her family. In 1955 she passed away at Double Bay, Sydney.

Melbourne's first women's cycling club

Sarah Maddock's long-distance ride to Melbourne in October 1894 helped to inspire the formation of Melbourne's first women's cycling club.

The Age newspaper reported February 15, 1895 that a Ladies' Bicycle Club had been formed in the state of Victoria: "The Austral Wheeling Club is the name chosen for a recently formed cycling club for ladies.

"The committee and office bearers were elected last night. The president, who corresponds to the captain of wheelmen's societies is Mrs. Brentnall, the 'pioneer' lady cyclist of Victoria; the vice-president, Miss Benzley, of Sunbury, who, it is stated, rides the 25 miles' distance from there to Melbourne in less than two hours.

"The committee are Mrs. Alex Muirhead (whose husband is well known as chairman of the Melbourne Bicycle Club); Mrs. Schwaeback, the wife of one of the founders of the League of Victorian Wheelmen; and Mrs.

Martin Knight, of the Warrawee Club. The secretary-treasurer is Mrs. Donald Macdonald, founder of the club, and honorary secretary of the Austral Salon.

"The ladies intend to make an imposing event of the first club run on 9th March, and will start from Parliament-place, Eastern Hill, to be afterwards their regular rendezvous for fortnightly runs.

"Following the example of the Austral Salon, gentleman are admitted as associates, but have no voice in the government of affairs, it is pointed out with cutting sarcasm, resembling the women of Victoria in taxation without the power of voting.

"About 12 ladies have joined the club. They will not wear rational dress, considering Melbourne not yet advanced enough for the innovation set by the ladies who recently astonished Healesville with the Rational Dress picnic. Any information of the club will be given by the secretary-treasurer, Queen's-walk, Swanston-street."

Doreen Middleton

By the 1930s, more woman cyclists were setting classic road race and long-distance records. Victoria's Doreen Middleton (born 11/03/1912) rode from Melbourne to Adelaide in 1931 covering 607 miles (976.9 km) in four days and 21 hours, then took only three days, 23 hours and 56 minutes to complete the return journey.

The National Pioneer Women's Hall of Fame said that: "Doreen Middleton aged 19 years, rode her bicycle from Melbourne to Adelaide (607 miles) in 4 days, 21 hours.

"The final 171 miles was over the formidable Coorong Desert and on to Adelaide. Two weeks later, she rode back to Melbourne in 3 days, 23 hours, 56 minutes and became the first person to ride both directions, a record which stands today."

However, another record attempt was ended by injury and bad weather. Launceston's The Examiner, December 5, 1931, said that Miss Doreen Middleton, the Victorian lady cyclist, left the Hobart post office in the early hours of last Saturday aiming to lower the existing women's unassisted record between Hobart and Launceston, which stands to the credit of Miss Madge Stewart, of Hobart.

"Nearing Oatlands the cyclist lost control of her machine and received a bad fall. When nearing Perth, Middleton was forced to retire." She encountered a severe head wind practically the whole journey and was also troubled with the cramp, the newspaper added.

Billie Samuel

Billie Samuel was perhaps the lightest woman cycling champion of this era. She made two attempts to break the women's long-distance cycling records from Melbourne to Sydney in June 1934 and from Sydney to Melbourne in July 1934. Born in Sydney, she was either 23 or 27 at the time (born 1911 or 1907), weighed six stone and seven pounds (41.5 kilograms) and was four foot and 11 inches tall. Incorrectly reported as the first woman to cycle between Melbourne and Sydney, she was trained by former 1920s-30s Australian road cycling champion and a Tour de

France cyclist, Ossie Nicholson. Samuel, a waitress, learned to ride a bicycle four months earlier. Poor weather and riding conditions hampered her attempt on Elsa Barbour's time riding in the Melbourne-Sydney direction. She tried again on her return journey.

The Sydney Morning Herald of July 5, 1934 said: "Miss Billie Samuel started her attack on the women's record from Sydney to Melbourne, held by Miss Elsa Barbour, at 10 o'clock yesterday morning. Her schedule will bring her to the Melbourne G.P.O. at 2 p.m., Saturday in 3 days 7 hours, about three hours faster than the present record."

She left Martin Place, Sydney on Wednesday, July 4 at 10.00am, riding a Malvern Star bicycle. With mostly favourable conditions, Samuel reached Melbourne in three days, one hour and 20 minutes, beating Elsa Barbour's record by a little over six hours.

Joyce Barry

In the 1930s, Joyce Barry of New South Wales set many long-distance road records including Sydney-Melbourne and Orange-Sydney, and the seven-day cycling record over a 35-mile circular course in Sydney. She also held the Australian quarter mile (402.34 metres) flying start track record of 33.4 seconds.

In September 1937, aged 18 years, she bettered Billie Samuel's 1934 Sydney-Melbourne record by nearly a whole day. Joyce Barry often rode with Hubert Opperman for her training and was sponsored by Malvern Star bicycles, when Opperman was Malvern Star's star rider.

In May 1938, Joyce Barry, then known as the New South Wales cycling champion, in an unassisted record attempt, broke the record for Launceston to Hobart and return. The Examiner newspaper reported that at times it appeared to officials that if Miss Barry lowered the record it would be by only a few minutes, but with an epic performance over the concluding 70 miles of the 240 miles journey, the girl cyclist regained lost vitality, and increased her speeds from 10 miles to 19 miles an hour.

"She arrived at the Launceston Post Office, where a big crowd awaited her, a little after 7.31 p.m., and broke the existing record by 2hrs, 53mins, 5secs. The previous record was held by Mrs. M. Price, of Hobart, her time being 20hrs, 25min, 35secs," the newspaper said.

Valda Unthank

Valda Unthank was a champion cyclist in Victoria during the 1930s and set many of new records on the road, and several tandem cycling records with Peggy Saker as her partner. "She broke numerous records for speed, distance and time spent riding, becoming a household name in the process," the State Library of Victoria said.

"In October 1938, Valda broke records for riding from Adelaide to Melbourne, travelling just over 760km in 33 hours and 39 minutes. She spent just 30 minutes resting during the ride and she didn't sleep." Later that year, Valda broke the record for time to ride from Launceston to Burnie (in Tasmania) and back. Her first attempt was marred by a crash and she was taken to hospital to recover.

Eleven days later, Valda was back on the bike and breaking records despite a shoulder injury. She set a new record for Launceston and Burnie and back and along the way, broke Joyce Barry's record for distance travelled in 12 hours, raising it to 319.3km.

"In 1939, Valda spent seven days and seven nights cycling between Melbourne and Mordialloc to set the record for distance travelled over a week. She spent a total of 15 hours resting for the entire trip," the State Library of Victoria said. She covered 2,309.4 kilometres during the week, which was a new record.

In early July 1940, Valda Unthank announced that after six years of cycling competition, she would retire from any form of competitive cycling for the duration of the war, but she would continue her activities of Red Cross and war work generally.

Edna Sayers

Edna Sayers held three NSW women's individual unpaced records for long distance rides in 1936 and was reputed to have achieved better times than many men in the Goulburn-Sydney race. In those days before women's cycling was an established sport, Edna lived, trained and rode with the Earlwood Cycling Club, probably on an unofficial basis as she was not allowed to compete against the men. She also rode at Henson Park, Marrickville.

Sayers was born in 1912, the eldest of six children of Alfred George and Elizabeth Mary Sayers. In October 1927 when Edna was aged 15, her mother died, and Edna took on responsibility for her siblings. Her father Alfred George Sayers was a cyclist. Sayers took up cycling and in 1932 aged 20, she was the first woman to win a race at the Canterbury velodrome. At this time, women cyclists could not compete in races such as the Goulburn to Sydney.

However, the Goulburn to Sydney race was held on public roads. Then in 1933, Edna decided to tackle the Goulburn to Sydney (Enfield) course on the same day as the professional men competed in the classic road race. Sayers started half an hour prior to the male professionals and lowered Lillian Thorpe's 1932 record to 7 hours, 41 minutes, 5 seconds.

The Truth newspaper, September 17, 1933 said: "SHE'S the fastest girl in town. Yes, at 20 years of age Edna Sayers is swift … too swift for most men. YESTERDAY she crowned a meteoric athletic and cycling career by cycling for 129 miles from Goulburn to Sydney in world's record time for a woman amateur.

"TRAILED by a detachment of exhausted male riders, Edna came to the finishing line smiling. After pedalling for 7hrs. 41mins & 5secs, she leapt from her machine and asked for a comb. 'Oh dear, my hair's awful,' she said. 'I washed it yesterday'."

Edna Sayers was a still a young woman when she broke the Goulburn to Sydney women's road record, racing on the same day as the professional men did in the road race on Saturday September 21, 1935, when the race had amateur and professional versions.

The Sydney Morning Herald reported on 23 September

1935 on the Goulburn to Sydney, usually a 132-mile race, that: "A girl cyclist, Miss Edna Sayers, also shared in the record-breaking feats on the course on Saturday, riding from the Goulburn Post-office to the Broadway, Enfield, officially timed, in 6 hours, 11 minutes, 30 seconds.

"She did not follow the complete course used by the racing men but came through the Cowpastures road from Narellan to Liverpool, effecting a reduction of perhaps a mile or so in the distance, and lowering her own record between the two points by more than an hour."

In 1936, Edna Sayers set three road race or distance records. Riding from Bathurst to Sydney over 134.5 miles (216.456km), she set the women's individual unpaced record of 8hrs, 38mins, 50.5secs. During her November 1936 record-breaking Canberra to Sydney ride over 197 miles (317.040km), her time was 11hrs, 8secs.

Riding in the 1936 Goulburn-Sydney race of 138 miles (222.1km), Sayers was reported to have set a new record of 7 hrs, 43mins, 8secs. She started 30 minutes before the men (professionals started first that year) so they would have passed her. At the time, the country roads were tarred with a hump in the middle, and the sides often got rough. But her road records still stood in 1981.

Edna Sayers moved to Budgewoi on the Central Coast of New South Wales in the 1970s where she established a women's cycling club and took cyclists out touring. A popular cycleway and pedestrian bridge over Saltwater Creek, Long Jetty, 18 kilometres south of Budgewoi, was named after Sayers in 1982. She died in 1996.

The City of Canterbury in Sydney unveiled a plaque on 20 September 2007 in honour of Edna Sayers (by Cr Robert Furolo, Mayor of the City of Canterbury). The plaque reads: Edna Sayers (1912-1986).

Irene Pyle

Another leading long-distance cyclist and record holder was Wangaratta girl cyclist Irene Pyle, who raced on the Wangaratta track in 1936 in match races against highly rated track cyclists like Beryl Matthews. Irene, known later by her married name of Irene Plowman, was reported to have broken the women's 50-mile road cycling record for a straight 50 miles course in August 1935.

Irene Pyle was described as a diminutive cyclist who stood a little more than five foot and no more than 8 stone in weight.

According to a report in Melbourne's The Argus newspaper on November 2, 1938: "GREAT RIDE BY GIRL CYCLIST SYDNEY TO MELBOURNE. Those who followed Irene Pyle, a Wangaratta girl cyclist, who left Sydney at 11.16 a.m. on Thursday and reached Melbourne on Saturday, commended her doggedness."

According to her trainer, Mr H. Arnall, Miss Pyle's time was 40hrs, 23mins which, he said, broke by 10hrs, 24mins the record made by Joyce Barry last year.

Mr Arnall said that for the first 50 miles Miss Pyle was one minute ahead of H. Opperman's record, although she had to climb the Razorback Mountain. At Tarcutta, 297 miles out, she was seven minutes ahead of Oppy's time.

The Sporting Globe reported on November 2, 1938 on Pyle's "Amazing Ride from Sydney", that was only 41 minutes behind Hubert Opperman's time: "Making a special appearance at the Globe's Charity Carnival at the Showgrounds on Saturday night, Miss Pyle received a great reception from nearly 40,000 onlookers as she did a tour of the track. Miss Pyle rode from Albury to Melbourne 1.5 hours faster than the great wheelman. Her courage and determination equalled that of Valda Unthank, who rode from Adelaide to Melbourne the previous week in the new record time, demonstrating the remarkable endurance of women cyclists."

Iris Bent

In May 1950, Australian Cyclist magazine named Iris Bent, "Australian champion of champions" and featured her on its front cover.

From Ballarat, Victoria, she was crowned the Champion-of-Champions three times at the national track championships, including sweeping the 1951 Australian Women's Professional titles in Bundaberg, Queensland for the third consecutive year, according to Australian Cyclist in February 1951, winning all five track titles.

In 1952 she won the national all-round track championship of Australia at Mt Isa, Queensland, after the Australian championships were reinstated. Described as Australia's fastest-ever cyclist, she was the daughter of Melbourne road cyclist George Bent and started track racing in 1945 at the age of 14.

Iris Bent, also know under her married name of Iris Dixon, won 25 Victorian cycling titles during her career. Beginning her career in 1945, the Victorian won 16 Australian titles on the road and track.

Cycling researcher and historian Monique Hanley, interviewing Dixon for Cyclingtips in 2016, said Sir Hubert Opperman described Dixon's performances "as the most outstanding showing by a Victorian woman cyclist in history". At age 85, Dixon was still riding three times a week with the 'Golden Oldies' at the Preston Cycling Club in Melbourne. She was inducted into the Cycling Australia Hall of Fame in 2016.

Margaret McLachlan

Margaret Miller, (later Margaret McLachlan), came from Sydney and took up competitive cycling as a 15-year-old and raced successfully on the track for six and a half years in the 1960s against men at the Dulwich Hill Cycling Club.

When 16, she caused a sensation by winning the club's annual Ron Jacobs' Memorial track event. Her name was recorded on the trophy for the 1962 race and she was the first woman to win the race. In 1966 the N.S.W. Amateur Cycling Union had restricted her to racing in club events.

The ACU then decided not to grant competitive membership to any women and cancelled Margaret's racing license under a clause denying a license to anyone it considers unsuitable.

According to the Women's Weekly magazine May 1967, Margaret, a cosmetician from Coogee was 21 and Mrs.

John McLachlan. Her fellow male members of the Dulwich Hill Bicycle Club disagreed with the Cycling Union's decision and protested on her behalf.

Margaret was introduced to cycling by her husband, John. John built Margaret a bike and they trained together. Margaret married John in 1965 and in the following season, won the Dulwich Hill club's first 26-mile handicap race. When she joined the men on their Sunday morning training rides to Picton and back (130 miles) and pedalled over Razorback Mountain to Picton, she was back in Sydney with the men by lunchtime.

McLachlan, concerned about the lack of public interest in cycling, decided to attempt to break Joyce Barry's Sydney to Melbourne 40 hours unofficial distance record.

She undertook a tough training program of riding 40 miles before work each morning and another 20 miles to and from work each day, 30 to 40 miles of racing on Saturdays and 100 to 130-mile road rides on Sunday.

McLachlan set off from the Sydney G.P.O. at 11.45am on June 16, 1966 followed by husband John and a timekeeper from the Dulwich Hill club in a car with bicycle spares and food. She arrived at the Melbourne G.P.O. at 10.12 p.m. June 18, in a time of 36 hours, 33 minutes, setting a new record for the distance for men and women. In 1968 she rode from Sydney to Newcastle in a new distance record time of 6 hours, 14.5 minutes.

From the 1980s-1990s to 2020, supported by strong national competition, Australian road cyclists led by Liz Hepple, Anna Wilson and Kathy Watt through to Sara Carrigan, Oenone Wood, Rochelle Gilmore, Chloe Hosking and Amanda Spratt produced international performances that equalled or bettered those of the top elite women cyclists from major cycling countries.

In the UCI women's elite road rankings from 2012-2020 Australia's women ranked as the fifth best road cycling nation edging towards fourth, amongst strong competition from Dutch, Italian, USA and UK cyclists. In the UCI women's road and WorldTour rankings since 2009, Gilmore, Hosking and Spratt were ranked in the top 10-20 cyclists three times. Gilmore ranked eighth in 2009, while Spratt ranked fourth in 2018 and Sarah Roy ranked 12th in 2020. The rise of our women road champions was helped by their performances at the Olympic and Commonwealth Games, UCI world championships, women's Tour De France, the Giro Rosa and Europe's classic road races, and the formation of Orica-AIS and Mitchelton-Scott women's world teams.

In 1958 the first official UCI road world championship for women was held at Reims, France when women raced over a much shorter distance than the men. The length of the women's race increased to 79km, 100km, and to 138.8km at Varese, Italy in 2008. In 1988, 16 women's road cycling teams first competed in UCI road cycling events. In 1997 Liz Tadich with silver was Australia's first women's cyclist to win a UCI road cycling medal.

Australia did not send women road cyclists to the 1984 Los Angeles Olympics and they first competed in the Olympic road race at Seoul in 1988, when Elizabeth Hepple, Donna Gould and Kathleen Shannon finished two minutes behind The Netherlands' winner, Monique Knol.

The women's Herald Sun Tour

The Herald Sun Tour has been a men's stage race since 1952. In 2018 launched was a two-stage race for women, the Lexus of Blackburn Women's Herald Sun Tour. The first stage is held over a mostly flat 94-kilometre course, while the 75 kilometre second and final stage includes a category 1 climb to Falls Creek (1700m). Its overall GC winners in the Tour's first three years came from the Mitchelton-Scott team, Brodie Chapman winning in 2018, and Lucy Kennedy in 2019 and 2020.

Lucy Kennedy (Mitchelton-Scott) won consecutive Herald Sun Tour titles on February 6, 2020 when she crossed the finish line in third place on the second and final stage at Falls Creek. However, the descent that was to open the stage was cut from the race due to the threat of inclement weather.

Only seven riders were in contention with four kilometres to go on the final climb to Falls Creek. But in the final 400 hundred metres as Kennedy attacked, she, together with Ella Harris (New Zealand national team) and Sarah Gigante (Tibco) fought for the stage win, while Arlenis Sierra (Astana) trailed. Harris fought back to win the stage from Gigante (same time) and Kennedy on three seconds in third place. Jamie Gunning (Specialized Women) was 11 seconds back in fourth place. But Kennedy claimed the overall GC win, with Jamie Gunning second in the GC, Arlenis Sierra third, Harris fourth and Gigante fifth.

In 2015 the Grafton to Inverell road race classic added a women's road race called the Grafton to Inverell des Femmes women's race. In 2017 a new women's course record was set by Tasmania's Holly Ransom (7:05:17).

The women's Tour Down Under

In 2012, the Adelaide and South Australia-based Tour Down Under hosted a series of women's street criterium races, the first time that female cyclists participated in the event. The annual women's race over four stages was established as part of the National Road Series in 2015, and in 2016 was granted UCI 2.2 status.

Now called the Santos Women's Tour Down Under, the race was upgraded to UCI 2.1 status for the 2018 event when elite international women's teams started their road season in Adelaide. In 2019, fifteen women's teams and ninety riders lined up for the event. In 2020 the Women's TDU was given the prestigious UCI ProSeries status.

Australian women have featured strongly in the overall winner's general classification and other classification results at the Women's Tour Down Under. In 2016, the GC winner was Katrin Garfoot, the Sprint and Young Rider winner Lauretta Hanson; in 2017, GC winner Amanda Spratt, Sprint winner Chloe Hosking; in 2018, GC winner

Amanda Spratt, Sprint winner Katrin Garfoot; in 2019, GC winner Amanda Spratt, Sprint winner Sarah Roy, and Young Rider winner Jamie Gunning.

Women's cycling teams in the winning team classification were Orica-AIS in 2016; Orica-Scott in 2017; and Mitchelton-Scott in 2018-19.

In 2020, three-time overall GC winner Amanda Spratt lost her Tour Down Under crown for the first time in four years on the final criterium race held over 25 laps of a 1.7 kilometre circuit on the streets of central Adelaide. USA national champion Ruth Winder (Trek-Segafredo) went into the final stage with a seven second advantage and did enough to win the overall Tour.

Deakin University Women's Road Race

The Deakin University Elite Women's Road Race is a one-day race held late January/early February each year. It follows a similar course to the Cadel Evans men's road race, running from Geelong and along the Great Ocean Road, then returning to Geelong.

In 2020, the Deakin University Women's Road Race was given UCI Women's WorldTour status and is the first women's road race on the UCI cycling calendar.

The Deakin University (Cadel Evans) Women's Road Race started in 2015 and was won by Australia's Rachel Neylan. Other early race winners were in 2016, Amanda Spratt (Orica-GreenEdge); in 2017, Annamiek Van Vleuten of the Netherlands (Orica-Scott); and in 2018, Chloe Hosking (Ale-Cipollini).

In 2019, Lucy Kennedy and Amanda Spratt (Mitchelton-Scott) claimed second and third places 19 seconds adrift of the winner Arlenis Sienna (Astana), who won the race in three hours, 7 minutes and 10 seconds.

The 2020 Deakin University road race over 121.5 kilometres featured a star-studded field of international cyclists. It was a held in rain-soaked, windy and difficult conditions when a race helicopter had to be grounded. An earlier breakaway was reeled in by the peleton.

At about 20km to go there was a crash coming down the Challambra Crescent climb on the final circuit at Geelong, with over a dozen cyclists crashing heavily and eight cyclists had to be taken to hospital.

However, 22-year-old German cyclist Liane Lippert (Team Sunweb) attacked at nine minutes and six minutes to go, making a winning break from a chasing group of three to win the race by 15 seconds at the Geelong finish.

The 2019 champion Arlenis Sierra (Astana) sprinted for second in front of Amanda Spratt (Mitchelton-Scott) in third place, while Chloe Hosking (Rally) was the next best placed Australian in sixth place.   The Swisse Queen of the Mountain jersey was won by Brodie Chapman (FDJ Nouvelle – Aquitaine Futuroscope).

Campaign for longer 'Tour de France Feminin'

The three European grand tours of the Tour de France, the Giro d'Italia and the Vuelta a Espana are men's events. Women's road cycling has no similar three-week races, while Italy's Giro d'Italia (Rosa), which runs over nine to ten stages, now the only grand tour road race for women.

In 1955, the first women's 'Tour de France', the Grand Boucle Feminine Internationale began, followed by the Le Tour Cycliste Feminine in 1984 with 18 stages over 1.066km, which ended in 2009 as a 4-day stage race. In 2014, a one-day race La Course by the Tour de France was launched and usually covers one of the same stages used by the men's grand tour.

One of the issues in international women's professional road cycling in recent years is the lack of a longer women's Tour de France stage race to replace the existing one-day La Course by the Tour de France. While the lack of a proper stage race was blamed on an absence of stable financial support and robust media coverage, and organisational issues, the push for a stage tour gained momentum in Europe, North America and Australia.

Among those calling for a longer women's Tour de France were some of the biggest names in cycling, such as Marianne Vos, Lizzie Deignan, Emma Pooley, Judith Arndt, along with former American triathlete and road cyclist Kathryn Bertine, who rode in La Course by the Tour de France in 2016.

Australia's Tracey Gaudry has the task of growing women's cycling worldwide as president of the Women's Commission for the Union Cycliste Internationale (UCI), cycling's world governing body. Ms Gaudry told ABC News in 2019 that the UCI would be very keen to see a staged race in France and is supporting all initiatives towards creating a major tour. She competed in the 1999

Tour de Feminin, two Olympic Games (1996, 2000), the 1998 Commonwealth Games and major road races.

The UCI said in 2019 that new initiatives it has introduced include more women involved in the sport's administration, increased media coverage of events and a new Commission devoted entirely to women's cycling.

In July 2020, Tour owners the Amaury Sport Organisation were reported to be looking to launch a new women's race with August the likely date.

Tour de France director Christian Prudhomme told Le Telegramme newspaper in late April 2020, "we are seriously working on a women's stage race project."

Battle of North, a women's Tour de France?

A new UCI Women's World Tour road race proposed for August 2021 is the 10-stage Battle of North, which is organized by the Ladies Tour of Norway, the Vargarda Sweden and the Danish Cycling Union. In 2020 it was promoted as the "Women's Tour De France".

The Battle of North, set to be raced in Denmark, Sweden and Norway over 11 days, was expected to feature all the best women's cyclists, offer live TV coverage and promote the three countries as a visitor destination.

Other issues outlined by cycling media are lack of sponsorship for women's (and men's) cycling teams, low or no wages for women pro cyclists and less prizemoney for women's road races. In 2017, Australian pro cyclist Gracie Elvin joined with three other cyclists to form The Cyclist's Alliance. The Alliance pointed out that almost half the women's UCI peleton raced for less than 5,000 euro a year, 17.5 percent were not paid, while 85 percent did not have a lawyer or agent check their contract.

A February 2016 survey of over 400 UCI registered women professionals found that 52 percent of the women's peloton work a second job to make financial ends meet; 51.6 percent paid back parts of their salaries to teams for costs, equipment, travel, and for trainers.

However, in January 2020 the UCI introduced a new team's structure for women's UCI WorldTeams and Women's Continental teams. UCI WorldTeams would receive a minimum salary (euros) of 15,000 in 2020, 20,000 in 2021, 27,500 in 2022 and parity with the men from 2023.

Former Australian track and road cycling champion Kate Bates said in 2020 that budget cuts to road cycling had hit women cyclists the most and could impact on their success, while she advocated for more equality for women in road cycling sport.

Australians on podiums at 'Tours de France'

After 2009-2010, the previous versions of the Tour de France Feminin stage races for women closed down, while the 10-stage Tour de l'Aude Cycliste Feminin was the last to close. However, the nine-stage Route de France Feminine was conducted from 2006 to 2016. Australia's only cyclist on the podium was former triathlete and Orica-AIS cyclist Carlee Taylor, who was third in 2012.

In 1988 Liz Hepple made cycling history as the first

Australian woman to be presented with a GC medal at the 900km La Tour de France Feminin (Women's Tour de France) stage race. Hepple claimed a GC third place when French road racing legend Jeannie Longo won the race and Italian legend Maria Canins was second.

The La Course by the Tour de France UCI WorldTour race launched in 2014 as a one-day race. Chloe Hosking won the race in 2016 and is the only Australian winner. On July 19, 2019, the La Course road race was held at Pau over a 121km circuit on the same course that the men rode in the earlier Tour De France individual time trial.

Mitchelton-Scott's Amanda Spratt attacked on the last lap of the hilly circuit with a solo breakaway and going into Pau led by 30 seconds. But Spratt was caught by the chasing bunch led by eventual winner Marianne Vos near the end of the last hill, a 70 metre, 17-degree steep ramp before a flat finish. Vos won from Canada's Lea Kirchmann and Denmark's Cecillie Uttrup Ludwig.

The Giro d'Italia (Rosa) grand tour

Established in 1988, Italy's 10-stage Giro d'Italia Donne (or Giro Rosa) is the only annual women's grand tour and major stage race on the women's elite cycling calendar.

In 2016 the grand tour became part of the new UCI Women's WorldTour. Earlier in 2013, the Giro Donne was rebranded to the Giro Rosa. The first edition of the Giro d'Italia Femminile in 1988 was won by Italian cycling legend Maria Canins, when Australia's Liz Hepple claimed second place in the general classification.

The Giro Rosa usually runs over 9-10 stages in Italy in early July. In 2013 the race was shortened to eight days, then returned to a 10-day tour.

At the 2019, 10-stage, 906-kilometre Giro Rosa tour held in Italy during July, Australia's Lucy Kennedy finished second on Stage 3 when overtaken on the line, while Amanda Spratt claimed five top 10 finishes during the tour and finished third in the general classification.

When Amanda Spratt claimed a GC third place in 2018, she was the only Australian cyclist to finish on the podium of the Giro Rosa since Kathy Watt took third place in 1994 and second place in 1990.

In late September 2020, the Giro d'Italia Rosa grand tour was dropped from the Women's WorldTour for 2021. The UCI revealed that the Giro d'Italia Rosa was downgraded to a 2 Pro-level status race. No official statement was provided by the UCI at the time but cycling media said a lack of live TV coverage was one issue.

Women's National Road Championships

One of the most important women's road events each year is the Cycling Australia (AusCycling) national road race championships (the RoadNats) held annually in January. In 1978 the first women's (amateur) national road championship was won by Linda Meadows, who also won in 1979 over a 25 kilometre course. The race was held around Australia and the distance increased to 100km in 1995, before it found a home in 2007 at the 102-kilometre Buninyong course at Ballarat in Victoria.

In 1991 the elite national women's individual road time trial debuted over a 29.3 kilometre course at Mt Buninyong and the women's road criterium started in 1994. Later, under 23 and under 19 women were added to the RoadNats. The winners of each category are awarded the green and gold Australian champion's jersey.

Featured in this chapter are Australia's elite women road cyclists who performed well internationally at the Olympic and Commonwealth Games, UCI road world championships and major international one day road classics, road races and grand tours.

Carla Ryan

Carla Ryan (born 1985) took up cycling in 2005 and won two national road time trial championships. Ryan won the Canterbury New Zealand Le Race road race in 2007. Ryan had success in Europe from 2008-12, mainly riding for Garmin-Cervello and won several race stages. She claimed three GC second place finishes at the Giro del Trentino Alto Adige in 2009 and 2010, and at the Tour de Feminin in the Czech Republic in 2012.

Kathleen Shannon

Kathleen Shannon (born 1964) won four elite women's national road championships in 1985-86 and in 1990-91 and rode professionally in France in 1987. Shannon represented Australia at the 1988 Seoul Olympic Games in the road race. In 1990, Shannon won the bronze medal in the Commonwealth Games road race at Auckland.

In 1992, Shannon finished a credible seventh in the Olympics road race at Barcelona, won by Kathy Watt.

Katie Mactier

Katie Mactier (born 1975), better known as a top track cyclist of the 2000s decade (see track cycling), won national road championships in 2001 and 2007.

Mactier rode for Australian and European professional teams from 2001 and won the Valedengo-Biella and Trofeo Guareschi road races in Italy, the USA's Nature Valley Grand Prix and Fitchburn Longsjo Classic. In 2006, she won Victoria's Jayco Bay Cycling Classic.

Elizabeth Tadich

Elizabeth Tadich (born 1976) came from Shepparton, Victoria. She took up track cycling at 13 and was selected for the Victorian track cycling team at 16. Tadich won the elite national road championship in 1995. Competing in Europe in the mid-1990s she was third in Germany's Schussenried road race and rode with the AIS team in the Giro d'Italia tour and Tour de France Feminin. Tadich won the Goulburn Tour and posted third places in the Canberra Tour and the 100km World Cup race at Sydney.

In 1997 when Tadich won the silver medal in a photo finish at the elite UCI road world cycling championships at San Sebastian, Spain, she made history becoming the first Australian woman to win a medal at the road worlds. She competed in road events at the 1998 and 2002 Commonwealth Games.

Alison Wright

Alison Wright (born 1980) was a road and track cyclist who rode for the Canberra Cycling Club. She won bronze at the 2002 Manchester Commonwealth Games in the 3000m individual pursuit. Competing at the national road championships, Wright won silver medals in the road race and the time trial between 1999 and 2001.

Wright represented Australia at the UCI road world championships three times, finishing fifth in 2002. Top results in European road classics and races include a win in the G.P. Citta di Castensao, third in the Trofeo Alfredo Binda (2003), second place in the Trophee d'Or Feminin and third in the Sparkassen Giro Bochum (2004).

Liz Hepple

Elizabeth (Liz) Hepple (born 1959) from Queensland was a champion road cyclist and triathlete who took up cycling at the age of 23. Hepple represented Australia internationally in events such as the La Tour de France Feminin, the women's road race at the 1988 Seoul Olympics, and in the triathlon at the 1990 Commonwealth Games held in Auckland.

Hepple didn't have a specialist cycling coach but rode with the (mostly male) riders in her club, the University of Queensland CC. "They would encourage me and push me to train hard with them. I raced in Queensland men's open A and B combined road races, and through this, got fit enough to be competitive in international women's races," she said. "My main sources of inspiration were other cyclists like Jeannie Longo (France), Maria Canins (Italy), and Rebecca Twigg (USA)."

She won the first ever Noosa Triathlon in 1983. In 1986 she claimed the silver medal in the national road race championships. Described by former national coach Shayne Bannan as having the right attributes to win the women's Tour de France, Hepple rode in the Tour de France Feminin International in 1986-1988, was fifth in 1986 and claimed a GC third in 1988 as part of an Australian team of six that included Donna Rae-Szalinski.

Hepple made cycling history as the first Australian woman to win a GC medal at La Tour de France Feminin in 1988, coming third behind two road cycling legends, France's Jeannie Longo and Italy's Maria Canins and was awarded the 'king of the mountain' jersey at La Tour.

She claimed another great result in 1988 with a GC second at the 10-day Giro d'Italia Donne (Rosa). She was twice named Australian Cyclist of the Year. Hepple represented Australia as a triathlete in 1989-1991 and won the World Cup Triathlon series in 1990. She started work as an athlete personal development advisor at the Queensland Academy of Sport.

Hepple said her best 4-5 performances in international cycling in major road races were third place overall in the 1983 Tour de France Feminin; second overall in the Giro d'Italia Donne in 1988; first on Stage 5 at the Giro d'Italia Donne in 1988; 12th place in the individual road race at the 1987 World Road Cycling Championships, Austria; and fifth overall at the 1986 Tour de France Feminin.

Hepple recalled some special and memorable performances including in difficult conditions. "In 1987 I was first in stage 1 of the Tour de Bretagne. I broke away and soloed to win on a course that included some dirt farm tracks with grass growing in the centre strip. In 1986 I placed third in a stage of Tour de France Feminin with a mountain top finish at the 2413 metre Col du Granon, near Briancon. The men's race was finishing soon after, so the women's entourage left before I had finished in the 'doping control' in the caravan at the summit. The men's tour had finished, and I was sharing the waiting room with Bernard Hinault and Greg Lemond!"

On opportunities for our top women road cyclists to be signed to international or European teams compared to the 1980s, Hepple believes there are many more opportunities and support for women to race now, from state road series, National Road Series, more international races and more professional women's teams.

"However, in 2020 there are many more female cyclists of a very high standard than in the 1980's and with a much greater depth in racing, so it is much more difficult to make an Australian team," Hepple explained. "There was no opportunity to pursue cycling as a 'profession' during the 1980's, as all the travel and equipment was largely self-funded (from working full-time in the off-season). That was the main reason I retired after three years of international racing.

"On the other hand, I was fortunate enough to be able to race the Women's Tour de France three times, when it was held at the same time and used the same roads (but shorter distance) than the men's Tour de France. An experience I feel exceptionally fortunate to have lived."

Anna Wilson

Anna Wilson (born 1971) came from Melbourne and was a champion road cyclist and time triallist in the 1990s to 2001. She won the UCI World Cup points score series in road cycling in 1999 and 2001 and claimed silver medals in two road world championships, helped by her determination and powerful sprint.

Wilson was one of the dominant figures of world road cycling during this time, according to a cycling bio in the Australian Cycling Hall of Fame. At 22, Wilson was seen as a late starter in competitive cycling in 1993 after riding the Great Victorian Bike Ride.

Talking about mentors and coaches, she started training with John and Vicki Beasley very early in her racing career: "They provided great knowledge and support and guidance the whole way, and we continue to be great friends," Wilson said. "I can remember the pain of the ergo sessions that I used to do in John's shop, and the motor-pacing John set up for me down the Western Highway, which I would do before riding from Footscray to Monash University for a day's classes. It was a time when my whole career was in front of me and I was just loving racing and training and the freedom of being on the bike."

She graduated from Monash University with a Bachelor of Science in 1992 and a Bachelor of Laws (honours) in

1995 and made the Australian cycling team for the 1996 Olympic Games at Atlanta, USA.

At the national time trial championships, Wilson won gold in 1997-98 and 2001, and silver in 1996, 2000 and 2002. Wilson also won the national road race championships in 2000 and finished second in 1997.

In 1998, she won the sprint points jersey in Italy's Giro d'Italia Donne (Giro Rosa) grand tour and finished 14th overall. At the first Tour de France Feminin in 1998, Wilson won the 122km, stage 6 at Allauch France. Representing Australia at the 1998 Commonwealth Games at Kuala Lumpur, Wilson won the gold medal in the road time trial and the bronze medal in the road race.

Wilson was almost unbeatable in 1999 when she won the UCI World Cup point score championships and the UCI women's road world cup, after winning around 20 road races or race stages riding for the Saturn professional team. She was the Australian Cyclist of the Year in 1999.

Representing Australia at the 1999 UCI road world championships, she claimed two silver medals in road events riding in the individual time trial and the road race. She was ranked number one in the world in 2000.

At the Sydney Olympics in 2000, Wilson came close to the medals after finishing fourth in the individual time trial and the road race. In 2000, she was the first cyclist to break the hour record under the 'new' UCI rules covering 43.5 kilometres. She married and became Anna Millward.

Wilson won the UCI World Cup points score for the second time in 2001. She dominated the season, winning five major road races and many race stages and in April 2001 was elated after claiming second place in the Belgian road classic La Fleche Wallonne.

Wilson also won a silver medal in the individual road time trial at the 2002 Commonwealth Games. However, injury cut her stellar road cycling career short and she retired. Wilson was inducted into the Cycling Australia Hall of Fame in 2016.

Looking back at her cycling career, Wilson said that her best 3-4 performances internationally when she won major races or medals during her cycling career were: "My two silver medals at the 1999 world championships in Verona are by far my best achievements and a wonderful memory for me. Behind that I would rate my 1999 win in the World Cup as it was a tough fought battle, and as I was very much the underdog against riders such as Diana Ziluite and Hanka Kupfernagel.

"Also, a key moment was my gold medal in the individual time trial at the Kuala Lumpur Commonwealth Games, coming after my disappointing result in the road race after pulling my foot in the sprint, significant for the fact that Kathy Watt was on the podium on a lower step."

Competing at major races against higher rated opponents or in difficult conditions, Wilson nominated some quite special performances: "I won the Powerbar tour in the USA in 1996 in my first year as a full-time cyclist, at a time when it was 13 days long, against all the major favourites and with the Australian national team.

"It was a special result in difficult circumstances and

because we were in the lead up to the 1996 Olympics and political tensions were running high in the team due to impending selection of the Olympic Games team.

"I won the same tour in 2000 (now the Hewlett Packard tour) with the Saturn team and the win was only secured when I lapped the field in the criterium on the second last day in a great battle move planned and executed by my team. I competed again in 2001 with Saturn on a day full of crosswinds. We were able to split the field apart and set up Judith Arndt for the win against Genevieve Jeanson."

Mary Grigson

Mary Grigson (born 1971) was a dual Olympian who boasts Australia's best mountain bike result in Olympic history with a sixth at the 2000 Sydney Olympic Games.

Mary Daubert (nee Grigson) is the only Australian female mountain biker to have won a World Cup race, which she did twice. She also won five national cross-country mountain bike titles in 2001-02 when at her peak.

She also won a 2002 Commonwealth Games bronze medal in the cross country. At the MTB world championships in 2001 she won a gold medal in the 24-hour mountain bike race and silver in the team relay. In 2016 Grigson was one of six inductees to the Cycling Australia Hall of Fame.

"When I was racing, I felt that women's mountain biking did not get much recognition so to be accepted into the Hall of Fame is an honour," Grigson said. "I was lucky to be part of a special time when Australia was working to make a debut on the international scene of mountain biking. I had a great coach, great support network with the Australian Institute of Sport and supportive teammates." She took up road cycling, competing from the late 1990s.

Kathryn (Kathy) Watt

Kathy Watt (born 1964) came from Warragul in Victoria and began her cycling career in 1985 as a 21-year-old. Watt had great all-round road racing and tactical ability and was a trailblazer, achieving many firsts in Australian cycling (also see track cycling).

Watt's greatest achievement on the road came at the 1992 Barcelona Olympic Games when she made history becoming the first Australian (male or female) to win an Olympic cycling road gold medal. She then added a silver medal in the 3000m individual track pursuit.

The Australian Olympic Committee described Watt's Barcelona triumph: "Watt's comparative anonymity, competing against cyclists with huge reputations, benefited her in the road race. Watt was not considered a threat, and while the heavyweights were duelling, she was able to slip away unnoticed from the main pack with one circuit to go. She took the lead and stayed in front, crossing the line 20 seconds ahead of the four-time world champion, France's Jeannie Longo-Ciprelli."

Her medal-winning performance at Barcelona is one of many highlights in a 20-year international career on the road and the track that included two Olympic Games, six world championships, and four Commonwealth Games.

Watt's long international career started and finished with victories in the Oceania Games road race in 1987 at her first appearance and her final appearance in 2007.

At the 1990 Auckland Commonwealth Games, Watt, a last-minute addition to the road team in her first headline-grabbing performance, unexpectedly won gold in the road race and followed it up with a silver medal in the 3000m individual pursuit, Cycling Australia said.

When the 1994 Commonwealth Games came to Victoria, Canada, Watt won three gold medals competing in the road race, the road team time trial, and the 3000m individual pursuit. In 1995, she won the bronze medal at the UCI road world championships in the individual time trial. At the 2006 Commonwealth Games in Melbourne, Watt won silver in the individual road time trial.

On the European road circuit from 1990, Watt was third in the GC at the Giro d'Italia (Rosa) in 1990 and claimed a GC second in the Giro Rosa in 1994 after winning three stages. She posted wins in three road races including the 2005 Chrono Champenois time trial. Watt won the Oceania time trial championship in 1997, the Canberra Stage Race tour in 1994, and the Tour de Perth in 2007.

In 2006 at age 41, Watt won the Australian road time trial championship, beating Olympic gold medallist Sara Carrigan by 33 seconds and world number one Oenone Wood. She was the winner of 24 Australian cycling titles, including four on the road, on the track and mountain bike racing. Watt was inducted into the Sport Australia Hall of Fame, and the Cycling Australia Hall of Fame in 2016.

Sara Carrigan

New South Wales cyclist Sara Carrigan (born 1980) started cycling in 1996 at the age of 15 and came from the town of Gunnedah. She won the women's road race at the 2004 Olympic Games in Athens becoming only the second Australian woman to hold the Olympic road gold medal since Kathy Watt at Barcelona in 1992.

Carrigan demonstrated her road cycling talents in 1999, posting top results in under 23 road races winning the Trophee d'Or Feminin in France, Germany's Thuringa Rundfarht, the Tour de Snowy in Australia, and in 2001 the sprint classification at the Giro della Toscana. She rode for European professional teams such as NED and Lotto. At the 2002 UCI road world championships, she was fourth in the road race and fifth in the time trial.

Carrigan won the national road time trial championship twice (in 2002-03) and was second four times. In 2003 she won a round of the UCI road World Cup at Geelong and two stages at the Tour de l'Aude in France.

At the 2004 Olympics in Athens, Australia's three cyclists in the event, Carrigan, Oenone Wood and Olivia Gollan decided that the objective was to get one of the three first over the line. Carrigan won the road race in a two-rider breakaway, proving too strong in the sprint to the finish with Germany's Judith Arndt.

"While Wood controlled a chasing bunch of six riders, Carrigan duelled for the lead with German champion Judith Arndt over the last lap, finally destroying her with a powerful finish," the AOC said. On the night of her great victory, the lights stayed on all night in Gunnedah. Taking a break from cycling she qualified for the 2004 Beijing Olympics road race, finishing 38th. In 2005 Carrigan claimed a GC third at the Vuelta Ciclista Castilla y Leon in Spain and in 2007 won the sprint classification at the Bay Classic Series. She was named Australian Female Road Cyclist of the Year in 2002, 2003 and 2004.

At the Commonwealth Games in Melbourne in 2006, Carrigan won a bronze medal in the individual time trial and played a crucial support role in the road race, won by Australia's Natalie Bates. Carrigan also represented Australia at eight road world championships and at the 2002 Commonwealth Games.

She received the Order of Australia Medal in 2005, was inducted into the Queensland Sporting Hall of Fame in 2012 and was an inaugural inductee into the Cycling Australia Hall of Fame in 2015.

After she retired at the end of 2008, she founded Sara Carrigan Cycling on the Gold Coast to provide cycling training and skills development for cyclists of all abilities.

Oenone Wood

Oenone Wood (born 1980) came from Newcastle and graduated as an electrical engineer. She took up road cycling at age 20 and was an AIS scholarship holder.

Wood burst onto elite road cycling in 2003, finishing second in the national road race championship (RoadNats) and won the RoadNats race in 2004 and 2008.

In 2004-2005 Wood also won the national road time trial

championship and in 2005 added the national criterium championship. Wood was selected in the 2004 Athens Olympics road cycling team and finished fourth in the road race, where she played an integral role in Sara Carrigan's gold medal win and came sixth in the road time trial. She was a dual Olympian and competed at Beijing in 2008.

Regarded as one of the world's best women's road cyclists of the 2000s, she won the UCI Women's Road World Cup point score in 2004-2005. In September 2005, she won the bronze medal in the women's road race at the UCI road world championships in Madrid on her 25th birthday. Germany's Regina Schleicher won the 126-kilometre race through the streets of the Spanish capital.

Wood paid tribute to her team-mates for setting her up with a chance to figure in the world's medals. "I'm happy with the result and the team made an awesome effort," she said, finding it hard not to be emotional. She said the team was racing in memory of road cyclist Amy Gillett.

One of Wood's best performances was at the Melbourne Commonwealth Games in 2006, winning gold in the individual road time-trial then claiming silver in the Games road race. Major Australian wins in 2004-05 include the Bay Classics Series, the 2004 Tour Down Under criterium series and two Geelong Tours.

From 2003 to 2007, she achieved success on the European road circuit with wins and places in one-day road classics in Italy, Germany, Spain and Switzerland that included: third place in La Fleche Wallonne classic in 2003; winning the UCI road World Cup and the points competition twice in 2004-05; winning many stages of the Giro d'Italia Rosa and the Giro Rosa points score in 2004; winning the Le Tour du Grand Montreal twice; sixth place in the UCI road world championships in 2006 and eighth place in 2007. Wood also finished second in the Tour of New Zealand in 2008.

In September 2008 Wood, who was only 28 years old, revealed she would retire from road cycling due to family reasons. She teaches maths and physics at high school.

Looking back at her best 3-4 international performances during her cycling career, Wood said these were: "In the 2004 World Cup Series, the 2005 World Cup Series, my 2006 Commonwealth Games individual time trial gold medal and road race silver medal, and my 2005 UCI road world championships bronze medal at Madrid."

Wood nominated special performances competing at major races, including against higher rated opponents: "My first win in Europe was against Nicole Cooke at (Italy's) Grand Prix Cavrie in 2003. That same year I finished third at Flèche Wallone and it was my first result at a World Cup event. In 2004, I won the Souvenir Magali Pache time trial in Switzerland. My time was faster than some of the men's field who raced on the same course."

On coaches or mentors that inspired her or helped her achieve her goals, Wood said: "I was very lucky to have a great coach in Kim Palmer to introduce me to the sport of cycling. Warren McDonald then took over coaching me when I joined the ACT Academy of Sport. Under his guidance I went from being a good local rider to a top level elite rider. I would never have had the career without having his guidance and support.

"My all-time favourite team director was (Germany's) Petra Rossner. I raced against her in 2004 and she became my team director in 2005. She was a brilliant tactician and could read a race and the capability of her riders to perfection. I have never raced as hard and with as much confidence as when I had Petra on the radio."

The Newcastle Herald reported on October 19, 2016 that Oenone Wood would be one of six inductees into the Cycling Australian Hall of Fame in November 2016.

Katrin Garfoot

Katrin Garfoot was another late starter who took up cycling in 2011 on the Gold Coast aged 29 when teaching at a local high school. Garfoot (born in Germany in 1981) had immediate success in local road racing and became an Australian citizen in 2013.

Garfoot placed second in the Canberra Women's Tour in 2012. In 2013 she dominated national road cycling winning the road race at the Oceania Continental Road Championship and the National Road Series. Joining the Orica-AIS world cycling team in 2014, she placed in several one-day races. Making her Australian team debut at the 2014 Commonwealth Games in Glasgow, she won the bronze medal in the road time trial. Garfoot won three consecutive national time trial road championships from 2016 to 2018, the 2017 national road championships and the Oceania cycling championships time trial in 2015-16.

At the UCI road world championships in 2014 she placed fourth in the individual time trial and at Doha in 2016 showed her great time trial ability by claiming the bronze medal in the individual time trial, becoming only the third Australian woman to win the elite medal along with Anna Wilson and Kathy Watt.

From 2014 to 2017, Garfoot, rode for the Orica-AIS and Mitchelton-Scott teams, scored many top ten results in major European road races and classics and was placed five times, and in 2016, won the Chrono Champenois European individual time trial championship in France.

At the 2016 Olympic Games in Rio, she was the highest placed Australian, finishing ninth in the road time trial.

Competing in the UCI road world championships at Bergen, Norway in September 2017, Garfoot claimed a bronze medal in the individual time-trial and a silver medal in the road race after being beaten in the road race by the Netherlands' Chantal Blaak.

However, Garfoot led home the bunch and last year's world champion Amalie Dedriksen to win silver. "Being 'over the moon' to win silver," she said on Twitter. "To win it against 3 dutchies was impossible, I think."

In 2018 at the Gold Coast Commonwealth Games she won gold in the women's individual time trial in 35mins, 08.09secs, when the average speed for the 25.5 kilometre race was 43.547km/h. Garfoot also finished third in the 2018 Tour Down Under and won the sprint classification.

Garfoot left the Mitchelton-Scott professional team in 2018 and the 36-year-old spoke of wanting to focus on family life. She said her biggest achievement was her two medals in the time trial and the road race medal at the 2017 road world championships in Bergen.

Natalie Bates

Natalie Bates (born 1980) is from Sydney and rode with the Paramatta Cycling Club and raced on the road and track. From a cycling family, she started riding when 10 and is the sister of track champion Katherine Bates.

In 1998 she won the bronze medal in the UCI junior road world championships at Bordeaux. Bates started riding on the elite women's international road circuit in 2003 and was sixth in the Geelong World Cup race.

Bates signed with UCI team Van Bemmelen – AA Drink from 2005. She competed in the road classics and major tours and was ninth in the Souvenir Magali Pache Lausanne time trial. In Australia she placed fourth in the national road race championship and won a stage at the Geelong Tour. In 2006, Bates won bronze in the national road time trial and placed fourth in the Geelong Tour.

She was selected to ride in the Commonwealth Games road race in Melbourne in 2006 and was a surprise winner of the gold medal by almost three minutes from Oneone Wood who claimed silver and Wales' Nicole Cook who took bronze.

In 2007 in the Czech Republic, Bates was seventh in the GC at the Gracia-Orlova stage race and competing in Canada in 2008 claimed a GC second place in the 5-stage Tour of PEI at Prince Edward Island.

Rochelle Gilmore

Rochelle Gilmore (born 1981) was a talented junior athlete who competed in BMX racing and track cycling. Gilmore, from Sutherland in Sydney, won silver at the world junior track cycling championships. At the national criterium championships in the early 2000s she won two under 23 and two elite championships and went on to become one of our best all-round road cyclists.

In 2001 in Italy she won the GP Carnevale d'Europa road race and a stage at the Giro d'Italia grand tour and in 2002 claimed the Bay Classic Series GC. On the track she won silver medals at the Commonwealth Games and the UCI track world championships.

Gilmore rode for the Ausra Gruodis team internationally in 2003. In Italy she was third in the Primavera Rosa, won a stage of the Giro Rosa grand tour and was third in Germany's Sparkassen Giro Bochum. In 2005, Gilmore won the Geelong World Cup and Italy's Trofeo Guaresci race and claimed second places in the Trofeo Liberazione and Nurnberger Altstadt World Cup race.

From 2007 up to 2011, Gilmore posted seven to ten, top ten finishes in major road races each year. In 2007 she won silver in the criterium at the UCI road world championships, won the national criterium title and three other criterium races. Gilmore also won the GP Bitburger Classic in Germany and the Oceania Games road race. In 2008 Gilmore won the Olympia Preis Bochum Criterium and placed second in the Sparkassen Giro Bochum, the GP Liberazione and the GP Comune di Fabriccio races.

Gilmore was ranked eighth in the UCI women's world rankings in 2009 riding for Team Lotto Belisol with wins at the Sparkassen Giro Bochum, the Omloop Door Middag-Humsterland, and the Cronulla International GP. At the Route de France stage tour she won two stages.

She was a prolific winner of stages competing in road tours, winning over 100 stages at major tours globally. Gilmore's top form continued in 2010 winning the Jayco Bay Classic series and Honda Insight GP Criteriums and a GC third at the Tour of Chongming Island. In the 2010 Commonwealth Games road race at Delhi, she won the gold medal in a sprint finish from England's Lizzie Armistead and Australia's Chloe Hosking.

After surviving multiple pelvis, back and rib fractures/injuries in mid-2010, she told The Sydney Morning Herald on December 11, 2011, she was aiming to win another (back-to-back) Jayco Bay Classic in Victoria.

Gilmore won the earlier Jayco Bay Classic series in 2011 and in 2012 placed second in the USA's Liberty Classic and Canada's GP cyclist de Gatineau. In 2013 she set up UK-based women's road teams Wiggle Honda/Wiggle High-5 and rode for the teams. She retired from competition in late 2015 and closed the team in 2018.

Tiffany Cromwell

Tiffany Cromwell (born 1988) is from South Australia was a top junior road and track and under 23 road cyclist. Cromwell broke through in 2008-09 with three wins in USA road races and won four silver medals in the under 23 and elite national road championships in 2008-2010 and silver in the 2012 national road race championship. She rode for Lotto, Orica-AIS and Canyon SRAM Racing.

Competing on the European circuit, Cromwell was second in Germany's Sparkassen Giro Bochum in 2010; second in France's GP de Plouay Bretagne World Cup race in 2012; won stages of the Giro Rosa grand tour in 2012 and 2016; and was second in Italy's GP Comune di Cornaredo race in 2014.

Among her best performances were winning the Omloop Het Nieuwsblad road race classic in Belgium in 2013 and placing third in 2016. She finished fifth in the UCI road world championships in 2014 and seventh in the La Course by Le Tour De France road race in 2016.   In 2015 she claimed second in the Chrono Champenois European individual time trial championship.

Cromwell represented Australia at the Commonwealth Games at Glasgow in 2014 and the Gold Coast in 2018. Talking to ABC News in 2017 about competing in the women's world tour, Cromwell said: "It takes a lot of sacrifice, a lot of determination, a lot of persistence, a little bit of luck as well."

Rachel Neylan

Rachel Neylan (born 1982) came from Sydney. She studied for a physiotherapy degree, took up rowing for 14 months and was the Australian Rowing Team's physio in 2007. Neylan joined the women's talent squad program at South Australia's Institute of Sport. In 2012 her road cycling career took off when she placed third in the Oceania Cycling Championships, won bronze at the national road championships and was fourth at France's Tour Cycliste Feminin Ardeche road race. She capped a good year on the WorldTour winning the silver medal in the road race at the UCI road world championships. Her best performance in 2014 was fifth in France's Trophee d'Or Feminine five-stage road race.

Neylan joined the Orica-AIS road team in 2015 and posted top results: winning silver in the national road championship, fourth in the Oceania road race championship, won the Cadel Evans Great Ocean Road Race, and won the GC at the Trophee d'Or Feminine stage race in France. "Standing of top of the podium winning UCI tour Trophee D'or in August 2015 was special and sentimental first ever European victory," she said.

In 2016 Neylan placed second in the Cadel Evans Road Race, won bronze in the national championship road race, and in France won the Grand Prix de Plumelec-Morbihan. She represented Australia at the Olympic Games, finishing 22nd in the Rio Olympics road race. In 2017 she placed second in Belgium's Erondegemse Pijl road race.

Riding for Team Virtu in 2019 she claimed a GC third at the Santos Tour Down Under and fifth in the Czech Republic's Gracia-Orlova tour. Neylan signed for the Chronos Casa Dorada women's team in 2020 and in late January, crashed and suffered a broken hand finishing 40th at the Race Torquay in Victoria, Australia. She recovered and rode in the UCI road world championships.

Shara Gillow

Shara Gillow (born 1987) took up cycling when 19 inspired by her road cyclist father David who represented Zimbabwe at the 1980 Moscow Olympics. From Queensland's The Sunshine Coast, she raced at elite level in 2008-09 taking second places in the Tour of Bright and the Canberra Tour. In 2010 she finished eighth in the UCI road world time trial championships and rode in the Giro Donne (Rosa) grand tour in Italy.

Gillow joined the Orica-AIS UCI road team in 2012 and represented Australia at the London Olympic Games. From 2011 she posted good results with wins in the Oceania championship road race, the Oceania time trial three times, and a GC second in the Women's Tour of New Zealand in 2012.

A top time triallist, from 2011 she won the time trial at the national road championships three years in succession, claimed a stage of the Giro Rosa and was third in Germany's Thuringen Rundfahrt tour. At the UCI world road championships in 2012, she won silver in the team time trial. Gillow had another strong year in 2013 with a second place in the Thuringen Rundfahrt, fourth overall in the Giro d'Italia grand tour, and bronze in the UCI road world championship team time trial.

She was Cycling Australia's elite women's road cyclist of the year in 2011 and 2013. Gillow placed third in the BeNe Ladies Tour in 2014 and placed sixth in the Commonwealth Games road time trial at Glasgow in 2014. Gillow won the national road time trial championship in

2015 and the bronze medal in the team time trial at the UCI world road championships. In Europe, she claimed a GC second in the Czech Republic's Gracia Orlova tour.

In 2017 Gillow joined the French professional team FDJ-Nouvelle Aquitaine – Futuroscope Cycling. She showed great form in European one-day races and classics and posted second places in Spain's Durango-Durango and the Grand Prix Morbihan in France, fifth places in the La Course by Le Tour de France and Fleche Wallonne classic, and sixth in the Strade Bianche classic.

Gillow placed sixth in the Flech Wallone classic in 2018 and in 2019 was fourth in the Durango-Durango road race. Also known as Shara Marche, she finished twelfth in the GC at the Tour Down Under in 2020.

Lauren Kitchen

Lauren Kitchen (born 1990) came from Armidale NSW. Selected under a road talent program in 2007-08, she finished seventh in the road race at the UCI junior world championships in 2007.

She competed with the national road team overseas in 2010-11 and raced in the Netherlands classics. Kitchen rode for Rabobank women's teams in 2011 taking second in the Berkelse Wielerdag one day race and won the under 23 national road time trial and criterium championships.

In 2013, Kitchen rode for the UK's Wiggle-Honda team, claiming four top ten road race finishes in Europe, including fifth in the Netherlands' 7-Dorpenomloop Aalburg. In 2014 after winning silver in the national road race championship and bronze in the criterium, Kitchen battled a leg injury that impacted on her road season.

In 2015, she won the Oceania road championships. Riding for the Hi-Tech team she won China's Tour of Zhousan Island, the Netherlands' Ronde van Overijssel road race and was second in the Tour of Thailand.

Kitchen posted a GC third at the Tour Down Under in 2016 and placed in the Netherlands' 7-Dorpenomloop Aalburg and Belgium's Trofee Maarten Wynants. She was fourth in the GC at the Tour Down Under in 2017.

At the national road race championship in 2018 she won silver. She joined French team FDJ Nouvelle Aquitane Futuroscope. Riding in France in 2018 Kitchen showed her growing one-day race tactical and sprinting ability with a third in the Le Samyn des Dames race and a win in the GP International d'Isbergues road classic.

In 2019 Kitchen claimed second place in the La Picto-Charantaise road race at Poitiers, France for FDJ Nouvelle Aquitane Futuroscope right in the backyard of the team's main sponsors and home of the team.

"While it isn't the biggest race on the calendar it's nice for me to be back on a UCI podium, it's been a solid season but without a big result," Kitchen said.

Returning to Australia in 2020 she rode in the Tour Down Under and was fifteenth in difficult conditions at the Deakin University road race at Geelong, when eight women crashed out of the race. In September 2020 riding for her team at the Grand Prix d'Isbergues classic in France, Kitchen took third place in a sprint finish.

Chloe Hosking

Chloe Hosking (born 1990, Bendigo, Victoria) grew up in Canberra and started cycling with her father aged 12 and rode with the Canberra cycling club. She won the national track under 19 scratch race title in 2008, then switched to road racing and represented Australia at the UCI junior road world championships.

When just 18 she moved to the Netherlands in 2009 and was signed by the Moving Ladies professional team and later rode for the HTC-Columbia team.

Hosking had immediate success in 2009, winning Shanghai's Tour of Chongming Island, The Netherland's Omloop Der Kempen road race, the Wellington Women's Race in New Zealand, and was third in Germany's Sparkassen Giro Bochum. In 2010 she won the under 23 national criterium championship, a bronze medal in the Commonwealth Games road race at Delhi, India, placed second in Belgium's GP Stad Roeselare and was third at the USA's Nature Valley Grand Prix stage race. In 2011 she finished sixth in the road world championships.

From 2009 to 2020, she amassed a long palmares in UCI, classic road races, stage tours and Australian road races with over 16 race wins, 20 places, 25 stage wins and many sprint classifications competing against the world's top road cyclists on the international circuit.

In 2012 Hosking's wins included the Drenste 8 van Dwingeloo and the Drenste Acht van Westerveld (in the Netherlands) and Halle-Buizingen (Belgium) road races, and a stage at the Route de France tour. In Australia she won the Jayco Bay Classic criterium series. In 2013 Hosking posted two second GC places at the Ladies Tour of Qatar and at Shanghai's Tour of Chongming Island. She won the Omloop van Borselle road race (Netherlands) in 2014 and posted a GC third at the Tour of Qatar, repeating the GC third in 2015. Other 2015 top results were third in Belgium's Gent-Wevelgem classic and a GC win in the Mitchelton Bay Classic Series.

Hosking, now recognised as Australia's best sprinter in road racing, had one of her biggest one-day road race wins in July 2016. Riding for the Wiggle High-5 team, she claimed victory in the one-day La Course by Le Tour de France, outsprinting Lotta Lepistö and the formidable Dutch champion Marianne Vos on the Champs-Elysees, becoming the first Australian woman to win on cycling's biggest stage in Paris.

Her other top results in 2016 included wins at the GC at the Tour of Chongming Island and at the GP Beghilli in Italy, second in the Madrid Challenge by La Vuelta, stage wins at the Giro Rosa and the Route de France tours, and seventh in the UCI world road championship.

In 2017, riding for the Ale-Cipollini team, she won the Drenste Acht van Westerveld road race again, posted a GC third at the Tour of Chongming Island, won a stage at the Tour of Norway and won the sprint points classification at the Tour Down Under and stage 3.

At the September 2017 UCI road world championships in Norway when Katrin Garfoot claimed silver in the road race, Hosking tweeted about the late addition of her and

Rachel Neylan: "I am immensely proud to have been a part of Australia's silver medal ride today, something that wouldn't have been possible without seven riders."

Her great form continued in 2018 with wins the women's Cadel Evans Great Ocean Road Race, the GC third and sprint points in the Herald Sun Tour, and a stage at the Santos Women's Tour. She won the gold medal in the Commonwealth Games road race, posted second places at Belgium's Driedaagse Brugge-De Panne road race and the Omloop van Het Nieuwsblad classic, and two third places in other road races.

In 2018, just weeks after a crash at 60kph during the Tour of Flanders in April, Hosking won gold in the road race at the Gold Coast Commonwealth Games from New Zealand's Georgina Williams and Wales' Danielle Rowe. Hosking made her move in the final 200 metres, sprinting to the line to claim the gold medal. Hosking said: "It's so special to have won on home soil. Lots of people say road cycling at the Commonwealth Games is not a big deal, but you know what? I'm Commonwealth champion and it's a big deal." Her Commonwealth gold medal was Cycling Australia's 'Moment of the Year'.

In 2019 she won the GC at the Tour of Guangxi and sprint points classifications at the Herald Sun and Santos Women's Tour. She started 2020 well claiming her second win in the Lexus of Blackburn Bay Crits series, won her first national road title in the criterium and was fifth in the national road championship.

Now 29 and riding for the USA's Rally UHC Cycling

team in 2020, her top results included fifth in the Santos Women's Tour after winning stage 1, sixth in the Deakin University road race and in February eighth in the Omloop Het Nieuwsblad road classic in Belgium.   In September 2020, Hosking won the GP d'Isbergues road classic in France in a sprint finish. She signed with the top ranked women's team Trek-Segafredo in October.

Sarah Roy

From Concord, Sydney, Roy (born 1986) was originally a triathlete who made a comeback to road cycling from 2009 following injury. She won the national criterium championship in 2014 and joined the Mitchelton-Scott team in 2015.

Roy posted seven top ten finishes in European road races in 2016, including second in Belgium's Keukens van Lommel Ladies Classic and third in the SwissEver GP Cham-Hagendom. In 2017 Roy had a breakthrough season claiming the team's first WorldTour victory at the UK's OVO Energy Women's Tour. Other top results were a win at the SwissEver GP Cham-Hagendorn race, third places in the GP de Plouay classic and Spar-Omloop van het Hageland, and a Tour of Chongming Island GC fourth.

2018 was another big year for Roy with six top ten finishes in major races and she won silver at the national criterium championship. Internationally, she won the Gooik Geraardsbergen Gooik road race in Belgium, placed second in the Netherlands' Salverda Omloop van de IJsseldelta road race, and she also placed fifth in the 2018

Commonwealth Games road race held on the Gold Coast.

The sprint leader for the Mitchelton-Scott team in 2019, Roy won the sprint points at the Tour Down Under. In January she won bronze in the national road race championship in a close finish with Shara Gillow and also won silver in the national criterium championship. Roy rode for Mitchelton-Scott in the Giro d'Italia in Italy in 2019 when her teammates finished first and third on the podium. She told Women Who Cycle: "It's easy for people to forget that cycling is a team sport when there is just one rider on the podium. When you are part of the team your contribution to the success is valued greatly."

In August 2019 Roy sprinted to a stunning victory in the first ever 120.7km one-day Clasica Femenina Navarra in Lodosa, Spain. Roy benefited from an impressive lead out from her Mitchelton-Scott teammates on the run into Lodosa and held off her rivals in the sprint for the line.

In 2020 she rode in the Jayco Herald Sun Tour and the Giro Rosa grand tour and in the Belgian one-day classics placed fourth in Gent Wevelgem and Driedaagse-De Panne, and fifth in the Tour of Flanders classic. Roy had a great start to 2021 when she won the elite women's road race at the RoadNats championships. Roy has a degree in sports science and is studying clinical physiology.

Gracie Elvin

Gracie Elvin (born 1988) was a champion cross-country mountain bike rider in 2008-09 winning four under 23 national championships and a World Cup mountain bike championship. Elvin, from Canberra, turned professional in 2012 and joined the Orica-AIS cycling team and later rode for the Mitchelton-Scott women's team. An AIS road cycling scholarship holder in 2012, she won the Oceania road championships.

Elvin won the elite women's national road race championship twice in 2013-2014 and was sixth in the Commonwealth Games road race in 2014. She claimed her first major race win at the 2015 Gooik-Geraardsbergen-Gook one day race in Belgium.

In 2016, she won the Gooik-Geraardsbergen race again, was second in the Netherlands' Ronde van Drenthe WorldTour road race and won the GC at the Mitchelton Bay Cycling Classic. Elvin was one of four cyclists who represented Australia in the 2016 Rio Olympics road race on a dangerous course that saw many bad crashes.

Elvin said in 2016 that her dad and family are one of the main reasons she is successful: "Finding the right coach and mentor is the most important thing you can do. You need someone who is 100 percent in your corner and cheering you on."

Riding for the Orica-Scott team in 2017, she made Australian cycling history taking second place at Belgium's prestigious one-day women's road classic Ronde van Vlaanderen (Tour of Flanders).

Elvin said: "I had my best result to date at my favourite race with a close 2nd amongst riders I've looked up to for a long time." She also placed second in the Dwars door Vlaanderen and posted six top ten road race results in 2017.

In 2018 Elvin posted second places at the Gooik-Geraardsbergen-Gooik road race and the Deakin University (Great Ocean Road) road race and in 2019 claimed a silver medal in the national road championship time trial.

Elvin won another silver in the national criterium road championship in 2020. She announced her retirement from road cycling in October.

Lucy Kennedy

Lucy Kennedy (born 1988) is from Brisbane and was a late starter to road cycling after earning a scholarship as a runner at the USA's Iowa State University and has degrees in civil engineering and commerce.

In 2015, in her own words, she "jumped in the deep end by racing in the Australian national championships". She was invited to the Australian Women's Development Team selection camp.

She described 2017 as a "breakthrough year" after winning bronze in the national road race championship and the Oceania Continental Championships time trial.

Kennedy was selected for the High5 development team and spent 10 weeks racing in Europe as the recipient of the 2017 Amy Gillet Scholarship. She won the GC at the Tour Cycliste Feminin de l'Ardeche in France.

Mitchelton-Scott signed Kennedy at the start of the 2018 season and said she was a talented climber and time triallist. In her first ever WorldTour race she was fifth in the Strade Bianche one-day classic in difficult conditions.

She placed fourth in the GC for the Tour Down Under and second in the national road championships time trial, won the Taiwan KOM Challenge race, and was fifth in the UCI world championships team time trial riding for Mitchelton-Scott.

Kennedy started the 2019 season with her biggest win in Australia in the 2-stage Jayco Herald Sun Tour, taking the final stage and overall GC win. She claimed second place the previous weekend at Geelong in the 2019 Deakin University road race, finished fourth in the national championships time trial and claimed a GC second in the Santos Women's Tour (Down Under).

She posted her first European road victory for the Mitchelton-Scott team in May 2019. After a solo attack in the 113-kilometre, Basque Country race the Durango-Durango. Kennedy powered on ahead and did enough to hold off the chase and take the race victory, 26 seconds ahead of Amanda Spratt in second. The duo used their numbers, allowing Kennedy to sneak away and hold on for the win, with Spratt patrolling the chase.

Kennedy said: "It's my first European win with the team, so it feels very special. It's an honour just to be given the opportunity so I'm glad I could make it count."

In July 2019 Kennedy claimed second place after an attacking ride and a duel for victory at the first edition of Spain's Emakumeen Nafarroako Klasikoa one-day race.

She won her second European one-day race in August 2019 despite puncturing and losing a minute to win the inaugural edition of the Clásica San Sebastián in Spain.

Kennedy rode in Italy's Giro Rosa 10-stage grand tour in July 2019 and finished a close second in stage three.

Following a sixth place at the national road championships time trial in February 2020, Kennedy won an impressive back-to-back GC victory in the Jayco Herald Sun Tour of Victoria riding solo over the last 15km to win. In Italy in 2020, Kennedy finished third in the team time trial at the tough Giro Rosa grand tour and posted a GC 31st, the best result by an Australian.

Amanda Spratt

Amanda Spratt (born 1987) started by riding a BMX at nine years. She took up competitive cycling at 12 helped by Penrith Cycling Club's junior rider's program. In 2004 she competed at the world junior track championships, the road world championships, and the Commonwealth Youth Games. From Springwood in the New South Wales Blue Mountains, Spratt is based in Varase, Italy.

In 2008, Spratt won the under 23 national road championship time trial. In 2011, she won the elite Tour De Feminin in the Czech Republic and made her Olympic Games debut in the road race at London 2012 when torrential rain and hailstones derailed her campaign.

Known for her climbing and all-round ability, from 2012 she raced with the Orica-AIS and later Green-EDGE cycling teams then the Mitchelton-Scott team. In 2012 she won the national road race championship at Buninyong and was third in the Netherlands' 7-Dorpenomloop Aalburg one-day race.

In 2013, Spratt won bronze in the UCI road world championships team time trial with the Australian team and went one better in 2014 winning silver in the team time trial. Spratt claimed her second European road race win in 2015 at Italy's Giro del Trentino Alto Adige tour. She posted eight top ten finishes in 2015, including third in the Ladies Tour of Norway, fourth in the Cadel Evans women's road race and fifth at the Santos Women's Tour Down Under.

She won her second national road race championship in 2016 and also won the Cadel Evans Women's road race. At the Rio Olympics on a difficult road course, Spratt did well to finish fifteenth around four minutes behind Dutch winner Anna van der Breggen. Spratt posted eight top ten finishes in 2016 including second in the Women's Tour of Thuringia stage race in Germany.

At the Women's Tour Down Under in South Australia in 2017, Spratt claimed the overall GC. She was second in the national road race championship and finished in the top ten in five major races, including the Giro Rosa grand tour (fifth) and La Course by Tour De France (sixth).

Spratt showed impressive form in 2018 including in the one-day classics riding for Mitchelton-Scott, with 14 top ten results and her second GC win at the Santos Women's Tour. Spratt placed first in Spain's Emakumeen Euskal Bira road race and Switzerland's GP Cham-Hagendorn one-day race; third in the Amstel Gold classic; third in the GC at the Giro d'Italia Rosa grand tour; and second in the Liege-Bastogne-Liege classic in Belgium.

In September 2018 she gave a road cycling masterclass in winning the silver medal at the UCI road world championships on a challenging UCI road world course at Innsbruck, Austria. She won silver over three minutes behind Dutch winner Anna van der Breggen and nearly two minutes ahead of bronze medallist, Italian Tatiana Guderzo, after riding courageously on her own for around 40 kilometres to the finish.

Spratt ranked fourth in the Women's WorldTour standings in December 2018 and was named Elite Female Road Cyclist of the Year at the Cycling Australia Awards and said her road world silver medal, "was definitely the highlight of my year and my career so far". Spratt told the Sydney Morning Herald she agreed with coach Gene Bates in 2018 to forgo the Commonwealth Games road race and media coverage that follows Games success to compete in Europe's biggest women's road races.

At the 2019 national road championships, Spratt won silver in the 104-kilometre road race and won the GC for Mitchelton-Scott at the four-stage Santos Women's Tour (Down Under) in mid-January after taking the lead in the second stage. With an attack on Mengler Hill, Spratt won the stage 39 seconds ahead of Lucy Kennedy. She increased her lead to 49 seconds on third stage and held the advantage on the final stage, claiming her third consecutive GC win in the Tour Down Under at Adelaide.

In early 2019, she finished second to Kennedy in the two-stage Jayco Herald Sun Tour and third in the Deakin University women's road race. Riding in Europe in late

March, she sprinted to take second place in Italy's Trofeo Alfredo Binda road race. At the Emakumeen Bira four-day race in Spain, Spratt finished just two seconds behind GC winner Elisa Longo Borghini. She also claimed an impressive GC third in Italy's tough Giro Rosa grand tour.

Spratt won bronze at the 2019 UCI road world championship in Yorkshire after a hard battle with Dutch gold and silver winners van Vleuten and van der Breggen and said: "I'm really proud to finish off with a bronze medal after a great team performance." She won Cycling Australia's 2019 Elite Female Road Cyclist Award.

In 2020, Spratt posted wins at the Lexus of Blackburn Bay Crits and national road championship, a GC third in the Santos Women's Tour and third in the Deakin University Women's Road Race. In September 2020 she crashed out of the Giro Rosa and was injured. Spratt, in the 2021 Olympics' Australian cycling team, told newspapers her focus was winning gold in the road race.

Grace Brown

Grace Brown, from Camperdown, Victoria (born 1992) concentrated on running at school and university and took up cycling in 2015 at the suggestion of her father. In 2017 she won the Mersey Valley Cycling Tour in Tasmania.

Brown was the recipient of the Amy Gillet Scholarship and rode on the European women's road circuit. In 2018 she was third and fourth in the national road race championship and time trial championship and posted a GC fifth at the Santos Tour Down Under.

She won the National Road Series in 2018 and the road time trial at the Oceania Road Championships.

Brown rode for the Wiggle High5 Team internationally in 2018 in races such as La Course by Le Tour De France, for Australia at the UCI world road championship at Innsbruck and was signed by Mitchelton-Scott for the WorldTour. In 2019 she demonstrated her time trial ability with a clear win in the elite women's national time trial title at Buninyong over a 29.5km course.

In 2019 she rode in Europe for Mitchelton-Scott and was fourth in the Giro Rosa team time trial. At the RoadNats championships in 2020-21 she won two silver medals in the time trial, bronze and silver in the road race and rode in the Santos Women's Tour.

With the team backing her time trial strengths, in September 2020, Brown put in a top performance placing fifth at the UCI road world time trial championship. In the Belgian one-day road classics she counter-attacked to claim second at nine seconds to winner Lizzie Deignan in the Leige-Bastogne-Liege Femmes. In October she posted her European debut win at the Brabanste Pijl. Mitchelton-Scott said three days later, Brown rode to "a superb solo victory at Brabanste Pijl, announcing herself as a serious contender in the hilly one-day classics".

Olivia Gollan

Olivia Gollan (born 1973, Maitland NSW) came from Newcastle. She was a late starter taking up road cycling at age 26. She rode in the Canberra World Cup in 2001 and in 2002, gained a scholarship with the AIS. In 2002 she rode in Europe, placing fifth in the Chrono Champenois Trophee time trial championship and second in a stage of the Giro d'Italia Donne grand tour.

Gollan developed into a top all-round road cyclist and in 2003 claimed a GC win at France's Trophee d'Or Feminin tour, a GC win at Switzerland's Tour de Berne, second in the Netherlands' Amstel Gold road race and a fifth in Belgium's La Fleche Wallone classic.

The Australian Olympic Committee said that Gollan won the Australian national road championship in 2003, silver in the road time trial and ranked in the top ten in the world.

"Gollan made her Olympic debut in the individual road race at the Athens 2004 Olympic Games, finishing 12th out of 67 riders. After three years with the Australian National Team, she turned pro in 2005 with the German squad Equipe Nürnberger Versicherung, the number one team in the women's ranks at the time," the AOC said.

Gollan posted seven top ten results in 2004 with a third in the Montreal World Cup, second in Italy's Trofeo Alfredo Binda road race, eighth and ninth in the GP Plouay and La Fleche Wallone road classics, and a GC ninth at the Giro d'Italia Donne (Rosa) grand tour.

In 2006 her results included a win at the Grand Prix de Santa Ana, a GC fourth in El Salvador's Vuelta Ciclistica, a stage win at Le Tour du Grand Montreal and a ninth place in the Commonwealth Games road race.

Gollan spoke about her difficulties adjusting to life in Germany and said she wanted to go back to Italy.

However, in 2006 she signed with Italian team Nobilli and was based at the small town of Novellara about ten kilometres from Bergamo, which was 50-60 kilometres from where the AIS were based in Barrese.

Gollan highlighted the importance of the AIS for the development of Australian women's cycling, for producing top-level female athletes and giving them the opportunity to race at their best on the world stage. "It's largely about getting the girls over there and giving those Australians with promise a chance to shine," she said.

In 2007 Gollan claimed a GC third at the Tour de Feminin Limousin in France and a GC second at the Tour de Prince Edward Island in Canada. She also rode in the European road classics and the Giro Rosa grand tour and stopped racing in 2008.

Brodie Chapman

Brodie Mia Chapman (born April 1991) grew up at Mt Glorius 40km north of Brisbane and started mountain bike racing when 17 in 2008. A late starter to road racing in 2015, she recovered after being hit by cars while cycling in 2014 and in 2017.

She competed in women's road racing in 2016-17 in national and Victorian road series events as an amateur placing second in the GC at the Tour of the South West, third in the Baw Classic, sixth in the GC at the Tour of Gippsland, and second in the Giro Della Donna race from Warburton to Mt Donna Buang.

In 2018 Chapman was the overall winner of the women's

Herald Sun Tour and won its mountains classification and placed sixth in the national road race championships. She was signed by professional team Tibco-Silicon Valley Bank in 2018 and was fifth in the Amgen Tour of California and won two stages at the Tour of the Gila in New Mexico.

Chapman posted top performances in 2019 including a GC third in the Herald Sun Tour and was sixth in the Deakin University Women's road race at Geelong. She won the Gravel and Tar La Femme race in New Zealand; won the GC at the Tour of the Gila in New Mexico; was second in the GC at the Colorado Classic; sixth at the Amgen Tour of California; won a stage at the Tour de Feminin in the Czech Republic; and placed ninth in road race classic La Fleche Wallone.

In October 2020 when she was signed by top French team FDJ Nouvelle-Aquitaine Futuroscope for the 2021-22 seasons, FDJ general manager Stephen Delcourt said that Chapman is one of the best climbers in the world.

She won the Race Torquay in 2020, was tenth in the Deakin University Women's Race, and rode in the UCI road world championships in Italy and in the Belgian road classics.

Jessica Allen

Jessica Allen is from Perth and was a top junior cyclist and under 23 road cyclist. In 2011 she won the gold medal in the individual road time trial at the UCI junior road world championships held in Denmark.

Allen won the Oceania road race championship in 2014 and the national road criterium championship in 2017 and rode for the Orica-Scott team in 2016-17 and later Mitchelton-Scott. She placed second in the GC at the Mitchelton Bay Classic series in 2017. In 2018-19 she rode in European road races and time trials and was second in the Ladies Tour of Norway Team Time Trial and became a 'super domestique' for the team. She was fifteenth at the Race Torquay in early 2020 and was described by Mitchelton-Scott as a real team player with a lot of experience.

Shannon Malseed

Shannon Malseed came from Narrawong, Victoria and broke through at under 23 level in 2015, winning the national road race and criterium championships. In 2016, she won the Oceania road championship and in 2016 was fifth in Canada's White Spot/Delta road race.

Malseed won the elite national road race championship in 2018 and riding for Team Tibco-Silicon Valley Bank, claimed second in the GC at China's Tour of Chongming Island and was seventh in the GC at the Santos Women's Tour. In 2019 she claimed second in the GC at the USA's Joe Martin Stage Race. In January 2020, Malseed crashed at the Lexus of Blackburn Bay Crits series in Victoria, suffering a fractured scapula, fractured vertebrae, and head injury but in May 2020 was training on the road.

Other cyclists and emerging champions who have won national road championships and performed strongly from junior and under 23 to elite level up to 2019-2020 include Alexandra Manly (see track cycling), Jaime Gunning, Ruby Rosemary-Gannon, and Sarah Gigante.

Jaime Gunning

Jaime Gunning, from the Balmoral Cycling Club in Brisbane, was the Australian and Oceania junior national time trial champion in 2017. She posted four second places in the under 23 national time trial/road race championships between 2017-2020. In 2019 Gunning was signed by Specialized Women's Racing domestic cycling team and was a GC sixth at the Tour Down Under. At the Herald Sun Tour in February 2020 she claimed a GC second, 12 seconds behind GC winner Lucy Kennedy.

Ruby Roseman-Gannon

Ruby Roseman-Gannon rides for the Brunswick Cycling Club in Melbourne. She was a top junior on the road and track from 2012 and was second in the under 19 national road championship in 2015 and third in the Oceania road championships in 2016. A neuroscience student at the University of South Australia, she joined Ara Pro Racing Sunshine Coast in 2019.

Roseman-Gannon was second in the elite national criterium championship in 2019-20, winning the under 23 criterium title both years. In 2020 she was a GC second behind Chloe Hosking at the Lexus of Blackburn Bay Crits and in 2021 claimed a GC third place at the Santos Festival of Cycling stage race.

Sarah Gigante

Sarah Gigante is from Melbourne and rides for the Brunswick Cycling Club. In 2017 she won the National Road Series and silver at the Oceania road championships in Canberra. In 2018 Gigante won the under 19 national road race and time trial championships, and Oceania road cycling championship. At the track world championships, she won the under 19 points race.

Gigante rode for the Roxsolt Attaquer team in 2019, was awarded the 2019 Amy Gillet Foundation cycling scholarship and studied science at the University of Melbourne. Gigante, when 18 in January 2019, burst onto elite women's road cycling, winning the elite and under 23 national road championships, 50 seconds ahead of Australian champion Amanda Spratt. The gold medal win came eight months after a club race crash when she broke her elbow, wrist, and shoulder. She told ABC News: "It's more than a dream, I wouldn't even dream this big."

In 2019 she also won the under 23 national time trial championship, the under 23 Oceania championship road race and time trial titles and the Spirit of Tasmania Cycling Tour.   In February 2020 she placed fifth in the GC at the Herald Sun Tour and rode in road races internationally for Team Tibco-SVB. In January 2021 Gigante claimed the GC at the Santos Festival of Cycling stage tour and in 2021 won her first elite national road individual time trial championship (28.6km) at Mt Buninyong, defeating defending champion Grace Brown.

In 2000, Anna Wilson was ranked number one in women's world road cycling. Photo courtesy Victorian Cycling Hall of Fame.

Kathy Watt winning the road race gold medal at the 1992 Olympic Games at Barcelona. Photo Graham Watson.

Michelle Ferris won silver in the sprint at the 1996 Atlanta Olympic Games. Photo courtesy Victorian Cycling Hall of Fame.

Julie Speight won Australia's first women's sprint medal at the 1990 Commonwealth Games. Ray Bowles photo.

Anna Meares' many track gold medals include 2 Olympic, 5 Commonwealth, and 11 Worlds' medals. Ray Bowles photo.

Australia's first bicycle race for women was held over two miles at the Ashfield Recreational Grounds, Sydney in 1888 and was won by Dot Morrell when women raced on high wheelers. Women's track cycling races became more popular in the 1930s and after the end of the second world war from 1946 (see Women Record Breakers).

In 1947 the Victorian Women's Professional Cycling Union (VWPCU) started and ran track racing successfully until 1954, when women's cycling in Victoria ceased after a dispute between the professional and amateur cycling associations. The Australian women's professional track championships started in 1949, while the national women's track championships restarted in 1952.

However, the women's national amateur track championships lapsed in the 1950s and in some states, women were left with club racing and sports carnival races. The reinstatement of women's national track cycling came in 1979-80 with the start of the national amateur track cycling championships.

In the 1980s only three to four titles were contested in the individual pursuit, sprint, one kilo time trial and scratch race. In 1979 Barbara Eason won the one kilo time trial at Devonport. In 1980 at Hurstville, Diane Brown won the sprint, Vickie Carne won the kilo time trial and Sian Mullholland won the scratch race, and in 1981 Vicki Carne won the sprint and the scratch race. Australia's state amateur cycling associations ran track cycling until the reunification of amateur and professional cycling between 1993 and 1995 when races were declared 'open'.

The first track world championship events for women were held at Paris in 1958 in the sprint and individual pursuit, but it wasn't until 2017 when the madison was added to the UCI women's track world championships that women achieved parity with the men's events, according to cyclinglegends (UK).

When the first women's cycling events were established on the Olympic program at Los Angeles in 1984, the Australian Cycling Federation chose against sending a women's track contingent to contest the Olympic events. Australia's women track cyclists competed at their first Olympic Games at Seoul in 1988 in the track sprint.

In 1987 the Australian Institute of Sport established a track cycling program in Adelaide with high performance programs for talented female cyclists.

Women's track cycling events at the Commonwealth Games started in 1990 with the 3000m individual pursuit and the women's 1000m match sprint, the points race was added in 1994, the 500m time trial in 2002 and the scratch race in 2010.

From the mid-1990s Cycling Australia became the national governing body for track racing and ran the TrackNats national championships from the 2000s, a pathway to be selected for Australia internationally at the Olympic Games, Commonwealth Games and UCI world track cycling championships. Among the winners of the women's elite TrackNats in its first decade from 1980 were Sian Mulholland (seven titles), Vicky Carne (three titles), Linda Orrow (four sprint titles), Donna Gould (two pursuit titles), also an Olympic road cyclist, Michelle Culyer (two titles), Julie Speight (11 titles to 1991), and Lucy Tyler (11 track titles) across the sprint, time trial, individual pursuit, and points. She also rode for the USA.

Later multiple winners of the TrackNats to the 2010s include Alayna Burns, a dual national track champion in 1999, who won the gold medal in the points race at the 1988 Commonwealth Games in Kuala Lumpur.

Belinda Goss was a four-time points race national track champion (2007-10) and scratch race TrackNats winner in 2010. Goss won three bronze medals in the scratch race at the UCI track world championships in 2008-09-10, and two Oceania Games track championships.

Megan Dunn was a gold medallist in the points race and scratch race at the 2010 Commonwealth Games in Delhi.

Melissa Hoskins, the 2015 TrackNats points race champion, won silver medals in the scratch race at the UCI track world championships in 2012 and the team pursuit in 2012-13, and a gold medal in the team pursuit at the 2015 track world championship at Yvelines, France.

Rikki Belder was the 500m time trial champion in 2015 and was a six-time national track champion in the team sprint up to 2018.

Julie Speight

Julie Speight (born 1966) was 15 when she started her track racing in 1980 with the Randwick Botany Cycling Club in Sydney. She competed at the national track cycling championships in 1983 when, only three national titles were made available to our top track women, winning the national sprint championships and in the same year, won the national road race and contested the world road championships. Speight won 11 national track titles from 1983: the sprint and time trial in 1983; the scratch race in 1985; the sprint, time trial and scratch race in 1988; the time trial in 1989; the point score in 1990; and in 1991 the sprint, scratch race and point score titles.

In 1988 at Seoul, Speight became the first woman to ride on the track for Australia at the Olympic Games, finishing fifth in the sprint. Then in 1990 she won Australia's first-ever women's sprint medal with a silver medal at the Commonwealth Games in Auckland.

Speight petitioned the NSW Cycling Union to hold a women's state championships for the team pursuit, before doing the same with the Australian Cycling Federation to include the points race as a national title for the 1990 nationals.

She told cyclingnews in November 2017 she was proud of having set an example for the likes of Michelle Ferris Anna Meares, who achieved success at the world titles and Olympic Games. "I felt really happy that I had fought so hard for women to be included in the track team. They are both such amazing riders and now because of them, little girls believe they can be Olympic cyclists. Women cyclists make excellent role models."

Speight retired from cycling in the early 1990s and was inducted into the Cycling Australia Hall of Fame in November 2017.

Kathryn (Kathy) Watt

Kathy Watt (born 1964) came from Warragul in Victoria. Her father was a marathon runner, and she took up running, winning the national junior 3km title. Watt switched to cycling in 1985 when 21 and went on to become one of Australia's best all-round track and road cycling champions (see road cycling).

Watt starred in the 1992 Olympic track individual pursuit elimination races and defeated another quadruple world champion, American Rebecca Twig in the semi-finals. Watt was beaten in the final of the pursuit by Germany's Petra Rossner. However, the Australian Olympic Committee said ACF coaching staff insisted that Watt train exclusively for the road race and she was unable to practice on the track for three months, until three days between the road and track events and often argued with head coach Charlie Walsh about this.

From 1988 to 2000 at the national track cycling championships, Watt won twelve elite track titles and gold medals, including eight 3000m individual pursuit titles, and points race, sprint and time trial titles.

In 1992 Watt won the individual pursuit and the sprint championships; in 1993 the individual pursuit, the sprint, and the time trial championships; and in 1994 the individual pursuit and the points championships. During this time, Watt competed against strong opposition from national track champions such as Julie Speight, Lucy Tyler-Sharman, and Michelle Ferris. At the 1990 Auckland Commonwealth Games, Watt won the silver medal riding in the 3000m individual pursuit. More success came at the 1994 Commonwealth Games at Victoria, Canada with a gold medal in the 3000m individual pursuit and two gold medals in road events.

Watt was involved in a legal dispute over who would ride in the individual pursuit at the 1996 Atlanta Olympics track events, after she was replaced several days before the event by Lucy Tyler-Sharman. Watt appealed to the International Court of Arbitration which ordered that Watt be reinstated in the race.

She ended her successful 20-year career on the track and road in 2008 and works as a cycling coach and personal trainer. Watt was inducted into the Sport Australia, Cycling Australia, and Victoria Cycling Halls of Fame, and was awarded the Order of Australia Medal.

Michelle Ferris

Michelle Ferris (born 1976) came from Warrnambool in Victoria and discovered her love of cycling in high school after taking part in a charity ride. At the inaugural junior national women's track cycling championships in 1992, she posted faster times than two elite women aiming for Barcelona Olympic Games selection. She was a scholarship holder at the Australian Institute of Sport.

At 18 Ferris won the silver medal in the sprint for Australia at the 1994 Commonwealth Games at Victoria in Canada. At the Kuala Lumpur Commonwealth Games in 1998, she won another silver medal in the sprint and became one of our best female sprinters on the track.

Ferris was one of the few cyclists to say publicly she was gay. She won 10 national track championships including the sprint and the 500m time trial three times in the one year, in 1996, 1997 and 1998; the time trial title in 1999; the 200m flying time trial (1998, 2000) and the sprint title in 2000.

At the UCI track cycling world championships, Ferris won seven medals: at Bogota in 1995 and Manchester in 1996 winning bronze medals in the 500m time trial; at Perth in 1997 winning silver medals in the sprint and the time trial; and at Bordeaux in 1998 winning another silver in the sprint and bronze in the 500m time trial. At Berlin in 1999, she won her third consecutive world track silver medal in the sprint after being edged out of a gold medal by French cycling great Felicia Ballanger.

Competing at the Olympic Games in 1996 at Atlanta then the Sydney Olympics in 2000, she won a silver medal in the sprint at Atlanta and a silver medal in the 500m time trial at Sydney.

The Australian Olympic Committee said that after posting the fastest qualifying time, Ferris proved her strength and tactical ability in the knock-out sprint duels, winning her way to the final where she lost to Ballanger. "Her result was the best recorded by an Australian cyclist at the Atlanta Games," the AOC said.

"Four years later in Sydney Ferris set a scorching personal best time in the women's 500m time trial, only to have Ballanger edge her out for the gold medal. Ferris also competed in the sprint, placing fourth." In 2018 Ferris was inducted into the Cycling Australia Hall of Fame. In a Ride Media interview in November 2018, she was described as a genuine pioneer for cycling in Australia. Ferris said: "I certainly didn't do it for the money because there was no money. But I would not change a thing. I would do it all over again because I loved it."

Katie Mactier

Katie Mactier (born 1975) took up competitive cycling in 1999 at age 24 with Melbourne's Carnegie Caulfield Cycling Club and held a scholarship at the Australian Institute of Sport. Better known as a top track pursuit and endurance cyclist of the 2000-2010s decades, she was an all-round road and track cycling champion who won two national road championships and rode as a professional road cyclist from 2002 to 2008 (see road cycling).

At the national track cycling championships, Mactier won gold in the 3000m individual pursuit four times between 2003 and 2007. Competing at the UCI track world cycling championships in 2003 in Stuttgart and in 2004 at Melbourne, Mactier won silver medals in the 3000m individual pursuit. She went one better winning gold for Australia in the individual pursuit at Los Angeles in 2005, then won three bronze medals in the individual pursuit at the worlds from 2006 to 2008.

The Australian Olympic Committee said that Kate Mactier had been competing as a track cyclist for about eighteen months when she won a silver medal, behind the indomitable Sarah Ulmer of New Zealand, in the 3000 metres individual pursuit at Athens 2004. Mactier was second in the event at the previous two world championships in 2003 and in 2004 behind Ulmer. The Australian Olympic Committee said. "In the ride-off for the gold medal both Ulmer and Mactier shattered the previous world record, the third time Mactier had set a personal best time during the competition.

"After Athens, Mactier became the world champion in the event in 2005 and won the bronze medal at the next three world championships. At Beijing 2008, she qualified seventh fastest but was beaten in the quarter-final by the gold medallist, Romero of Great Britain."

At the 2006 Commonwealth Games in Melbourne, Mactier claimed the gold medal for Australia in the 3000m individual pursuit.

Mactier, now Katie Henderson, was inducted into the Cycling Australia Hall of Fame in November 2017.

Mactier said that her silver medal at the 2004 Athens Olympics followed by her 2005 world championship win and her win at the 2006 Melbourne Commonwealth Games are probably her three greatest achievements.

Anna Meares, Queen of the track

Anna Meares (born 1983) started cycling at 11 with older sister Kerrie Meares. Growing up in Middlemount then Rockhampton in Queensland, she was a member of the Rockhampton Cycling Club. She won a scholarship to the Queensland Academy of Sport in 1998 and was later based at the Australian Institute of Sport in Adelaide.

From 2003 to 2016, Meares competed at the elite women's national track championships winning 25 national titles and gold medals, including nine sprint, three team sprint, six 500m time trial, six keirin (sprint), and one 200m flying time trial titles. Meares held Olympic, world, Commonwealth and national records and became Australia's greatest female track sprinter, having all the qualities of a top track sprinter in speed, power, and tactical ability.

Her first international success came in 2002 at the Commonwealth Games in Manchester, winning bronze in the sprint when sister Kerrie Meares won the gold medal. She won more Commonwealth Games medals at Melbourne in 2006, taking gold in the 500m time trial (setting a new Games record) and silver in the sprint. At the Delhi Commonwealth Games in 2010, Meares won gold medals in the 500m time trial and the sprint in new Games record times and the team sprint with Kaarle McCulloch. In 2014 at Glasgow she won more Games gold in the 500m time trial and a silver in the sprint.

Meares set new records for women's track cycling at the Olympic Games winning a gold medal in the 500m time trial at Athens in 2004 and a bronze medal in the sprint; a silver in the sprint at Beijing in 2008; gold in the sprint and bronze in the team sprint (with Kaarle McCulloch) at London in 2012; and bronze in the keirin at Rio de Janeiro in 2016. At the Athens Olympics Meares was Australia's first track gold medallist and the first woman to break the 34-second barrier in the 500m time trial, and also claimed world and Olympic records. The Queensland Sporting Hall of Fame said that Meare's performances were not all about class. "She was a gold medallist for courage too. Seven months out from the 2008 Olympic Games she crashed at 65 km/hr and broke her neck. She was back on the bike ten days later on route to a very special silver medal in Beijing."

At the London Olympics in 2012, AOC historian Harry Gordon said Meares faced the daunting task of taking on defending Olympic title holder Victoria Pendleton competing at her last Olympic event and dealing with a parochial home crowd cheering for their champion. "Despite crossing the line second by the narrowest of margins in the opening race of the final, Meares was awarded the win after Pendleton was deemed to have moved out on her Australian rival in the final straight. Meares rode the second race to perfection letting Pendleton take the lead before eventually wearing her down to win her second Olympic gold medal," Gordon said.

She was also the first Australian cyclist and athlete to win a medal at four Olympic Games, and the first Australian cyclist to win six Olympic medals.

Anna Meares also has an incredible record of 12 appearances at the UCI track cycling world championships from 2003 at Stuttgart to 2016 at London, winning four gold medals in the 500m time trial, three golds in the keirin sprint, three in the team sprint, and one in the sprint and accumulated 27 medals overall.

Meares faced one of her biggest challenges before the

2016 Rio Olympic Games and said: "Most people were unaware that just to get to Rio I had six cortisone injections through my spine."

In her new book, Anna Meares Now, Meares pays tribute to her main coaches, Reg Tucker, Martin (Merv) Barras, and for the last nine years of her career, Garry West, a former track pursuit champion and coach of Japan and the USA. She formed a special bond with West while she was recovering from a broken neck in 2008 and when West took charge of Cycling Australia's track program. West was diagnosed with Motor Neurone Disease (MND) and died a year after the Rio Olympic Games.

In her book, Anna Meares Now, Meares said about her bronze medal in the keirin at the 2016 Rio Olympics: "Considering all that went into it, that bronze was as much a success as any gold I have every earned."

The Anna Meares Velodrome in the Brisbane suburb of Chandler was named after her. She was the winner of the Australian Cyclist of the Year award in 2008 and 2012.

Anna Meares retired from competitive cycling in October 2016. She was inducted into the Queensland Sporting Hall of Fame in 2018 and was awarded the Order of Australia Medal.

Kerrie Meares

Kerrie Meares (born 1982) came from Rockhampton, Queensland and started track cycling with younger sister Anna at Mackay. She was a member of the Rockhampton Cycling Club and broke several state and national records in the junior track sprint. Representing Queensland at the national track championships in 2001-2009 she won 15 titles that included the 500m time trial, the sprint (four), the team sprint (seven), the keirin and the scratch race.

Selected for the 2002 Commonwealth Games in Manchester, Kerrie won gold medals in the 500m time trial and in the sprint. At the Commonwealth Games in Melbourne in 2006, she won bronze medals in the sprint and the 500m time trial.

Meares was named the Queensland sportswomen of the year in 2002. She was a contender for the 2004 Olympics track team but pulled out due to injuries from track crashes earlier that year.

The Commonwealth Games Association said in August 2017 that Kerrie Meares, one year older than Anna, launched the family dominance winning the inaugural 500m track time trial at the 2002 Manchester Commonwealth Games. "Fifteen years and four Games later, only Meares sisters have won this event."

At the UCI track cycling world championships in Ballerup in 2002, Meares won a silver medal in the sprint and bronze in the 500m time trial. She also found success competing in the Oceania Games track championships, winning seven track titles starting from Melbourne in 2004 to 2007 at Invercargill.

She retired from cycling and with former track cyclist partner Emily Rosemond, runs the Track Cycling Academy in Brisbane where Kerrie coaches and mentors the next generation of young cyclists.

Katherine Bates

Katherine (Kate) Bates (born 1982) is from Sydney and started track racing at 10. She rode for the Parramatta Cycling Club and is the sister of road cyclist Natalie Bates. When 16 in 1999, she won a silver medal in the junior 2000m individual pursuit at the world track cycling championships. She won seven TrackNats national track championships, winning the individual pursuit in 2001 and 2005, the scratch race in 2005-2006, and the points race in 2001, and 2005-2006.

Bates represented Australia with distinction at two Olympic Games and two Commonwealth Games. At the Manchester Commonwealth Games in 2002, Bates won gold in the points race and silver in the individual pursuit. When the Commonwealth Games came to Melbourne in 2006, Bates won her second gold medal in the points race and silver in the individual pursuit.

She placed fourth in the 3000m individual pursuit at the 2004 Olympic Games at Athens and represented Australia on the road and track at the 2008 Beijing Olympics.

At the UCI track world cycling championships, Bates posted top performances in the points, individual pursuit, and the scratch race between 2001 and 2011 winning eight medals, including a gold in the points race at Palma de Mallorca in 2007; four silver medals, one in the points race at Bordeaux in 2006, and silver medals in the points race, individual pursuit and scratch race at Los Angeles in 2005; and bronze medals in the individual pursuit in 2002 and the points race in 2006.

In 2005 and 2006 she was third in the Geelong World Cup and in 2011 won the scratch race and individual pursuit at the Oceania track championships.

Bates rode as a professional for leading European cycling teams from 2002 to 2011. Her top road results included a third in the Amstel Gold road classic in 2002, a GC win at the Geelong Tour in 2003 and second in the national criterium championship. In 2007 she won the GC in the Bay Classic series and claimed a GC third at the Tour du Grand Montreal. She won the national road race championships in 2006.

Bates said that her best career performances included her best-ever Olympic result of fourth in the individual pursuit, and her world track championship gold medal in the worlds points race in 2007, which she said was the highlight of her career.

After a hip injury in Italy derailed her career, she retired in 2011 and worked for SBS Television as a cycling commentator.

When Bates was inducted into the Cycling Australia Hall of Fame in 2019, she said she was honoured to stand shoulder to shoulder with some of cycling's legends.

Bates told Cycling Australia: "I want to acknowledge and thank the village of people who helped me through my career, with special mention to my family for their unwavering support, and my coach Gary Sutton for his patience and belief in me."

She added that, "anything I achieved, I did so because of the team behind me."

Josephine Tomic

Josephine Tomic (born 1989) came from Subiaco, Perth. She and started road cycling at 14 and rode for Northern Districts Cycling Club. Competing at under 17 level in 2004, she won the individual pursuit at the national track championships and won the New Zealand Oceania Tour.

At the UCI under 19 track world championships in 2007, Tomic set a world record for the 2000m pursuit winning the gold medal and won gold in the track points and the road time trial.

Tomic went on to win 10 elite TrackNats championships in from 2008 to 2012, three in the individual pursuit, five in the team pursuit for Western Australia, and one in the points race and omnium.

At the elite UCI track world championships, Tomic won a gold medal in the tough omnium event at Pruszkow in 2009 and bronze in the team pursuit. She won gold in the team pursuit at Ballerup in 2010 and at Melbourne in 2012, won a silver medal in the team pursuit.

She represented Australia at the 2012 Olympic Games in London in the team pursuit when the Australian team finished fourth.

Tomic also competed as an elite road cyclist and rode in Australia and Europe in 2008-2012 and for the Lotto Ladies Team in 2010. Her top results include the GC at the Tour de Perth in 2008, GC second in the Bay Criterium Series in 2009, and winning the under 23 national road time trial championship in 2009. She was inducted into the Sport Australia Hall of Fame in 2009.

Kaarle McCulloch

Kaarle McCulloch (born 1988) comes from Sydney and started cycling while in high school after switching from athletics as a promising middle-distance runner. She won a bronze medal at the 2006 UCI junior track world championships and rode for the St George Cycling Club.

McCulloch, a sprinter, competed in the elite TrackNats championships and in 2008 at Sydney won the sprint, 500m time trial and keirin sprint. She went on to win 15 national track championship titles up to 2019 with two in the sprint, three in the team sprint for New South Wales, three in the keirin, and seven in the time trial.

Representing Australia at her first Commonwealth Games at Delhi in 2010, McCulloch won a silver medal in the 500m time trial and a gold medal in the team sprint with Anna Meares. She teamed with Anna Meares again in 2012 at the Olympic Games in London, winning a bronze medal in the team sprint.

She missed the 2014 Commonwealth Games due to a knee injury. At the Commonwealth Games in 2018 at Brisbane, McCulloch won gold medals in the 500m time trial and in the team sprint (with Stephanie Morton), silver in the keirin and bronze in the match sprint.

McCulloch became one of our best and most successful track sprint champions. Competing at the UCI track world championships from 2009 at Pruszkow, she won gold in the team sprint with Anna Meares. McCulloch repeated her team sprint win at the track worlds at Ballerup in 2010 and at Apeldoorn in 2011, she teamed with Meares and added two more gold medals. Competing in the team sprint, McCulloch won silver at Melbourne in 2012, bronze at Yvelines, France in 2015 with Anna Meares, and silver at Hong Kong in 2017 with Stephanie Morton.

At the UCI track world championships at Pruszkow in 2019, McCulloch claimed three medals: gold in the team sprint with Morton for her fourth world team sprint gold and world rainbow jersey, silver in the keirin, and bronze in the 500m time trial. Cycling Australia said: "The stellar form of Kaarle McCulloch continued with the Sydney cyclist completing a set of medals, winning a surprise silver in the keirin final."

Despite injuries, she won silver in the team sprint with Stephanie Morton at the 2020 track world championships at Berlin. Now 32, McCulloch is in Australia's Cycling Team for the 2021 Tokyo Olympics and with Morton's retirement, will concentrate on individual track events.

Stephanie Morton

Stephanie Morton (born 1990) is from Adelaide. She started cycling aged 15 and rode for the South Coast Cycling Club in Adelaide. In 2011 she became a tandem pilot for para-cyclist Felicity Johnson and the duo won gold at the 2012 London Paralympic Games in the kilo time trial tandem event.

At the TrackNats championships in Adelaide in 2013, Morton won the sprint and the keirin, and the team sprint with South Australian sprinter Rikki Belder and the duo won five team sprint golds for South Australia. From 2013 to 2018, Morton won 13 TrackNats national championship with three in the sprint, six in the team sprint, and four in the keirin. In 2014 and 2017, Morton won the keirin, sprint and team sprint titles at the Oceania track championships.

Competing at her first Commonwealth Games at Glasgow in 2014 Morton defeated her idol Anna Meares to win the sprint gold medal and she also won silver in the 500m time trial.

Returning to the Commonwealth Games at Brisbane in 2018, Morton defeated New Zealand's Natasha Hansen in the women's sprint final. She blitzed the sprint events winning three gold medals in the sprint, keirin and team sprint, and silver in the 500m time trial.

A Commonwealth Games GC2018 report said that Stephanie Morton made history on several fronts: "She became the first woman to defend a Commonwealth Games individual sprint title, and the first Australian woman to win individual sprint gold medals at two Commonwealth Games (Glasgow 2014 and GC2018)."

Now Australia's number one female track sprinter, she competed at the UCI track world championships in 2017 at Hong Kong, five weeks after fracturing her shoulder in the TrackNats keirin. Morton won silver in the team sprint with Kaarle McCulloch and silver in the individual sprint.

In 2018 at the track world championships at Apeldoorn, Morton was Australia's only women's medallist winning silver in the sprint. Selected for her fifth UCI track worlds championship at Pruszkow in 2019, she won silver in the sprint and gold in the team sprint with Kaarle McCulloch.

At the 2020 UCI track world championships in Berlin, she claimed team sprint silver with McCulloch and her first world medal in the keirin with bronze. Leading into the track worlds Morton and McCulloch were carrying injuries. Morton said: "I think we are the happiest silver medallists you have ever met. We had to go through some pretty dark clouds to even look at the rainbows here."

Morton, who studied for a Bachelor of Justice, announced her retirement in November 2020 and will concentrate on her post-racing career. She told Cycling Australia she has a lot of favourite moments in the past fifteen years.

"Winning three gold medals in front of a home crowd at the Gold Coast Commonwealth Games would have to be up there, along with becoming world champion in 2019 (in the team sprint) with Kaarle," Morton said.

Annette Edmondson

Annette Edmondson (born 1991) is from Adelaide. She started cycling at 13 through a South Australian Institute of Sport high school talent program with brother Alex and rode for Norwood CC. From 2007 she won ten junior Oceania and national track titles in sprint and endurance. At the TrackNats from 2011 she won 18 national titles including the individual pursuit (3), points race (4), scratch (4), omnium (3), madison (3) and team pursuit.

Edmondson made her Olympic Games debut in 2012 in the team pursuit at London when the Australian team was edged out in the gold medal and bronze medal ride offs.

Riding in the first ever Olympic track omnium event at London, she claimed a bronze medal in the tough six-event race. At the 2018 Rio Olympic Games, a training crash on the eve of the Games hit Australia's team pursuit chances, while Edmondson was eighth in the omnium.

She competed at two Commonwealth Games beginning at Glasgow in 2014 claiming a gold medal in the scratch race and silver in the individual pursuit. At Brisbane in 2018, Edmondson won gold in the team pursuit with Alex Manly, Amy Cure, Ashlee Ankudinoff and Georgia Baker, and the bronze medal in the individual pursuit.

At the 2012 UCI track world championships in Melbourne, Edmondson won silver medals in the omnium and in the team pursuit with Melissa Hoskins and Josephine Tomic. At Minsk in 2013 she won silver in the team pursuit and bronze medals in the individual pursuit and omnium. In 2014 at Cali, Colombia, she won bronze medals in the team pursuit and omnium. The Australian Olympic Committee said at the 2015 UCI track worlds at Yvelines, Edmondson made history alongside Hoskins, Amy Cure and Ashlee Ankudinoff in the team pursuit.

"The quartet won world championship gold and broke the world record," the AOC said. "Edmondson backed this result up with gold in the omnium to become a dual world champion."

Now one of our best track endurance cyclists in the fast, relentless pace and precision riding of the team pursuit, at the 2019 track world championships at Pruszkow, Edmondson, riding with Ankudinoff, Cure, Manly and

Baker, claimed another gold medal for Australia in the 3000m team pursuit. During the 2019-20 World Cup season, Edmonson won two gold medals in the madison with Georgia Baker, won team pursuit gold and silver and was selected for the 2021 Tokyo Olympics track team. At the 2020 UCI Track World Championships in Germany, she was fifth in the team pursuit.

Edmondson competed on the road from 2012 winning races including the Towards Zero Race, the GC at China's Tour of Chongming Island and the 2021 RoadNats elite women's criterium championship.

Amy Cure

Amy Cure (born 1992) is from Penguin-West Pine in Tasmania and joined the Mersey Valley Cycling Club. She went on to win UCI junior track world championships in 2009 in the scratch race and in the individual pursuit, the team pursuit and scratch race in 2010 and went on to be one of our best all-round track cyclists.

At the elite TrackNats championships Cure won silver in the individual pursuit in 2013, then 10 gold medals with wins in the in the individual pursuit in 2014-15; the team pursuit for Tasmania in 2014-15; the 25km points in 2017-18; the 10km scratch in 2017-2019; and the omnium championship in 2017.

Representing Australia at the Commonwealth Games at Glasgow in 2014, Cure won a silver medal in the scratch race and bronze in the 3000m individual pursuit. In 2018 when the Commonwealth Games track events were held in Brisbane, she claimed two gold medals for Australia in the scratch race and in the team pursuit.

Cure made her Olympic debut at the 2016 Games in Rio. A high-speed training crash affected her chances in the team pursuit and the Australian's finished fifth.

She competed at her first elite UCI track world cycling championships at Apeldoorn in 2011 placing fourth in the team pursuit. At Minsk in 2013, Cure won her first medals at the worlds with silver in the individual pursuit and team pursuit. In 2014 at the Cali track world championships Cure won a gold medal in the points race and bronze medals in the individual pursuit and team pursuit. At Yvelines, France in 2015, she teamed with Ashlee Ankudinoff, Annette Edmondson, and Melissa Hoskins to win gold in the 3000m team pursuit setting a new world record time of 4mins, 13.683secs.

She became one of Australia's most successful track champions after winning three medals at the 2017 track world championships in Hong Kong. Cure won silver in the team pursuit, bronze in the omnium, and bronze in the madison teaming with Alexandra Manly.

Cycling Australia said: "Cure made history by becoming the first person in track cycling history to win a medal in six different world championship events."

In 2019 at the UCI track worlds at Pruszkow, she won a gold medal in the 3000m team pursuit and a silver in the madison riding with Georgia Baker. At the Berlin worlds in 2020, Cure finished fifth in the team pursuit before a crash halted her podium chances in the omnium.

On the road, Cure won around six elite road races in Europe and Australia and rode for the Lotto-Soudal and Wiggle High5 teams from 2014 to 2017. Cure's 13 career world championship medals (3 gold, 5 silver, 5 bronze) ranks second all-time for Australia's female track cyclists behind Anna Meares (27), Cycling Australia said.

She announced her retirement from international cycling on June 19, 2020 and said, "It's one of the most difficult decisions I have had to make."

Ashlee Ankudinoff

Ashlee Ankudinoff (born 1990) comes from Menai, Sydney. She was a hockey player and emerging triathlete who joined the St George Cycling Club at age 15 and took up road cycling.

In 2008 she switched to track endurance cycling and at the UCI junior track world championship, won gold in the individual pursuit and team pursuit.

Ankudinoff has accumulated TrackNats championship titles since 2010, including four titles in the omnium in 2010, 2012, 2015, and 2018; the individual pursuit in 2016 and 2018; and the 25km points race in 2018-2019.

Between 2009 and 2016 she won nine gold medals at the Oceania track championships and her coaches at the time included Brad McGee and Jason Batram.

Competing at the elite UCI track world UCI track world championships, at Pruszkow in 2009, Ankudinoff won bronze in the team pursuit. At Ballerup in 2010 she won her first elite gold medal at the track worlds in the team pursuit riding with Sarah Kent and Josephine Tomic, despite riding with a chronic back injury. At Melbourne in 2012 she won bronze in the individual pursuit. In 2015 at Yvelines, Ankudinoff won her second gold in the team pursuit in world record time (4:13.683) riding with Annette Edmondson, Amy Cure and Melissa Hoskins, ending Great Britain's four-year dominance of the event. At Hong Kong in 2017 she won silver medals in the individual pursuit and team pursuit.

In 2019 at the track world championships at Pruszkow, she claimed an historic double victory winning two gold medals riding in the individual pursuit, and in the team pursuit with Cure, Edmondson, and Georgia Baker. In 2020 at Berlin Ankudinoff was fifth in the team pursuit but crashed out of the omnium event.

The Australian Olympic Committee said Ankudinoff is "the only female cyclist to win four endurance world titles and now has Olympic glory in her sights."

At the Commonwealth Games in Brisbane in 2018 she won gold in the team pursuit with Baker, Cure, Edmondson and Alexandra Manly, and was fourth in the 300m individual pursuit. Making her Olympic track debut at Rio de Janeiro in 2016, Ankudinoff was fifth in the team pursuit.

She was selected in the Australian Cycling Team in track endurance events at Tokyo 2021. In December 2019 she told the St George & Sutherland Shire Leader newspaper: "I definitely would not be riding if I had ticked all my goals off and the Olympic gold is definitely one."

Ankudinoff was named the 2019 women's Elite Track Cyclist of the Year at the Cycling Australia awards.

Alexandra Manly

Alexandra Manly (born 1996) came from Kalgoorlie. After her family moved to the Adelaide Hills, she took up cycling at 14 through the South Australian Sports Institute talent identification program and rode for Central Districts Cycling Club. From 2012 to 2018 Manly competed on the road at the national and Oceania road championships at junior and under 23 level, winning four gold medals in the road time trial championships and two in the road race championships. She rode for Orica-AIS and Mitchelton-Scott professional road teams from 2015.

In 2015 competing at elite level she claimed gold in the team pursuit at the Track World Cup and in 2016 won the team pursuit at the Oceania track championships. In 2016-2018, she won three TrackNats team pursuit titles for South Australia and the madison title in 2017 riding with Danielle McKinnirey.

At the 2018 Commonwealth Games in Brisbane, Manly won a gold medal in the team pursuit with Ashlee Ankudinoff, Amy Cure and Annette Edmondson in a new race record and also was fourth in the 25km points race.

Manly won silver in the team pursuit and bronze in the madison teaming with Amy Cure at the UCI track world championships at Hong Kong in 2017. At the track worlds held at Pruszkow in 2019, Manly won a gold medal in the 25km points race and another gold in the team pursuit with Ankudinoff, Cure, Georgia Baker, and Edmondson.

The UCI website said that Alexandra Manly delivered Australia's sixth world title in the women's points race, after taking a lap on the field midway through the race, and scoring points in the final sprint to jump ahead of Lydia Boylan of Ireland by one point. "The plan worked out perfectly," Manly said. "I conserved energy at the start but still managed to get points. I knew I had to go for a lap, as I knew I would need a big chunk of points if I wanted to be in the mix for the medals. I just needed to stay composed for the final sprint, and I did."

Manly rode with the Michelton-Scott cycling team in the European road classics and tours up to 2019. She was selected for the Australian track cycling team for the Tokyo Olympics in 2021.

Georgia Baker

Georgia Baker (born 1994) is from Launceston, Tasmania. She was an all-round athlete who represented her state at netball and in the triathlon, before trying out in a talent identification program with the Tasmanian Institute of Sport. She focused on cycling and rode with Northern Districts Cycling Club near Launceston.

In 2011 Baker represented Australia in the team pursuit at the UCI junior track world championships at Moscow, winning a gold medal with Taylah Jennings and Emily Herfoss. She repeated the team pursuit win in 2012 at the UCI junior track worlds at Invercargill, New Zealand, winning gold with Jennings and Kelsey Robson.

Competing at the elite TrackNats championships, Baker was in Tasmania's winning team pursuit in 2014-15 and won the madison in 2016 with Danielle McKinnirey and in 2020 with Ashlee Ankudinoff.

In 2017 Baker was diagnosed with an abnormal heart rate (supraventricular tachycardia) that occurred two years after her father died of a heart attack, aged 44. Although non-life threatening, the then 23-year-old underwent surgery to prolong her cycling career. Two weeks after surgery she resumed training.

She courageously bounced back at the 2018 Commonwealth Games in Brisbane in the team pursuit, winning a gold medal with Ashlee Ankudinoff, Amy Cure, Annette Edmondson and Alexandra Manly.

Competing at Pruszkow in the 2019 UCI track world championships, Baker won a gold medal in the team pursuit with Ankudinoff, Manly, Edmondson and Cure, and won silver in the madison teaming with Amy Cure.

In 2020 at the Berlin track worlds, Baker finish fifth in the team pursuit in a disappointing world's campaign for the Australians, when she was impeded by a knee injury.

Baker showed great form during the 2019-20 UCI track World Cup season winning three madison gold medals (two with Edmondson) and gold and silver medals in the team pursuit.

Baker also competed on the road from 2014 riding for teams such as Wiggle-Honda/High5, Orica-Scott and TIS Cycling. She will compete on the track at her second Olympic Games at Tokyo in 2021.

Rebecca Wiasak

Rebecca Wiasak (born 1984) comes from Geelong and was a Victorian athletics champion in the under 20, 800 metres and competed in her age group at the 2009 world triathlon championships on the Gold Coast. She moved to Canberra in 2003 and trained for athletics at the AIS and was a university media and law graduate.

A late starter to track cycling in 2010, in 2011 she won the individual pursuit at the NSW championships and the TrackNats individual pursuit title in 2017. In 2012 she trained with the Australian track endurance squad and in the 2013-14 World Cup series won the individual pursuit.

Wiasak represented Australia at three UCI track world cycling championships, winning a gold medal in the individual pursuit at Yvelines in 2015; at London in 2016 she won her second track worlds gold medal in the individual pursuit and was fifth in the team pursuit; and at Hong Kong in 2017 she won silver in the team pursuit.

At the Commonwealth Games in Brisbane in 2018, Wiasak won a silver medal in the 3000m individual pursuit when 34, setting a new Australian record that bettered her previous 2015 national record set in France.

She was cut from the track endurance program in 2018. In 2018 and 2019 Wiasak won the RoadNats national criterium championship and finished a close sixth in 2020. In 2011 she won the GC at the Geelong Tour. Wiasak rides for the USA-based Fearless Femme professional road cycling team and in 2019, won three USA races and was placed five times.

Emily Petricola

The four-time reigning world champion in para-cycling, she won the C4 pursuit, omnium and scratch race at the 2020 track world championships in Canada. Petricola was aiming for selection for the 2021 Tokyo Olympics.

Paige Greco

Greco won gold in para-cycling in the C3 3000m individual pursuit at the 2020 track world championships, almost equalling her 2019 world record, when she won world titles in the individual pursuit and time trial.

Maeve Plouffe

Maeve Plouffe started cycling when 14 and rode for the Port Adelaide CC. In 2018 at the elite TrackNats championships Plouffe won the team pursuit with South Australia. In 2019 she won individual pursuit, team pursuit and madison titles and in October, gold and silver in the World Cup team pursuit. In 2020 she made her elite track worlds debut at Berlin in the 3000m individual pursuit and is in the 2021 Olympics track cycling team.

From 2018-19 other champions emerged at the elite Track Nats championships, including Tasmania's 2018-2019 champion **Macey Stewart** (one madison, one omnium); Queensland's 2018-2020 champion **Kristina Clonan,** (two madison, one sprint and one keirin); and Victoria's 2019-2020 champion **Caitlin Ward** (two time trial, one sprint and one keirin). Ward also won the 500m time trial title in 2016.

Darryn Hill, Shane Kelly & Gary Niewand celebrate their team sprint gold medals win at the 1996 track world championships, with coach Charlie Walsh. Graham Watson photo.

Dean Woods, team pursuit gold medallist at the 1984 Olympic Games at Los Angeles, won three gold medals at the Commonwealth Games. Ray Bowles photo.

Australia's first road world champion, Jack Hoobin, wins the 1950 world amateur road championships held in Belgium. Photo courtesy the AusCycling Victoria History Archive.

Clyde Sefton, Australia's first Olympic Games road race medallist, won silver at Munich in 1972. Ray Bowles photo.

Despite the break from racing in 1939-46 due to the Second World War, Australia's top road cyclists from the late 1940s produced world-class performances. Up to the 1990s they were helped by strong competition in tough, classic one-day road races such as the Warrnambool to Melbourne, the Goulburn to Sydney, the Grafton to Inverell, the Beverly to Perth in Western Australia, stage tours such as Australia's longest stage race the nine-day Sun Tour of Victoria, Tasmania's Tour of the North and a busy calendar of state road races.

Some of our best road cycling champions made fastest time in the Warrnambool road classic and from the 1930s-1970s include Dean Toseland, Billy Guyatt, Russell Mockridge, George Goodwin, Barry Waddell, Graeme Gilmore, Kerry Hoole, Keith Oliver, and Hilton Clarke.

In the Goulburn to Sydney (professional and amateur) classics three-time winners were: Hubert Opperman, Ken Ross, Alfred Strom, R.W. 'Fatty' Lamb, Charles Winterbottom, Rodney Crowe, and Fred Kerz, while Kerry Hoole and Robert Leach won five times.

From the late 1940s to the 1990s our trailblazing road cyclists found success in Europe, at the Olympics and world championships and include Russell Mockridge, Jack Hoobin, Clyde Sefton, Michael Wilson, Phil Anderson, Allan Peiper, and Neil Stephens.

The Herald Sun Tour

The Herald Sun Tour has been staged for 67 years and has become an international road race that generated media exposure for Victoria and Australian road cycling. Backed by the Herald Sun newspaper, the Herald Sun Tour is Australia's oldest professional stage race.

The Sun Tour of Victoria started in 1952 as a professional road race over nine stages and was the first professional stage race held in Victoria since the 1934 Centenary Thousand Classic. An estimated 500,000 people throughout Victoria saw the 'Sun Tour' as it was known then. Of the 56 starters, only 18 finished the six-day event throughout Victoria. The winner was Keith Rowley, a Maffra sheep farmer (42hrs, 57min, & 55sec), beating his brother Max Rowley by 49 seconds to win.

From the 1950s to the 1980s the Sun Tour has been won by many of Australia's top road cyclists including: George Goodwin; Russell Mockridge; Hec Sutherland; John Young (twice); Peter Panton (twice); Bill Lawrie; Barry Waddell (five times), Keith Oliver; Graham McVilly (twice); John Trevorrow (three times); Peter Besanko; Don Allan; Clyde Sefton; Terry Hammond (twice); Shane Sutton; Gary Sutton; and Neil Stephens.

The Sun Tour, now the Jayco Herald Sun Tour, is a five-stage race for men each February that boasts an honour roll of past winners that includes from the 1990s many of Australia's top international road cyclists in Bradley McGee, Baden Cooke, Stuart O'Grady, Robbie McEwen, Cadel Evans, Jack Bobridge, Nathan Haas, Simon Clarke, and Cameron Meyer that gave Australian riders great credibility and interest globally.

In February 2020, Mitchelton-Scott rider Jai Hindley

won the GC at the Jayco Herald Sun Tour, adding his name to an impressive Sun Tour honour roll. In 2018, a women's tour started, called the Lexus of Blackburn Women's Herald Sun Tour (see women's road cycling).

The Grafton to Inverell

Our top road champions have also chalked their names on the Grafton to Inverell road classic's honour roll. From 1961 the Grafton to Inverell Amateur Cycle Classic in New South Wales was Australia's toughest and longest one-day road cycling race covering 228 kilometres with over 3,300 metres of climbing.

The race developed into one of Australia's top three one-day road cycling classics. The Grafton to Inverell classic started as a handicap race and changed to a mass start race in 1979. Organised by the Inverell Cycling Club, its winners were Australia and New Zealand's best road cyclists and sometimes top international road cyclists.

Among the Grafton to Inverell winners and fastest time winners were: 1960 Olympics road cyclist Alan Grindall; Jim Lloyd (twice); Don Wilson (twice); Kevin Morgan; John Trevorrow (twice); Remo Sansonetti; Gary Sutton; Wayne Hammond; Michael Lynch; Andrew Logan; Stephen Fairless; Jamie Drew; David McKenzie; Robert McLachlan; Mark Jamieson; Sean Lake (twice); and Neil Van der Ploeg in 2017 in a new course record of 5:46:20.

The Commonwealth Bank Cycling Classic for amateur cyclists was another pathway that opened doors for our road cyclists to ride in Europe (see end of this chapter).

The first official Australian Amateur Road Championships started in 1928 while in the late 1940s to the 1990s era, men's road cycling champions usually had two main road racing championships as pathways.

Road cyclists came through their state amateur and professional ranks to compete in the Australian Amateur Road Cycling Championship and the professional long-distance road championships, which later became the Australian (Professional) National Road Championships.

Strong competition on the state and national road racing calendars helped to prepare the top Australian road cyclists for the road world championships, the Olympic Games, the Commonwealth Games, the tough European road circuit in countries such as France, Belgium and Italy, and in the UK, and later success at the Tour De France, the other European grand tours and the one-day road classics.

National professional road race championships

Track cycling superstar Russell Mockridge started and finished his career on the road and won the Australian amateur road race title in 1947, the start of his incredible cycling career in Australia and internationally.

At this time, the title of long-distance professional road champion of Australia from 1947 to 1949 was awarded at the 150 miles (240 km) mark at the Warrnambool to Melbourne Classic.

In 1948, the Australian 150 miles road championship was won by Keith McFarlane (Footscray, scr) from Graham Stabell (Footscray) and Max Rowley (Maffra), the brother of Keith Rowley. Graham Stabell won the Warrnambool Blue Riband for fastest time in 1951-52 and took the silver medal as runner-up in the national road championships four times (1948-49) and 1951-52).

In the 1949 Melbourne to Warrnambool road classic, the outright winner and fastest time were claimed by scratch man Alby Saunders, 27 of Footscray. Saunders sprinted brilliantly to take the honour from Graham Stabell and Eddie Smith (South Australia).

Saunders time, 6hrs, 12mins, 10secs, was a new record and broke the previous fastest set by R. W. (Fatty) Lamb off scratch (6:21:18) in 1932.

Earlier, Saunders outsprinted Stabell and Smith for the Australian 150-mile professional road championship. Saunders won two Australian national road race titles (1949, 1953) and won another fastest time in the Melbourne to Warrnambool in 1953.

In the 1947 to late 1990s era, only Russell Mockridge (1956-58) and John Trevorrow (1978-80) won three elite professional national road race championships joining road champions such as Hubert Opperman. Mockridge and Trevorrow also won one Australian amateur road championship each. The first National (professional) Road Race Championships were held in Sydney in 1950.

Keith Rowley

Keith Rowley won the first National Road Race Championship over 125 miles at Caringbah, Sydney in 1950. Rowley was born in 1919 and in October 1947, was a 46-year-old Maffra farmer who had won the 150 kilometres (sprint point) and claimed the Australian professional road title held in conjunction with the 31st Warrnambool to Melbourne road race. He also recorded fastest time of 6 hours, 57 minutes and 43seconds.

He placed second in the Tour of Gippsland in 1948 and the 1949 long distance road championship of (187 miles). In 1950 Rowley was third in the general classification (GC) for the Tour of the West.

Keith Rowley had another great year on the road in 1952 winning the GC at the inaugural Herald Sun Tour six-stage road race in Victoria when total prizemoney was 1,500 pounds.

The Sunday Herald reported in 1950, CYCLING TO ROWLEY. "Victorian Keith Rowley won the first official Australian professional cycling championship over 125 miles at Caringbah yesterday. Rowley, one of two brothers in the contest, raced away from Harold Johnson, of New South Wales, over the last 300 yards. He won by 50 yards in 5 hours, 55 minutes, 20 seconds."

His brother Max Rowley was also a top calibre road cyclist during 1948-1952 and won the Blue Riband for fastest time in the 1950 Melbourne to Warrnambool.

John Beasley (Snr)

John Beasley (Snr) was a top road cyclist of the 1950s and the son of 1920's road cycling ace J.J. (Jack) Beasley. Jack Beasley broke Snowy Munro's 100-mile road record set in 1909, before he claimed second place in the Road

Championships of Australasia in 1923, held during the 165-mile Melbourne-Warrnambool road classic. John Beasley won two Melbourne-Wangaratta road races (1950-51); the Australian National Road Championships in 1951; the GC for the Tour of the West in 1951; and was second in the Goulburn to Sydney classic in 1954.

Beasley was one of the first Australian professional road cyclists to ride in Europe after World War II. He rode in the 1952 and 1955 Tour De France grand tours but did not finish both tours hindered by tyre replacement issues in 1952 and food poisoning in 1955 and rode in both tours without proper support. In 1952 he finished 28th in the Paris-Nice road stage race.

Eddie Smith

Eddie Smith, who was born in Canberra, was listed as a South Australian, a Victorian and a New South Welshman in various classics, was another top road cycling ace of this era and rode for the Malvern Star cycling team. He won the gold medal for the 125-mile Australian National Road Championships twice, in 1954 and in 1955. In 1954, he had to dismount six times and use four different bikes to record the win at Ringwood, Melbourne.

In 1954 Smith won a great victory in the Goulburn to Sydney classic road race. Newspapers reported in September that Australian professional road champion Eddie Smith won the 128-mile Sydney Goulburn cycling race in race record time, beating Victorian John Beasley by eight yards with a powerful final sprint. He posted a time of six hours and nine seconds for the distance, which smashed by one minute, 51 seconds the record set by 1953 race winner Roger Arnold. Only 29 of the 100 amateur and professional cyclists who started finished the race.

Smith also won the Warrnambool-Melbourne road classic and the Blue Riband for fastest time in 1955. He created a new Warrnambool race record (6 hrs, 4 mins, 55secs) and won nearly 800 pounds in cash and trophies.

Russell Mockridge, road cycling sensation

Edward (Russell) Mockridge was a cycling sensation who won major races in Australia and internationally on the road and track. He was born on 18 July 1928 in South Melbourne. Mockridge attended the Geelong College and worked as a cadet journalist at The Geelong Advertiser. He was short-sighted and wore spectacles when he raced. After winning his first race in Geelong in 1946 riding a roadster so convincingly, it was thought he had taken a short cut and became known as the "The Geelong Flyer".

He won the Australian amateur road championship (201km) in 1947. A report in the Argus newspaper, 1 Sept 1947, said: "Victorians won the senior and junior Australian amateur road cycling championships at Centennial Park (Sydney) yesterday, Russell Mockridge (Geelong), an outsider, winning the senior race. Mockridge's win over the 125-mile course gave him first selection of six road riders for the 1948 Olympic Games in London. The others chosen are Hoobin (Vic), Caves (Qld), Nestor (SA), Williams (NSW), and Cook (NSW).

"Covering the 125 miles yesterday in 5hrs, 52mins, 55secs, Mockridge defeated Caves, Nestor, and Williams in that order. Mockridge began road riding only a few months ago and his ride yesterday was his fifth race in open company and his first win. Jack Hoobin, the favourite, fell after covering 16 miles, and was taken to hospital with a broken wrist. E. Ridings, another Victorian, fell in the same mishap and had to retire.

"RIDES IN SPECTACLES. Inexperience nearly cost Mockridge the race. At a furlong to go Mockridge was forced to the side of the road. But riding round the field he won by a wheel from Caves and Nestor. He rides with spectacles strapped to his head with sticking plaster. The course was the same as that used for the 1938 Empire Games, but the distance was doubled." Mockridge competed at the 1948 London Olympic Games in the road race and the team pursuit. In the road race, Mockridge suffered from several tyre punctures in the 194.6-km race and finished 26th in a field of 101.

Mockridge turned professional in 1953 and riding in France won the Tour de Vaucluse and in 1954 was fifth in the Grand Prix of Monaco. He also competed in track and six-day track racing (see track cycling).

In 1955 he became the first Australian to finish the Tour De France since Hubert Opperman in 1931. He rode with Victoria's John Beasley for a Luxembourg team. Mockridge was 64th of the 69 who finished the 1955 Tour out of 130 who started, despite issues such as food poisoning, a knee injury and chronic bronchitis.

Returning to Australia in 1956, Mockridge posted fastest time in the Melbourne to Warrnambool classic in 1956 (6hrs, 6mins, 12secs), a race record averaging a world record 44km an hour. Victorian road ace and rival George Goodwin bettered the record two years later. But it wasn't until Wayne Hildred's fastest time in 1980, then Dean Woods fastest time in 1990 (5hrs, 12min, 26secs) that Mockridge's and Goodwin's times were lowered.

Mockridge also won the Sun Tour (Victoria) in 1957 with a breath-taking ride, three national elite road race titles (1956-58), and 12 national championships during his short career. Tragedy occurred on September 13, 1958, when shortly after the start of the Tour of Gippsland, Mockridge was struck by a bus and killed on the Princes Highway at Clayton, Melbourne.

Already an international cycling star, he was 30 years old. Mockridge was an inaugural inductee into the Cycling Australia Hall of Fame in 2015. In 2018, Geelong's new home of cycling at the Belmont Criterium Track was named the Russell Mockridge Pavilion, in honour of one of the city's greatest ever sportsmen.

In 1921 the first men's amateur world road titles were held in Copenhagen, followed by the first professional road titles in Nurberg, Germany in 1927.

Jack Hoobin, our first road world champion

In 1950, Australia gained its first world road racing champion in the amateur ranks. Jack Hoobin, a well-performed Victorian road cyclist who was selected for the

1948 Australian Olympic road race, stormed home to win the 110-mile (177km) world amateur road championship in a sprint finish at Moorslede, Belgium on Sunday, 20 August 1950.

From Victoria (born June 23, 1927 in London, UK) Jack Hoobin is best known to the cycling public for his breakthrough win. But the 22-year-old Hoobin was no 'flash in the pan' success. He started cycling when four years old and was soon racing with the Cheltenham cycling club in Melbourne. In 1945 when 18, he enlisted in the Army near the end of World War II he rode a daily 100km round trip from his home to the Balcombe Camp.

In 1947, cycling pundits saw the first glimpse of Hoobin's potential as he made fastest times or wins in Victorian Amateur Cycling Union 50, 75 and 100-mile races and pushed his bike uphill to the finish line after puncturing to win one race.

Jack Hoobin was named to the 1948 Australian Olympic team on the strength of his wins in the 1948 Victorian Championship and the 125-mile Sun Classic on the Broadmeadows circuit. Despite a series of punctures, he finished sixth (the first Australian) in the 124-mile Olympic road race at London's Great Windsor Park. Hoobin was also a highly accomplished track cyclist. He placed second over 10 miles in the 1948 Australian Amateur Track Championship and was third in the 5-mile Track Championship.

In 1949 he placed seventh in the world amateur road championship road race after illness restricted him and he was praised for his courage. When 22 in 1950 he tried again coached by six-day and road cycling great Alf Strom. Australian Cyclist magazine said Hoobin showed good sense in coming over to Belgium in 1950 to stay with Alf Strom three weeks before the big race. Despite crashing in a warm-up race in the week just before the big event, he was patched up by Alf Strom and Roger Arnold. He became acquainted with the circuit and settled down in readiness for the big day.

On the final circuit of the race only 10 riders remained. In the final sprint the Italians led out at a furious pace and near the finish, the two favourites Varnajo and Ferrari, rode elbow to elbow with less than a furlong to go and they looked easy winners. Then Hoobin came from the back like a jet plane and hit the front in a last desperate 100 yards sprint to win by a wheel. Hoobin, unknown to the Continental crowd and not listed in the official programme, received a tremendous ovation. Hubert Opperman, who had been elected to the Victorian Parliament, cabled his congratulations to Hoobin.

Jack Hoobin overcame the blatant blocking tactics of the strong European teams to outsprint French champion Robert Varnajo and the 1947 world champion Ferrari of Italy in the upset of the decade, according to his bio in the Sport Australia Hall of Fame.

In 1952 Hoobin placed third in the inaugural Sun Tour behind the Rowley brothers Keith and Max. He later took up golf and played in the Victorian pennant competition. Jack Hoobin was inducted into the Sport Australia Hall of

Fame in 1991 and the Cycling Australia Hall of Fame in 2017. He passed away at the age of 72 in 2000, just weeks before he was to attend the Olympic Games in Sydney.

Barry Waddell, 'Iron Man' of the road

Barry Waddell was a real 'iron man', a multiple winner of major road classics and a dominant cyclist of the 1960's era. In 1954 when only 17 years old, Waddell (born 1936), a West Australian, was beating top track cyclists in Western Australia. After moving to Melbourne in 1956, Waddell won the 5,000 metres and the 10-mile Australian professional track championships in 1957 and became a top rider on the six-day cycling circuit in Australia.

He took out the national road title with his fastest time in the Warrnambool road race in 1964, following a third place in 1958. Waddell won the general classification for the Herald Sun Tour five times, from 1964 to 1968 and the elite national road championships in 1964 and 1968.

Waddell also won the Blue Riband for fastest time in the Warrnambool-Melbourne road race three times (1964-65 and 1968). In 1965, Waddell bettered Hubert Opperman's record when he completed the Adelaide-Melbourne 545-mile (877.091km) distance in 22 hours and 55 minutes.

In 1985 Waddell was reported to have won the Melbourne to Lakes Entrance road race one weekend, completed his record-breaking Adelaide-Melbourne long-distance record on the Tuesday, made fastest time in the Warrnambool-Melbourne road race on the following Saturday, competed at a three-day track carnival in Port

Pirie and then started in the Herald Sun Tour stage race (which he later won), all within two weeks.

He also competed in 17 six-day track races, winning five gruelling six-day races with partners Ian Campbell (twice), Sid Patterson, Joe Ciavola, and Ian Stinger.

Barry Waddell's elite cycling career ended around 1971, but he competed in and won the first World Veteran's title in Austria in 1975. Waddell operated a cycling shop on the Burwood Highway in Melbourne until 2011 when he was 74 years old. He was twice awarded the prestigious Sir Hubert Opperman medal the 'Oppy'. Since 1958, when Russell Mockridge took out the inaugural 'Oppy' medal, it's also been won by cyclists of the calibre of Peter Besanko, Stuart O'Grady and Cadel Evans.

Ray Bilney

Ray Bilney was a top road cycling champion from Victoria and came from Ballarat, winning the first of his three Australian amateur road race titles in 1964 (1964-1966). He showed he was one of the best road cyclists of his era when just 18, he finished fourth in the 1964 Olympic Games men's road race held in Tokyo and won the 4-stage, 804km Tour of Tasmania in 1965.

Bilney competed in the 1966 and 1970 Commonwealth Games in road cycling, winning a silver medal in the road race held in Edinburgh in 1970 won by New Zealand road ace Bruce Biddle. While competing in the UK in 1970, Bilney also rode in three Scottish road race classics, posting a win and a second place.

Bilney held the Australian Cyclist of the Year award in 1965-1966, winning the coveted Sir Hubert Opperman Trophy. In 2014 he was inducted into the Victorian Cycling Hall of Fame.

Donald Wilson

Donald Wilson came from Geelong Victoria and in 1966 won the 4-stage, 804-kilometre Examiner Tour of Tasmania amateur road race. In 1967 he won two New South Wales classics: the amateur Grafton to Inverell (handicap) road race off scratch and posted the fastest time, and the amateur Sydney to Goulburn (handicap) road race and the fastest time. He finished in 14th place in the individual road race at the 1968 Summer Olympics in Mexico City.

Wilson also rode in Europe in 1961, 1969 and 1973 where he posted placings and stage wins in road races including a third in the Ronde van Sweden and won the UK's Vulcan CRC-APR road race.

In 1975, Wilson was third in the GC for the Herald Sun Tour in Victoria and in 1975 and 1977, won the elite national road championships. Wilson was still competing in and winning Victorian criteriums and road races in 1979-1980, such the Sandown Raceway road race in 1980, and at Bendigo, Swan Hill and Taralgon.

Kerry Hoole

Kerry Hoole was one of the best performed road cyclists of the 1960s and 1970s. From Goulburn in New South

Wales, Hoole is famous for setting the fastest time in the 116-mile (186.7km) Goulburn to Sydney professional road race five times, from 1965-68 and in 1972 (Milperra, Sydney to Goulburn direction).

Hoole won the elite national road championships in 1966 and 1973 and finished second three times and third four times between 1962-1972. In 1969 he set the fastest time off scratch in the 1969 Melbourne to Warrnambool classic road race. He also rode in five Herald Sun Tours in Victoria, with two fourth placings his best results.

Graham McVilly

Graham McVilly rode with great success on the road and track and came from Hobart, Tasmania. He won the Tasmanian amateur road championships in 1969 and turning professional in 1969, won the state's professional road championships. McVilly finished second in the Herald Sun Tour of Victoria in 1969-70 and won the national road championships in 1970 and 1971.

Turning to track cycling, he won the Latrobe Wheel in 1970, the Austral Wheel race in 1971 and the Werribee three-day road race. McVilly won the Herald Sun Tour of Victoria three times (1971-73) and the West Australian road championship in 1971. He was awarded the Sir Hubert Opperman Trophy as the Australian Cyclist of the Year in 1971-72.

After being selected to represent Australia in the world road cycling championships, McVilly travelled to Europe in 1973 and he spent two seasons riding with leading road cycling teams Gitane and Peugeot. In 1979, he won the Grafton to Inverell road classic and claimed fastest time. McVilly topped the rankings for Australian Road Cyclist of the Year in 1970, 1971 and 1973. At the 2001, 50th Anniversary of the Sun Tour, he was honoured as one of three Legends of the Tour. He was inducted into the Tasmanian Sporting Hall of Fame.

Clyde Sefton, our first Olympic road medallist

Clyde Sefton (born 1951) came from South Purrumbete in the Otways region of Victoria and showed his rare cycling talent as a junior riding with the Camperdown Cycling Club. At 16 years of age he won the Dandenong to Morwell road race and the Melbourne to Colac amateur classic off scratch.

After Sefton finished fourth in the 1972 Australian national road championships, he lined up two days later for the selection race for the 1972 Olympic road race in Munich, West Germany on September 7, 1972 and impressed the Olympic selectors. Now 21 years old and a full-time builder, Sefton was guided by Melbourne-based coach Ken Trowell who developed training for Sefton with sessions in the hills of The Dandenongs.

Prior to leaving for the Olympics, the Australian team of Sefton, John Trevorrow, Don Allan, and Graeme Jose had to devise their own training schedules. They paid their own way to Munich, helped by local fundraising efforts and had to ride their own bikes.

Clyde Sefton said that in the Munich Olympics road race

and later in his career he rode against the best European road classic and Tour de France cyclists. At Munich he faced the likes of current (1971) world title holder French champion Regis Ovion and other national champions. But Sefton was not deterred by talk from his teammates about all the European champions in the race.

"I'd never read about European champion cyclists at home so was probably a bit naive in this way when the rest of the team knew all about them. But I feel it played to my advantage as far as not taking any notice of them, staying positive and going out there to win," he said.

Before the race, the Australian Olympians were faced with the terror of the Black September attack on the Israeli team. On September 5, 1972, eight Palestinian terrorists climbed a fence and raided the Israeli team barracks in the Olympic Village.

The road race was delayed by two days and cyclists were not allowed out of the village to train, but Clyde went on a training run regardless.

According to race reports, during the 190km race, Irish Republican protestors targeted the Irish riders, disrupting their chances several times, but Sefton managed to get onto the back of a breakaway bunch of 23 riders.

After several laps of the race circuit, the Netherland's Hennie Kuiper made a move off the front while two Dutch teammates blocked for him. Soon the race stretched out like a long ribbon. After Kuiper established a big lead, Sefton teamed up with three Commonwealth riders including New Zealand's Bruce Biddle, UK riders Phil

Edwards and Phil Bayton, and Spain's Jamie Heulamo. On the last lap of the circuit, the chasers cut Kuipers three-minute lead to about 25 seconds. But helped by his Dutch team, Kuipers jumped to a 45 second lead about four kilometres out to win on a flat road to the finish.

In the last 200-300 metres, Sefton outsprinted Biddle, Heulamo and Bayton to win the Olympic silver medal for Australia becoming the first Australian to win an Olympic road medal. Biddle was third and Huelamo fourth, but Huelamo was later disqualified for taking a prohibited substance. Kuipers went on to win major European road classics, finishing second in the Tour De France and was the professional world road champion in 1975.

Looking at some of the quite special performances of his career where he won major races or medals against higher rated opponents or in very difficult conditions, Sefton said: "In the Olympic Games road race I beat a lot of top European road cyclists who went on to be road classics and Tour de France/grand tour stage winners, such as French world road race title holder Regis Ovion, and cyclists like Fedor den Hertog (Dutch road champion), Italy's Francesco Moser (3-time Paris-Roubaix winner) and Belgian champion Freddy Maertens (twice world champion, winner of multiple road classics).

"I rode in Italy as a professional against the best road cyclists in the world and there were 90 top riders in Europe you had to beat to get onto the podium instead of about five riders in Australia. There are a lot more Australians riding in Europe today and they have better training, support and professional coaches." His European road racing career started in 1973 in the UK, where he rode in the Tour of Britain, won the GC for the Tour of Scotland and in London, the Lester Young Memorial race.

After initially missing selection in the 1974 Commonwealth Games cycling team, Sefton travelled to New Zealand in February with the Australian team where he won the Commonwealth Games road race gold medal at Christchurch.

Sefton rode in Italy as an amateur in 1974-75-76 and was reported to have rode for Dutch teams and Italian teams such as Fiorella, G.S. Mobili and Alfa Lum. In 1974 he won the Coppa della Place road race in Liguria, two stages of the amateur Giro Ciclistico d'Italia and was second in the Trofero Carteuropa in Toscana (Tuscany). In 1975 he won the Firenze (Florence) to Viareggio road race in Toscana and was second in the Bassano-Monte Grappa road race in Veneto.

Sefton won the national amateur road championship in 1976 and competed in the Montreal Olympics in 1976 in the men's road race (28th) and the teams time trial (ninth). After turning professional in 1976 he won the GP Ezio del Rosso road race in Toscana.

He competed in Italy as a professional from 1977 to 1980 and rode in the Giro Lombardia in 1977 and in 1978 claimed two GC second places in the Giro della Romagna and the Giro del Piemonte at Torino. He continued to race in Italy for several more seasons, but an eye cataract operation affected his performances. Other significant results in road racing came when Sefton won Australia's national road race championships in 1981 and was second to Terry Hammond in the 1983 road championship. Sefton also won road races including at Leongatha, Yarrawonga, and the Tour of Echuca, and was fourth in the GC at New Zealand's Tour of the South in 1981.

Competing in the Herald Sun Tour of Victoria, he was second in the GC in 1978 and 1982, and finally won the gruelling Sun Tour in 1981. "As a professional I was planning on retirement then, but had never competed in Australia as a professional for a full season so did in '81 when I won the Tour of Hunter NSW, the Australian road championship and the Herald Sun Tour. Part of the prize for this was a trip to Italy so I went back in '82 for one more season (1982-83)," Sefton said.

Back in Australia in 1983 he finished second in the GC for the Griffin 1000 West tour and claimed a win and two places in Victorian road races. He capped his brilliant career by winning the Melbourne to Warrnambool road classic before he retired. Sefton was inducted into the Cycling Victoria Hall of Fame in 2017.

Looking back at his best 3-4 performances internationally Sefton said this would include being the only Australian male to win a road race medal at the Olympic Games. "My silver medal at Munich in 1972 is one of my more notable ones and it was noticed around the world," he said. "It was a good stepping-stone for racing in Europe that would be my best performance. Another is winning two stages in the amateur Giro d'Italia, (the Giro

Ciclistico) in 1974 and the Firenze to Viareggio road race, one of Italy's longest one-day amateur road races. And my gold medal in the Commonwealth Games at Christchurch on one of the most difficult road course or circuits used in the Games."

On cyclists, coaches or mentors that helped inspire him to achieve his goals he said: "Before the Munich Olympics I had Ken Trowell. He coached me for six months and helped train me with set tasks and rides in The Dandenongs. A good coach makes all the difference. Eddy Merckx won most races he started in and he inspired me to do better in a lot of my races. I believe I was lucky to make a living out of bike riding and had a brilliant career. I appreciate it more today than when I was riding."

Michael Wilson

Tasmanian road cycling champion Michael Wilson (born 1960) was one of the first Australian amateur and professional road cyclists who landed in Europe in the 1980s aiming to break into professional road cycling and ride in the grand tours and one-day classics.

Wilson, born in Adelaide, grew up on Tasmania's north-west coast. He represented Tasmania in 1977 winning the Australian junior road championship that year and was the national track pursuit champion in 1978. He became the youngest ever winner of Tasmania's (Sanyo) 4-day Tour of the North in 1978, after finishing third in 1977 behind Gary Sutton and Arch Sansonetti. He won the Tasmanian 200km road race title in 1978.

In 1978, Wilson claimed the fastest time in the Grafton to Inverell amateur road cycling classic and was awarded fastest time in the Goulburn to Sydney amateur road classic the same year. Wilson won the Australian Amateur Road Cycling Championships in Adelaide in 1979.

He represented Australia at the 1980 Moscow Olympics finishing eleventh in the 100km teams time trial and 25th in the individual road race, the first Australian to finish.

Wilson decided to try his luck in Europe and was noticed by Italian team Alfa Lum, which signed him for three years. Known for his climbing and time trial ability, in Italy in 1982 he won the Memorial Gastone Nemcicni road race and was third in the Giro del Piemonte.

In 1982 he rode in his first Giro d'Italia grand tour, winning stage 2 and coming 43rd overall and was the first Australian professional to win a stage of the Giro. In 1983 he placed third in the Giro di Romangha in Italy and rode in the Giro d'Italia, finishing 61$^{st.}$ Wilson also rode in his first Tour of Spain (Vuelta Espana) in 1983, where he broke away and won the final stage into Madrid well ahead of Laurent Fignon, who was part of the team that helped Bernard Hinault win the Vuelta Espana. Fignon went on to win the 1983 Tour de France.

Among Michael Wilson's many wins, placings and top ten finishes in European road races and tours between 1984 and 1990 were winning the Trofeo Matteotti road race; second in the Giro dell'Emillia; in 1985 eighth in the GC at the Giro d'Italia; seventeenth in the GC at the Giro d'Italia in 1986; second in the Trofeo Baracchi one-day race in 1985-1986; third in the Grand Prix des Nations in 1988 and 50th in the GC at the Tour de France the same year. Other results include third in the Rund um den Henninger Turn and the Temse Ooost-Vlaandren, and second in the Tour du Nord Ouest in Switzerland.

In 1989 he rode in the Tour de France, won stage 3 at the Tour de Suisse and won a stage of the Tirreno-Adriatico tour, and in 1990 was fourth in the GC at the Tour de Romandie.

Wilson rode in nine grand tours between 1982 and 1989. Wilson retired in 1991 and operated a hotel at Latrobe, Tasmania and later a vineyard at Legana near Launceston.

Neil Stephens, the 'super domestique'

Neil Stephens came from Canberra and was the youngest of three cycling brothers who rode for the Queanbeyan Cycling Club. Stephens (born 1963) began cycling at the age of eight and was winning club road titles in the early 1970s, while brother Brian won major road races and represented Australia in Switzerland in 1983.

In 1981, riding for New South Wales, Stephens finished second in the 100km Australian professional cycling title in South Australia and in 1982 won the Australian professional junior road cycling championship.

He finished second in the GC for the Midlands Tour in Victoria in 1985. In 1986, Stephens won Australia's toughest stage road race, the Sun Tour of Victoria and was second in 1987 and 1998 and third in 1990. He set world professional hour and 20km records in 1987. Stephens also won two national road race championships (1991 and 1995) and won the Tour of Tasmania in 1985.

In 1986 at the Sun Tour, after Neil Stephens and his team captain, Allan Peiper led the field in the middle of the race with Stephens 40 seconds ahead, Stephens refused to give ground to second placed Peiper and held his lead in the Sun Tour for the last three days to go on and win the Tour. Stephens said it was one of the toughest events he's competed in. When the organisers abandoned the Falls Creek part of the route due to heavy snow, the cyclists had to ride up Mount Hotham instead.

He made his first visit overseas in 1984 finishing second in a road race in England. In 1986, Stephens gained a contract with Santini Chierre Conti Galli in Italy for up to six months of each year and raced with the team in Italy and Belgium, the UK, and the USA.

Successes in Europe included first place in the GP Villafranca de Ordizia road race in Spain in 1991, the first of his four wins in the race, including 1993-94-95, and first in Spain's Trofero Calvia road race (Vuelta a Mallorca) in 1992. Stephens rode in 11 grand tours for nine stage wins in Europe and rode for teams such as Peugeot Michelin, Festina-Lotus and ONCE, and became known as a highly valued 'super domestique' that supported the team's top cyclists.

In 1992, he became the first Australian to race in all three grand European tours of the Tour De France, the Giro d'Italia and the Tour of Spain (La Vuelta). Stephens placed tenth in the UCI world road championship road race held in Switzerland in 1996 and won stage 17 of the Tour De France in 1997. He raced professionally during 1997-98 when he was caught up in the controversy of the Festina EPO doping scandal in the 1998 Tour De France. Stephens said later he believed that he was being given injections of vitamin supplements.

Stephens became a sports director of cycling teams such as Liberty Seguros-Wurth and was director sportif for GreenEdge (now Michelton Scott) cycling for eight years until September 2018. Soon after he joined UAE Team Emirates as a director sportif, alongside Allan Peiper.

Allan Peiper

Allan Peiper came from Alexandra, Victoria (born 1960) and started cycling on the road and track at age 12. He represented Australia at the junior world cycling championship on the track and road in 1977-78, winning bronze and silver medals in the points race.

Peiper was a real trailblazer for Australian road cycling moving to Belgium in 1977 when 17, long before the Australian Institute of Sport supported young cyclists.

He lived in Ghent and rode on the junior amateur road circuit. In 1978 he won 10 races and placed second 25 times riding as a 'professional junior' but returned to Australia in mid-1979 due to hepatitis. Peiper recovered by late 1980 ready to tackle road races, helped by mentoring from former Great Britain Olympic track pursuit rider Peter Brotherton, who was building frames in Melbourne. In a successful return to road racing in 1981, Peiper won the

Dulux Tour of the North Island in New Zealand. He returned to Europe in 1982 and rode for the Paris-based French ACBB amateur team, winning 14 races, including the Grand Prix des Nations time trial.

Rupert Guinness said in his Tour de France book, Aussie, Aussie, Aussie, Oui, Oui, Oui, that for Peiper, on his return to Europe, becoming a team leader for Peugeot was new and difficult. "But you have to, and in the time trial be positive and somehow explode," Peiper said. When he missed selection for the Commonwealth Games road team he signed with the professional Peugeot team for the 1983 season and started winning more races, including the short time trial prologue stages at the start of tours winning three in 1984, along with GC wins at the Tour of de l'Oise, the Tour of Sweden, the Tour de Picardie, and a stage of the Criterium Dauphine. In the UK, he won the Harrogate Criterium at the Great Yorkshire Classic in 1983 and won the Kellogg's Criterium three times (1984-86).

On his Tour de France debut in 1984, he was third in the prologue and finished 95th. In 1985 he won a stage of the Paris-Nice race and was 86th in the Tour de France. Back in Australia in 1986 he won three stages of the Herald Sun Tour. Peiper joined Dutch Panasonic team in 1986 and rode in the 1987 spring classics. He won the GP Raymond Impanis in 1986, the Grand Prix d'Isbergues and the Circuit des Frontieres road races in 1987. In 1988 at the road world championship, Peiper was tenth after being in the first five riders at the last 100 metres. He also won the GC at the KBC Driedaags race.

He continued to ride in the Tour de France but did not finish the 1987 and 1990 tours and came in at 126th in the 1996 Tour. In 1990 he won a stage of the Giro d'Italia and a stage of the Tour de France in the team time trial. Peiper rode in 10 grand tours: in the Tour de France five times, the Giro d'Italia four times and the Vuelta a Espana once. Peiper's palmares includes wins in around 20 European and UK elite road races, classics and criteriums, and 35 first places including stage wins.

From 2005, Peiper became a sport director of major European teams including Davitamon Lotto, HTC Columbia, Garmin Sharp, and BMC Racing. In 2019 he joined UAE Team Emirates as the lead director of sport.

Phil Anderson

Phil Anderson (born 1958, London) emigrated to Melbourne with his parents from the UK. He graduated from Melbourne's Trinity Grammar in 1975. Phil took up cycling with the Hawthorn Cycling Club where other aspiring champions were Alan Peiper, and Tom Sawyer, who became a top professional six-day cyclist.

Anderson won the Tour of North Island in New Zealand in 1977. In 1978 he won the Australian team time trial championship in Brisbane and won a stage of the USA Coors Classic road race. At age 19 in 1978, Anderson won the gold medal in the Commonwealth Games road race held in Edmonton, Canada.

He moved to France in 1979, joining ACBB, the top French amateur road racing club in Paris and won the amateur Grand Prix des Nations time trial. In 1980 he rode in the French and European classic road races, finished tenth in the Paris-Tours race and was second in the GC for the Etoile des Espoirs race. Anderson originally rode for the Peugeot-Michelin team in 1980-83, then Panasonic-Raleigh, TVM, and the Motorola team.

In 1981 Anderson won the Tour de L'Aude in France and the Tour de Corse. When he rode in his first Tour de France in 1981 and finished tenth in the GC, it was the highest finish by an Australian cyclist in the Tour. On the mountainous sixth stage in the Pyrenees after his French team leader fell back, the team director told Anderson to try and hang on at the front of the race. Anderson ended the day as the first Australian and non-European to wear the race leader's yellow jersey (the Maillot Jaune). After he fought for second place with Tour de France legend Bernard Hinault, he finished third, 27 seconds adrift of stage winner Lucien Van Impe, but taking a 17 second lead on Hinault. The Age newspaper quoted mentor Ted Sanders: "It's like a 19-year-old cricketer from Rome taking 10 wickets at Lords."

Anderson told ABC Radio: "So hang on I did and got to the last climb and I stayed up with Bernard Hinault. Belgian rider, Lucien Van Impe, an excellent climber, rode away and so we came in a couple of minutes later, but I had enough time from some good days previously, that I climbed into the yellow jersey, and I had no idea of what the yellow jersey represented. But really, you're sort of at the highest level of the sport."

More Tour de France glory was to follow. In 1982 he claimed fifth in the GC at the Tour de France, won Stage 2 of the race and wore the Yellow Jersey for nine days. He was also first in the Youth Classification and third in the sprint Points Classification and his fifth place was the highest place in the GC achieved by an Australian. In 1983, Anderson finished ninth in the GC at the Tour de France and was tenth in 1984, fifth in 1985, 39th in 1986. 27th in 1987 and 45th in 1991. He rode in 13 Tour de France tours and three Giro d'Italia tours. He was seventh in the GC at the Giro d'Italia in 1987, won stage 17 at the Giro d'Italia in 1989 and a stage in 1990. He also placed ninth at the UCI road world championship in 1983.

Between 1983 and 1992 Anderson posted many wins and placings in major races including in the road classics. Among these were winning the Netherlands' prestigious Amstel Gold Race, the Paris-Tours classic, Italy's Milan-Torino classic, the Grand Prix d'Isbergues in France, and Frankfurt's Rund um den Henninger Turm. He posted second and third places in the Liege-Bastogne-Leige classic, second in the Tour of Flanders classic, the Gent-Wevelgem and the Milano-Torino, and third in the Paris-Bruxelles race and the GP Eddy Merckx.

His major tour wins included the general classifications at the Tour du Suisse, the Criterium du Dauphine tour, Tour de L'Aude (twice), the Tour de Romandie, the Tour Mediterranean (twice), the Tour of Britain (twice), the Tour of Ireland twice in 1989 and 1992, the Tour of Denmark, and at the Tour of Sweden.

Anderson held the second highest ranking of any cycling professional in Europe in 1985 with 3037 points.

Editor-publisher of National Cycling magazine John Drummond summed it up in November 1985 when he said under the headline, "THE MASTER RETURNS, NO BRASS BAND FOR CYCLING HERO", and that Anderson, "had carried the flag successfully for Australia in an otherwise bleak year for Aussie sport." Anderson, then 27, had returned to holiday in Australia with his American-born wife Anne and nine-month-old son Loren.

Phil Anderson was 39 points ahead of second placed Irishman Sean Kelly in the 1985 Super Prestige Pernod, professional cycling's best cyclist of the year award. But he was forced to withdraw from the final race (the Tour of Lombardy) due to muscular damage sustained in falls during a heavy season and lost the award to Kelly.

In his fifteenth year competing in Europe in 1993, he was still in good form, winning the GP Impanis race in Belgium, the GC at the Tour of Sweden and the Kellogg's Tour of Britain, while he finished 84th in the GC at the Tour de France.

In 1994 in his last year of European racing, Anderson placed in road races in Italy and was 69th in the GC at the Tour de France. He concluded his career on the road with a gold medal in the team time trial at the 1994 Commonwealth Games held in Victoria, Canada.

Anderson was awarded the Medal of the Order of Australia in 1987 and a Centenary Medal in 2011, and was inducted into the Sport Australia Hall of Fame in 2010, and the Cycling Australia Hall of Fame in 2015. Looking back on his brilliant career on the road and some of his best performances in international cycling, Anderson nominated: the Commonwealth Games gold medals in the 1978 road-race (200km) and the 1994 team-time-trial (100km); the 1979 Grand Prix de Nations amateur time-trial; the 1981 Tour de France Yellow Jersey (1 day) and the 1982 TdF Yellow Jersey (9 days) plus the stage win in Nancy; the 1985 GP Zurich, 1985 Dauphine and 1985 Tour of Switzerland victories; and the 1991 TdF stage win in Quimper.

"I rode 13 Tour de France's, finishing each including five times in the top ten," he added.

On winning against higher rated opponents or in difficult conditions that he believed were quite special performances, he said: " I considered each of my wins to be against a handful of contenders, sometimes teams full of riders with more ability than myself. Behind every race, there is always a point where the race is won or lost, sometimes it's tactical or a cunning move against better riders, but there is always a story."

Anderson was inspired or helped by several mentors and coaches. "When I started in the Hawthorne club, Ted Sanders (David Sanders' father) gave me time, assisting with the basic principles of training," he said. "One of his pearls of wisdom was to ride with the best riders you know and learn from them. I chose to spend time with Sal and Remo Sansonetti. A couple of years later Gerald George from Melbourne introduced me to the ACBB club in Paris.

"Gerald bought me an air-ticket and a spot on this elite amateur outfit. Riding for the ACBB in France in 1979 gave me the opportunity to be seen on the European stage. The pro-teams are always scouting for young talent and back during that era, they looked at results in the top amateur events. Teams are definitely more international now, accepting of foreign riders not just a domestiques, but as team leaders and captains."

When Anderson turned professional in 1980, he missed out on competing in Olympic Games road events at Moscow but said he has no regrets. "It would have been nice to do an Olympic Games, but even Olympic gold didn't carry any weight or respect as a professional. Since 1996 (two years after I retired) that changed and elite riders can now compete. The Olympic road race is another event on the UCI calendar every four years."

Donald (Don) Allan

Don Allan (Born September 1949) started riding with the Blackburn Cycling Club in Melbourne and is another top road cycling professional who rode in Europe in the 1970s with distinction. Allan won the Examiner Tour of the North/Tour of Tasmanian in 1970 (5 stages) and again in 1972 (7 stages). He was paralysed in a car accident in 1970 but fought his way back to health and was selected for the 1972 Munich Olympics for the individual road race and team trial.

Allan was offered a contract with the Dutch professional team Frisol and won many race stages at top road races in

Europe, including at the Tour of Scotland, the Tour of Austria and the Peace Race in France, and won criterium and road races in Belgium and the Netherlands.

Don Allan made Australian road cycling history twice. For being the first Australian cyclist to finish the Tour De France in 1974 since Russell Mockridge in 1955. Allan courageously rode in the Tour De France in 1974-75 and was also the first Australia to win a stage in the Vuelta a Espana in 1975 winning the stage at Bilbao, riding for Frisol. His brother David Allan won the Sun Tour and two Melbourne to Warrnambool classics.

In 1976 Don finished a creditable ninth at the UCI road world championships held in Italy. He is well known as a champion six-day cyclist with 17 six-day track racing wins, including 15 wins teaming with six-day cycling ace Danny Clark. A leg injury forced Allan's retirement.

John Trevorrow

John Trevorrow (born May 1949) is another road cycling champion of the 1970-1980 era who achieved success in Australia's road classics. Born in Melbourne, Trevorrow won the Australian amateur road race title in 1970.

He was selected to ride in the 1970 Commonwealth Games at Edinburgh winning the bronze medal in the road race. Trevorrow later finished third in the Inverness-Elgin road race in Scotland. He represented Australia at the 1972 Summer Olympics in Munich where he finished 17th in the 100km time trial and 32nd in the men's road race.

John Trevorrow made fastest time twice (1970-71) in the

Grafton to Inverell amateur (handicap) road classic. He went on to win three elite national road championships in 1978-1980 and three of Victoria's gruelling Herald Sun Tours, Australia's biggest road and stage race at the time, in 1975, 1977 and 1979.

When he won the Sun Tour in 1975, Trevorrow won seven stages including the final time trial stage. He won eight stages in 1977 but not the GC. In the 1979 Sun Tour, Trevorrow again won eight stages and this time claimed the GC win. In 1979, Trevorrow won the first pro-am 4-stage (810km) 'Examiner' Tour of the North in Tasmania.

Trevorrow raced in Europe for professional cycling teams in 1973, 1978-79, and 1981, where he was placed in the general classification in several road races and in race stages in the UK, Belgium, and Switzerland. He rode in six-day races in Australia and won the 1981 Melbourne Six riding with Paul Medhurst.

Trevorrow spoke about his best performances in Australia and internationally, mentors and breaking into European pro teams in the 1970s. "It's funny how you rate things. At the time of the event and in hindsight. Without doubt the three biggest thrills for me in Australia were: Winning my first Australian road title in Geelong. I was 20 years of age. It was the first national title I had competed in and with it came selection in the Commonwealth Games in Edinburgh 1970.

"I was told that Dick Paris from NSW was the man to watch in a sprint. I wondered who he was as we approached the final few miles. Then fellow Victorian Ray Bilney started to jostle me for the wheel that I was sitting on and I realised it was Paris. The second one was in 1975 winning my first Sun Tour, the biggest cycling event in Australia and I had grown up with the riders staying in our house. I had a great duel with my Olympic teammate Don Allan who rode the Tour de France that year.

"Thirdly it was winning the Australian Professional Road Title at Sandown in 1980. It meant I had won three pro titles in a row and joined the legendary Russell Mockridge who also won an Amateur Aussie title at his first attempt before winning three pro titles on a trot."

Internationally Trevorrow said his favourite was a sprint victory for fourth place that rates high because of who he beat: "It was the Grand Prix of Dortmund and I won the sprint from a large breakaway group beating Roger De Vlaeminck and Sean Kelly. The bunch was swarming across the road about a kilometre to go and just avoiding a parked car. Unfortunately, the guy behind me went through the back window of that car and ended his road racing career. That was Patrick Sercu, probably the greatest all-round cyclist of all time.

"I was fortunate to have a father who raced at the top level. He had raced off the scratch mark with one of the absolute legends of the sport in Sid Patterson on the track and rode off scratch with our first world road champion Jack Hoobin on the road. Dad had an amazing knowledge of how the body worked and how to best prepare. I would never have made it to any high level of performance without his input."

Trevorrow said it was hard to break into a European team back in the 70s: "Most of the teams predominantly wanted riders from their own country and the wages were pretty low. A handful of Aussies made it into pro teams, but I really only played at it. The real pros at that time were Don Allan, Garry Clivelly and Michael Wilson who were all well respected. Then came Phil Anderson who I raced against in my final year 1981. I rode against him in a couple of races in Belgium and then I went off to the Giro while Phil rode his first Tour de France. He started his quick climb to the top of the sport. After that teams started to look at Aussies a little differently."

Gary Clivelly

Gary Clivelly represented Australia at the 1975 World Amateur Road Titles in Colombia, finishing fourth, one of the best world road cycling performances by an Australian. From Brisbane, he turned professional from 1975-1991 and rode in Italy for the Magniflex team in 1975-77. He was ranked as Italy's top amateur cyclist in 1975 after winning 11 road races.

In 1976 he placed in major Italian road races such as the G.P Camalore, the G.P. Alghero and the Giro della Provincia di reggio in Calabria. He placed third in two stages of the Vuelta a Espana in 1977 and finished seventh in the GC for the Vuelta. Clivelly returned to Australia in 1978 disillusioned with European professional cycling. He appears not to have competed at national level until 1989, when he won the Australian national road championship.

Remo Sansonetti

Remo Sansonetti was born in Italy and grew up in Melbourne where two of his brothers Sal and Arch also took up road cycling. Remo, one of the best performed amateur road cyclists of the 1970s, won the Australian Amateur Road Cycling Championships three times in 1973, 1975 and in 1976, and was also selected to ride in the 1976 Montreal (with brother Sal) and 1980 Moscow Olympic Games in the road race and time trial.

At the 1974 Commonwealth Games held in Christchurch, New Zealand, Remo Sansonetti took the bronze medal behind two of the top road cyclists of the era, Australia's Clyde Sefton and Britain's Phil Griffiths. He won the Examiner Tour of the North four-day stage race in Tasmania three years running in 1974-75-76. In 1976, he won the Grafton to Inverell road classic and set the fastest time. He also set the fastest time in the 1979 amateur Goulburn to Sydney road classic.

Peter (Bulldog) Besanko

Peter Besanko won the Blue Riband for his three fastest times in the Melbourne to Warrnambool classic off scratch when it was still a handicap race and before it became a massed start (scratch) race in 1996. From Melbourne, he won his first Warrnambool road race in 1984 and backed up with victories in 1989 and in 1992 when aged 37. He also claimed three third placings and a second place in the Warrnambool from 17 attempts. All of Besanko's wins came off the elite scratch or back mark.

In September 2015, The Standard newspaper in Warrnambool, Victoria reported that, the most successful rider in Melbourne to Warrnambool Cycling classic history, Peter Besanko would wave the chequered flag at the finish line of the Melbourne to Warrnambool road race on October 17, 2015, as the iconic event celebrates its 100th edition. Besanko said that the Melbourne to Warrnambool was his major cycling priority and he treated the road race like the Cox Plate group 1 classic for racehorses. "I always worked myself up for it," he said.

When 21 years of age, Besanko won the 1976 elite national road championship and won the road title again in 1984. Besanko also won the nine-day Herald Sun Tour of Victoria in 1976, was second in 1981 and 1984, and third in 1979 and 1982. Besanko won the Sir Hubert Opperman Cyclist of the Year award in 1979, 1981 and 1984 and rode his last Sun Tour race in 1996 when 41.

Besanko rode in Belgium professionally in 1983 and scored one win, two seconds and a third in elite Belgian road races. He also rode in Belgium in 1985, where he finished a credible 30th in the World Road Championships held in Italy, just one minute behind the winner.

The Bank Classic, Australia's amateur stage tour

The gruelling 15-stage Commonwealth Bank Cycle Classic amateur road tour launched in 1982 and ran for 19 editions down Australia's east coast each October until 2000. National Cycling said in 1985 the Bank Classic attracted 12 international cycling teams and started with a

Brisbane prologue. The cyclists rode 14 stages down the New South Wales Coast to Sydney and finished with a criterium at Coogee.

The Commonwealth Bank Classic was organised by Phill Bates, at the time a Sydney cycling promoter, coach, cycling shop owner and Cycling Australia director. The race had as its major sponsor the Commonwealth Bank of Australia. The race gained daily news coverage on all five national television networks, including ABC and SBS.

"The Bank classic was a special event – something that we needed in Australia at the time. The event was held after the Commonwealth Games in Brisbane in 1982 and we used many of the countries that were here for the Games to be part of the race. I also brought in the USA to give it a little bit more of an international flavour," Bates said. "At the time, the Herald Sun Tour was a professional race in Victoria which promoted the sport there, but very little was seen in parts of Australia.

"The most important aspect of the Bank Classic was the international component in its early years and racing from point to point from Brisbane to Pier One in Sydney." Bates said that the Bank race was tough event, especially when it had two stage days – generally a road race and then a criterium with 15 stages usually the normal length.

"Although when the Bank Classic raced from Brisbane to Canberra, then in 1987 from Brisbane to Albury, followed by the bicentennial race in 1988 when it went from the Gold Coast to Melbourne – the race was over 1800 kilometres," he added.

"The stages, especially when you had two stages finishing with a criterium did make the event that little bit tougher – the Milk race in England also did twilight criterium events," Bates said. "It was not just tough on the riders but also for the crew setting up the stage finishes and criterium circuits as well as the media."

The Bank Classic was a great pathway for riders to head overseas and become noticed and for many the start of their professional careers. "I think Steve Hodge was the first trailblazer in that department and went on to head the Festina team," he said. "There were many opportunities and friendships born from the Bank Classic and invitations extended to Australians to compete in overseas countries here for the Bank Classic. When the Bank Classic kicked off Cycling Australia would struggle to issue 10 international licences a year and at the height of the Classic, we were up over 350 international licences!"

Some cycling writers described the race as Australia's Tour de France. But Bates said: "It was never the Tour de France or for that matter any other pro tour event but in its day attracted the best amateur riders in the world including many world champions, Olympic champions and the cream of world amateur cycling. For me, staging the event was a natural thing to do and one thing I was keen to do is leave a great legacy."

Following the success of the first year in 1982 Bates increased the nations taking part that grew steadily to 9-10, as well as 5-6 Australian teams. "In 1984 we had Eros Poli, an Olympic champion and Olympic bronze medallist Roy

Knickman, along with our own four Olympic gold medallists so was very special. It was also the year that ABC joined with SBS to undertake a big coverage and the finish live on ABC from Coogee with a crowd of close to 20,000. Road cycling in this country had been born."

The 1985 event attracted 12 overseas teams and four Australian teams and in the early years the Bank Classic had just four-man teams then was built it up to five-man teams – ideal for the style of race. "It was not completely dominated by internationals and when Andrew Logan won the race, he had to beat the Dutch team, all of them being current world champions," he said. "It was interesting to see the likes of Nico Verhoeven win stages in the Bank Classic then win stages in major classics including the Tour de France the following year.

"Matt Bazzano's win in 1989 was against one of the best possible fields, - world road champion Joachim Halupczok from Poland and the last ever East German team to ever compete and between them they had won thirteen world and Olympic Games gold medals. Matt Bazzano made the Commonwealth Games team off that win. Darren Smith did the same after his second in 1991 to Thomas Liese and made the Olympic team in 1992."

The 1988 Bicentennial Commonwealth Bank Classic was mooted as a $1.8 million event with over $100,000 in prizemoney held over 2500km, but Bates said costs were a little more than that and when you consider the media coverage, it was quite huge. "In 1988 I travelled to the Milk race as a guest of the National Dairy Council, following Phil Liggett's intervention and I wanted to improve the technical aspects of the event," he said. "Our media was quite amazing and can never forget turning up for the start of the Milk Race in 1988 on Westminster Bridge, I was confronted by all five Australian networks asking the questions as to why I chose the Milk race to improve the Bank race and not the Tour de France.

"I was also hell bent on getting Phil Liggett to head my media coverage of the Bicentennial event. What a race it was, and Phil was the icing on the cake. The CBA had the media coverage valued at more than $16 million. We were live for four hours in St Kilda on Channel Nine's Wide World of Sport." Bates packaged the Bank Classic's TV and gained media coverage on all the networks.

It was announced that the 2000 Commonwealth Bank Cycle Classic's 19th edition would be its last. Bates said it was mutually agreed between himself and the Bank. For Bates it was not just chasing the dollars (the Bank rarely made up more than 35 percent of the budget). "Sponsors were critical for its success, the organisation in travelling the coast, the team's support, coordinating the television, clothing, and the personnel who became like family," Bates said. "It was a tough and relentless gig and a huge undertaking. However, it was a great 19 years of unbelievable promotion for the sport."

The Bank Classic attracted the top world amateurs including world champion and 1993 winner Jan Ulrich, the 1997 Tour De France winner, Uwe Ampler, George Hincapie, Jens Voight, Jeremy Hunt and Erik Zabel.

In 1983 Melbourne road cyclist Gary Trowell was the first of four Australians to win the Commonwealth Bank Classic. He also represented Australia in the road race and teams time trial at the 1984 Los Angeles Olympic Games and was an under 23 national road champion. He rode professionally in Italy in 1989.

Andrew Logan from St George CC won the 1986 Bank Classic. The race was held over 17 stages including a criterium in Canberra, with a prologue at the start on the Gold Coast. Logan also won the 1986 Grafton to Inverell road cycling classic (massed start).

Matt Bazzano from St George CC was the 1980 national road race champion. He won the Bank Classic in 1989 riding for the Hampshire Homes team with Brett Dutton, Clayton Stevenson, and Barney St George.

In 1996, Sydney road cyclist Nick Gates claimed the Bank Classic GC riding for the Giant-AIS team over 14 stages. In 1996, Gates won the 200-kilometre national road championship at Centennial Park, Sydney and was second in the GC at the Tour of Tasmania in 1997. From 1997 to 2008 he rode in Europe for professional teams. Gates rode in two Tour De France tours (2003-04), two Giro d'Italia tours, the Vuelta a Espana, rode in Germany where he won several road races and was placed in others, and claimed a GC third at the Tour of Japan in 1999.

Australia's track cyclists have a long tradition of success internationally and at the world amateur and professional track cycling championships from the 1900s up to the 1980s. When the Australian Institute of Sport opened a high-performance track cycling unit in Adelaide in 1987 it helped our track cyclists' international performances against top track cycling nations who were using a more science-based approach to the sport.

From the 1990s our track sprinters and endurance cyclists produced great performances at the UCI world championships, the Olympic Games and Commonwealth Games. Among our best were sprinters and time triallists Shane Kelly, Darryn Hill, Ryan Bayley and Matt Glaetzer, endurance and all-round track champions Brad McGee, Stuart O'Grady, Michael Hepburn, Peter Dawson, Leigh Howard, Luke Roberts, Cameron Meyer, Graeme Brown, Brett Aitken, and Sam Welsford.

In the present era of Australia track cycling in the last two to three decades, our elite male track cyclists have been 'bringing home the bacon' for Australian cycling. They have outperformed their road cycling colleagues in terms of winning races and numbers of medals won at the last five Commonwealth Games since 2002 to Queensland in 2018 and the last five Olympic Games since 1996 to Rio de Janeiro in 2016.

Australia a top track cycling nation

At the UCI track world cycling championships up to 2020, Australia is the fourth ranked nation in numbers of gold and silver medals won behind France, Great Britain and the Netherlands, and fifth overall for medals won.

From 1988 to 2019 (32 years) Australia's male cyclists competing at the UCI track world championships won 44 gold medals and world championships with 13 in the team pursuit, five in the individual pursuit, five in the points, three in the omnium, two in the madison and two in the scratch race (30 gold medals); five in the sprint, two in the team sprint, four in the keirin, and three in the time trial (14 gold medals).

Australia's team pursuit men were ranked number one up to 2013, then number one or two to 2019 and only missed medals five times since 2002, including in 2020.

Our track cyclists have a great record on the world stage and have justified their continued support for state, national and international cycling events and championships.

Darryn Hill

From Western Australia, Darryn Hill (born 1974) was an accomplished BMX rider who successfully took up cycling on the track as a teenager. At the junior world titles in Colorado in 1991, he won a bronze medal in the sprint. At the national track championships in the 1990s, Hill won six national sprint championships, four keirin sprint tiles and two team sprint titles.

Hill, who was powerfully built and renowned for his explosive speed, with Gary Neiwand, led Australia's track sprint attack against the top track cycling nations at the UCI track world championships in the 1990s.

The pinnacle of Hill's career came at the 1995 UCI track world championships in Colombia where he won the gold medal in the sprint. In the qualifying round he posted a time of 9.926 seconds for the flying 200m, becoming the first Australian to break the 10-second barrier.

He won a silver medal in the sprint at the 1994 UCI track world championships in Palermo, won a sprint bronze medal at the track worlds at Manchester in 1996, then added a second world gold medal riding with Gary Neiwand and Shane Kelly to win the team sprint. In 1997 at the track world championships in Perth, Hill added a bronze in the team sprint.

The Australian Olympic Committee said that Darryn Hill combined with Sean Eadie and Gary Neiwand to win the bronze medal, behind France and Great Britain, in the inaugural staging of the Olympic team sprint at the 2000 Sydney Olympics.

At the Commonwealth Games at Victoria, Canada in 1994, Hill won silver in the time trial and bronze in the sprint and at Kuala Lumpur in 1998 claimed a gold medal in the sprint.

Hill was the Oppy Medal Cyclist of the Year in 1995 and was inducted into the Western Australia Institute of Sport's Hall of Champions in 2009.

Shane Kelly

Shane Kelly (born 1972) grew up in a cycling family at Ararat, Victoria. He won the kilo time trial at the national track championships as a junior and in 1989 gained an AIS scholarship at Adelaide and was coached by Charlie Walsh until 2020. Kelly went on to win eight national track championships from 1990 to 2008 including three in the time trial, six Oceania track cycling titles, and in 1994 and 1998, two gold medals at the Commonwealth Games in the kilo time trial in 1994 and 1998.

Kelly, one of our best ever exponents in the 1,000 metre 'one kilo' race against the clock and a top track sprinter, started his Olympic career at Barcelona in 1992, losing by just 0.946 seconds to Moreno of Spain in the 1000m time trial to take the silver medal. Kelly, a five-time Olympian, in 1996 at Atlanta was the reigning world champion and hot favourite to win the time trial gold medal, the Australian Olympic Committee said, but his foot slipped off a bike pedal whilst starting and his race was over.

In 2000 at the Sydney Olympic Games, Kelly won the bronze medal in the kilo time trial. At the 2004 Athens Olympics, Kelly won the bronze medal in the keirin event behind clear winner Ryan Bayley and Escuredo, after he held pole position in front of Ryan Bayley behind the motorbike for five laps of the eight-lap event.

Kelly won 14 medals at the UCI track world championships: gold in the kilo time trial in Colombia in 1995; gold in the kilo at Manchester in 1996 and gold in the team sprint; gold in the kilo at Perth in 1997; silver in the kilo at Hamar, Norway in 1993; silver medals in the kilo and team sprint at Bordeaux in 1998; silver in the kilo at Berlin in 1999; silver in the kilo at Stuttgart in 2003; and five more bronze medals from 1994 to 2006. In September

2002 The Age newspaper said that Kelly won a medal at every track world championship contested since 1992.

Kelly was the Oppy Medal Cyclist of the Year in 1996 and in 2004 was awarded the medal of the Order of Australia. He retired in 2008 and later became a coach at the Victorian Institute of Sport.

Sean Eadie

Sean Eadie (born 1969) came from Sydney and started cycling when 10 years old. He rode for the Bankstown Cycling Club and became a professional in 1990. Called the 'gentle giant', he won nine Australian track cycling titles, mainly in the sprint and team sprint, several Oceania sprint titles, World Cup sprint and keirin titles.

Success came in the UCI track world championships. At 1997 at Perth, Western Australia he won bronze in the team sprint; at Antwerp, Belgium in 2001, Eadie won silver in the team sprint; and at Ballerup in 2002, he claimed gold in the sprint and a silver in the team sprint.

At the 2000 Olympic Games in Sydney, he combined with Darryn Hill and Gary Neiwand to win the bronze medal, behind France and Great Britain, in the inaugural staging of the 'Olympic' team sprint. When the Olympic Games returned to Athens in 2004, Eadie, Ryan Bayley and Shane Kelly finished fourth in the team sprint.

Competing at the 2002 Commonwealth Games in Manchester, Eadie won a gold medal in the team sprint and a silver in the sprint, breaking the Commonwealth Games record for the flying 200 metres and posting a time of

10.145 seconds. When the Commonwealth Games came to Kuala Lumpur in 1998, Eadie won silver in the sprint.

Representing Australia at the 2004 Athens Olympic Games, controversy erupted after a package containing peptides was sent to Eadie from San Diego. He denied involvement but was knocked out in the sprint event.

Ryan Bayley

Ryan Bayley (born 1982) started competitive cycling in Perth Western Australia at 15 and later rode for the Albany cycling club. In 2000 he won the sprint and team sprint at the junior track world championships in Italy. Bayley credits his early experience riding BMX and motocross as helping his initial success on the track.

At the national track championships in the 2000s he won the 200m flying time trial title and the teams sprint in 2001, and sprint titles in 2003 and 2007.

Competing at the 2001 UCI track world championships at Antwerp, Belgium, Bayley won gold in the keirin after a crash knocked teammate Jobie Dajka and other fancied riders out of the final and he said he walked away an unexpected world keirin champion. Bayley had more success at the track world championships winning silver medals in the team sprint at Antwerp in 2001 and at Copenhagen in 2002, bronze in the sprint at Melbourne in 2004, and bronze in the team sprint at Bordeaux in 2006.

Bayley achieved double gold winning two gold medals at the 2002 Commonwealth Games at Manchester in the sprint and team sprint.

While Bayley was known for his 'junk food' eating habits, Cycling Australia said that 'Flyin Ryan' launched himself into sporting folklore as the first Australian track cyclist to win two individual gold medals at the same Olympics at Athens in 2004.

AOC historian Harry Gordon said that while Russell Mockridge won two golds in Helsinki in 1952, one was in the tandem with Lionel Cox. "In the Athens individual sprint, Bayley won gold overwhelming world champion, Theo Bos, of the Netherlands, 2-1 in the final. Bos won the first of their three encounters and looked well placed to take the second when Bayley summoned up enough fast-twitch force to throw his bike across the line, a trick he learned as a junior BMX champion. In the final shoot-out he passed Bos on the last curve to win," Gordon said.

In the keirin event at two laps to go after the motor bike reeled away, Jose Escurado hit the front. But at one lap to go Bayley unleashed a big sprint to easily win the eight-lap keirin that gave Australia the top track-cycling nation status at Athens.

Bayley said the keirin, partially paced by motor bike, suited him: "It's a lottery, like dodgem cars. It's insane."

At the 2006 Melbourne Commonwealth Games, Bayley won gold medals in the sprint and keirin. In 2008 after an unsuccessful Olympics he retired in June 2009. Bayley was Cyclist of the Year in 2004 and Track Cyclist of the Year twice. Bayley was awarded a Medal of the Order of Australia and inducted into the Sport Australia Hall of Fame in 2015 and the Cycling Australia Hall of Fame.

Jobie Dajka

Jobie Dajka (born 1981) came from Adelaide and in 1999 burst onto international track cycling winning the junior world track championship with gold in the sprint, bronze in the one kilo time trial, and gold in the team sprint with Ben Kersten and Mark Renshaw.

Dajka won elite keirin and sprint titles at the Australian track championships in 2001 and the keirin again in 2005. When 17, Dajka won silver in the team sprint at the 2001 UCI track world championships at Antwerp. Other top results at the track worlds were: at Ballerup in 2002 with gold in the keirin, silver in the sprint and the team sprint; at Suttgart in 2003 with silver in the sprint and the keirin; and in 2005 at Los Angeles with bronze in the sprint.

At the Commonwealth Games in Manchester in 2002, Dajka won gold in the team sprint and bronze in the sprint. His career began to unwind when he was sent home from a pre-Olympic Games training camp in 2004 accused of lying to investigators during an alleged doping affair involving sprint cyclist Mark French.

Dajka was banned in June 2005 for three years after an assault on Australia's national track coach Martin Barras. A comeback was flagged in 2006. Adelaide newspapers reported on April 2009 that the 27-year-old was found dead in in his home and that his death was not suspicious.

Ben Kersten

Ben Kersten (born 1981) came from Wollongong, south of Sydney. He rode for the St. George Cycling Club and was an AIS scholarship holder. Kersten won gold in the one kilo time trial and silver in the team sprint at the 1998 junior track world championships in Cuba. At the 1999 Athens world junior track championships, he won gold in the one kilo time trial, gold in the team sprint and bronze in the sprint.

In 2003, Kersten won the senior kilo time trial title at the national track cycling championships in Sydney and is credited with nine national track cycling titles between 2003-2007. He was an all-round track champion and won many track titles in the Oceania Games and World Cup.

Kersten specialised in the one kilo time trial 'race against the clock' and in 2006 claimed the silver medal in the kilo time trial at the UCI track world championships at Bordeaux. He also won the gold medal in the kilo time trial at the 2006 Commonwealth Games in Melbourne.

Kersten won national and Oceania keirin titles and he later switched to road cycling. From 2009 he won around seven road races and criteriums in Australia and the USA, including the USA Criterium Title and a GC third at the Tour of the Murray River. In 2012 he took up the role of sprint development coach at the NSW Institute of Sport, then head endurance coach, and later was appointed head road cycling coach.

Shane Perkins

From Melbourne, Shane Perkins (born 1986) was the son of professional track cyclist Daryl Perkins and he took up cycling in 1999. Perkins became known for his top sprint performances from 2003 in the junior and elite national track championships, winning seven elite track titles.

Perkins won the junior sprint and keirin titles at the 2004 track world championships at Los Angeles but tested positive for methamphetamine after the keirin. He was cleared on unintentional use of a nasal inhaler with a stimulant.

At the elite track world championships, Perkins won bronze in the team sprint at Bordeaux in 2006; silver in the sprint at Copenhagen in 2010; and a gold medal in the kierin at Apeldoorn in 2011.

Perkins credited his mental toughness for his 2011 keirin win after a quad tear impeded his sprint ride. At the Melbourne track worlds in 2012 he won team sprint gold alongside Matt Glaetzer and Scott Sunderland, edging out the French by one thousandth of a second for gold, despite the team being dubbed a "work in progress".

He made his Olympic debut in London in 2012 placing fourth in the team sprint and won the bronze medal in the individual sprint. In 2006 at the Commonwealth Games in Melbourne, Perkins won a bronze medal in the team sprint and in 2010, returning to the Commonwealth Games at Delhi he won two gold medals competing in the individual sprint and the team sprint.

In 2016 Perkins was a surprise omission from the national track program prior to the Olympics. He became a Russian citizen in 2017 and won Russian keirin and team sprint titles, while Russian cyclists are allowed to compete under a 'Russia' banner at the 2021 Olympics.

Matthew Glaetzer

Matthew Glaetzer (born 1992) comes from Adelaide where he rode for the Central Districts Cycling Club. Glaetzer was a dual junior world champion in 2010. From 2011, he won 11 senior national track cycling titles, mainly in the sprint, team sprint and keirin.

At the 2017 World Cup competition in Manchester, Glaetzer was the first cyclist to break the 1:00 minute mark in the one kilo time trial on a sea level velodrome. At the Commonwealth Games at Glasgow in 2014, Glaetzer won gold medals in the keirin and bronze in the team sprint and was fifth in the sprint.

When the Commonwealth Games track cycling came to Brisbane in 2018, he won more gold medals in the keirin and the one kilo time trial, and bronze in the team sprint. He redeemed himself after his shock loss in the men's sprint finals by winning gold the next day in the one kilo time trial, setting a new Australia one-kilometre track record of 59.340 seconds.

Leading Australia's sprint attack at the Olympic Games at Rio 2016, Glaetzer went down to Russia's Denis Dmitriev by 0.044 seconds in the ride off for bronze. Glaetzer represented Australia at the UCI track world championships winning his first world medal with a bronze in the team sprint at Apeldoorn in 2011 with Dan Ellis and Jason Niblett, when Great Britain, France and Germany were the top track sprint nations.

At the track worlds at Melbourne in 2012, Glatzer won gold in the team sprint riding with Perkins and Scott

Sunderland in a close contest with the French team. In the (match) sprint at the UCI track world championships in London in 2016, Glaetzer won silver behind Great Britain's Jason Kenny. At Apeldoorn in 2018 he claimed his first gold medal in the sprint beating Britain's Jack Carlin. The Australian Olympic Committee said: "At the 2018 World Championships, Glaetzer claimed a memorable maiden individual world title victory in the sprint and claimed silver in the kilo time trial."

Opening the 2018-19 World Cup he grabbed three sprint gold and one silver, but at the 2019 track world championships was fourth in the sprint and the keirin.

Glaetzer revealed in November 2019 that he had thyroid cancer but was recovering from thyroid cancer surgery. In December during the 2019-2020 World Cup he won bronze at New Zealand in the keirin, silver in the keirin and bronze in the sprint at Brisbane. He missed the 2020 track world championships due to a leg injury and is in the Australian cycling team for the 2021 Tokyo Olympics.

Scott Sunderland

Scott Sunderland (born 1988) came from Busselton Western Australia and held scholarships with the AIS and WA Institute of Sport. From 2004 he accumulated 16 championship wins in under 17/junior track cycling and at the UCI junior track worlds in 2005-06, Sunderland won five medals including gold in the kilo time trial and silver in the sprint. Known for his sprinting ability, he won seven gold medals at the UCI track World Cup up to 2014.

Sunderland also won a gold medal in the team sprint in the UCI track world championships at Melbourne in 2012.

At the Commonwealth Games at Delhi in 2010, Sunderland won gold medals in the one kilo time trial and in the team sprint with Daniel Ellis and Jason Niblett, and a silver medal in the sprint. At Glasgow in 2014 he defended his Commonwealth one kilo time trial title with a brilliant performance to win the gold medal, setting a new Commonwealth time of 1mins, 00.675secs after his Games record fell to New Zealand's Matthew Archibald.

He told ABC News: "It's always hard being a reigning champion with a record as well, so to come out and execute that time tonight was something special." Sunderland switched to road racing. In 2015 he won the Melbourne to Warrnambool road classic and in 2017 signed with the IsoWhey Sports Swiss Wellness team.

Brett Aitken

Aitken, (born 1971) came from Adelaide and was affiliated with the Adelaide Cycling Club. In 1989, he won bronze in the junior world championship points race and silver in the team pursuit and was an AIS scholarship holder. Aitken won 10 national track championship titles to 2000, including three in the madison and the points race, and four in the team pursuit riding for South Australia, and also won national road series and criterium titles.

In 1990 and 1991, Aitken won bronze medals at the world track championship in the team pursuit. He went on to win gold at the track worlds in 1993 in the team pursuit with Stuart O'Grady, Tim O'Shannessy and Billy-Joe Shearsby. In 1994, at the track worlds in Palermo, Aitken won bronze in the team pursuit and at the Commonwealth Games, won a gold medal at Victoria, Canada in the team pursuit, and in 1990 a silver medal at Auckland.

Aitken rode at three Olympic Games, winning two Olympic medals in the team pursuit with a silver in 1992 at Barcelona and bronze in 1996 at Atlanta. Aitken teamed with Scott McGrory after he and McGrory were selected to ride in the in the inaugural staging of the madison event at the 2000 Sydney Olympic Games.

The madison duo won the gold medal in the madison at the Sydney Olympics, riding a perfect race over 240 laps or 60 kilometres when sprint points are taken every 10 laps. The duo racked up points and won the race with 26 points from Belgium on 22 and Italy on 15 points.

Well before the madison race, Aitken and McGrory faced family adversity. "It was arguably the most remarkable performance against adversity of the Games and gave Australia its first track cycling gold medal since the team pursuit at Los Angeles 1984," the Australian Olympic Committee said.

Aitken abandoned his Olympic quest in early 2000 after his one-year-old daughter was diagnosed with a developmental disorder but his wife, friends and McGrory convinced him to continue.

From 1991 he competed on the road internationally winning road races, tour stages and criteriums. In 2013 when he was 42, Aitken retired from state competition due to a cardiovascular condition. He joined the South Australian Sports Institute as a cycling coach and was inducted into Cycling Australia Hall of Fame.

Scott McGrory

Scott McGrory (born 1969) came from Victoria and started track cycling at Albury-Wodonga and later at the Gold Coast and was an AIS scholarship holder. He won five national track cycling titles: two in the team pursuit (1991-92), two in the madison (1995-96), and the points race in 1993, and the national road championships in 1994. When 18, McGrory won bronze in the 4000m team pursuit at the 1988 Seoul Olympic Games.

In 1996 he won silver in the madison at the track world championship at Manchester. At the 2000 Sydney Olympics he won a gold medal in the inaugural madison event riding with Brett Aitken, but also faced adversity before the event. In another cruel twist McGrory's infant son died 10 weeks before the Games. How they both helped each other through this is quite unbelievable, the Australian Olympic Committee said.

McGrory said it was a privilege to be able to represent Australia at the Sydney Olympic Games, 12 years on in the prime of his career. "It was extraordinary to win the first Olympic gold medal on the track for Australia in 16 years," he said. McGrory and Aitken were named the Oppy Medal Cyclists of the Year for 2000.

He competed on the road in Europe from 1994 and from the late 1980s on the track he won around 17-20 six-day races. He joined the Victoria Institute of Sport as a coach from 2008 and was a director of the Sun Tour. He was inducted into the Cycling Australia Hall of Fame in 2019.

Stuart O'Grady

Stuart O'Grady (born 1973) came from a cycling family in Adelaide and started track cycling while at high school. When 18, he made his Olympic debut at the 1992 Olympic Games in Barcelona 1992, winning silver in the team pursuit with Brett Aitken, Stephen McGlede and Shaun O'Brien. O'Grady was an AIS scholarship holder.

O'Grady competed at every Olympic Games over a remarkable 20-year period from 1992 to 2012, joining an elite club of six-time Australian Olympians and has an impressive four medals on his Olympic record, the Australian Olympic Committee said. In 1996 at the Atlanta Olympics, O'Grady won the bronze in the points race and bronze in the team pursuit with Aitken, Brad McGee, and Dean Woods. An all-round road and track champion, at the 2004 Athens Olympics, he won his first Olympic gold medal teaming with Graeme Brown in the madison race.

In the Commonwealth Games, at Victoria, Canada in 1994 he won gold medals in the team pursuit and 10-mile scratch, silver in the points race, and bronze in the individual pursuit; at Manchester in 2002 he won gold in the team pursuit and the road race; and at Kuala Lumpur in 1998 won silver in the road time trial.

At the UCI track world championships, O'Grady won a gold medal in 1993 at Hamar, Norway in the 4000m team pursuit; won bronze in the team pursuit at Palermo in 1994; and claimed his second gold in the team pursuit and bronze in the individual pursuit at Bogota in 1995. From 2005 he concentrated on road cycling. (see road cycling).

Brad McGee

Bradley McGee (born 1976) came from Sydney, the youngest of four cycling brothers. When 16 at the UCI junior track world championships, he won the individual pursuit in 1993-1994 and the team pursuit. In the 1990s he won four national track titles in the team and individual pursuit. McGee was one of our best and most successful track pursuit cyclists. At the 1995 UCI track world championships he won gold at Bogota, Colombia in the 3000m team pursuit; in 2002 at Copenhagen, he won gold in the individual pursuit; and in 2008 at Manchester won bronze in the team pursuit.

At the 1994 Commonwealth Games at Victoria, Canada, McGee won gold medals in the individual pursuit and team pursuit; in 1998 he repeated the gold medal wins at Kuala Lumpur; and in 2002 at Manchester claimed his third Commonwealth gold in the 4000m individual pursuit in a new Games record of 4mins, 16.358secs.

He competed at four Olympics from 1996 to 2008. "McGee was the only cyclist to win medals in the individual pursuit at three Olympic Games and won more track cycling medals than any other Australian until Anna Meares won her sixth medal at Rio 2016," the Australian Olympic Committee said.

McGee claimed gold at the 2004 Athens Olympics in the team pursuit with Graeme Brown, Brett Lancaster, and Luke Roberts in a world record time of 3mins, 58.233secs, and silver in the individual pursuit. He won bronze in the team pursuit and individual pursuit at Atlanta in 1996 and bronze in the individual pursuit at Sydney in 2000. After a successful career as a road cyclist on the European tour, he retired in late 2008, becoming director sportif for a road cycling team (see road cycling).

Graeme Brown

Graeme Brown (born 1979) grew up in Launceston and Hobart and spent his high school years in Sydney. He rode for the Randwick Botany Cycling Club in Sydney and was mentored by NSWIS coach Gary Sutton. Success came early when he won the under 19 team (Olympic) sprint at the 1996 national track championships and team pursuit at the under 19 track world championships. From 1999 to 2003, Brown won national track titles in the points race, the team pursuit, and in the madison with Mark Renshaw.

At the 2002 Commonwealth Games in Manchester, he won gold medals in the scratch race and in the 4000m team pursuit when the Australian team set a Commonwealth Games record of 3mins, 59.583secs.

Brown's endurance and sprint ability helped his goal of being an Olympic champion. At the Athens Olympics in 2004, Brown joined Russell Mockridge (Helsinki) and Ryan Bayley (Athens) as the only cyclists to win two gold medals at one Olympics. At Athens in the team pursuit final, Brown rode with Brett Lancaster, Bradley McGee, Luke Roberts, and Peter Dawson and Stephen Wooldridge (both preliminaries) for Australia's first team pursuit gold since Los Angeles in 1984.

The Sydney Morning Herald said Stuart O'Grady was controversially chosen to replace Mark Renshaw in the 50km, 200-lap madison at Athens with Brown. But O'Grady and Brown won Australia's second madison gold since Sydney 2000, accumulating an extra lap on the field and 22 sprint points taking the madison from Switzerland (15 points) and Great Britain (12 points).

At the UCI track world championship in Stuttgart in 2003, Brown teamed with Peter Dawson, Brett Lancaster and Luke Roberts to win the team pursuit gold medal. At Manchester in 2008, Brown won bronze in the team pursuit. He was an accomplished road cyclist winning road races in Australia and Europe. After his last two seasons with Australia's Drapac, he retired around 2016.

Luke Roberts

Luke Roberts (born 1977) is from Adelaide. From a cycling family, he started cycling at the age of 13 was an AIS scholarship holder and turned professional in 2002. In 1994-95, Roberts won the team pursuit at the junior track world titles and gold in the individual pursuit. From 1996 he added five national track titles in the team pursuit/individual pursuit and in 1999 was first in the individual pursuit World Cup rankings.

Riding in the relentless pace and precision riding of the

four-man, 16-lap, 4000m team pursuit and the individual pursuit, Roberts was one of our best track endurance champions winning seven gold medals in the team or individual pursuit at the UCI world championships, Olympic and Commonwealth Games.

He was part of the gold medal team pursuit at the 1998 Commonwealth Games at Kuala Lumpur and won silver in the individual pursuit. At the Commonwealth Games at Manchester in 2002 he won gold in the team pursuit.

At the UCI track world cycling championships, Roberts won seven medals with gold in 2002 in the team pursuit and silver in the individual pursuit at Ballerup; gold in the team pursuit and silver in the individual pursuit at Stuttgart in 2003 and gold and silver again at Melbourne in 2004; and in 2008 bronze in the team pursuit at Manchester. He was named the Male Track Cyclist of the Year in 2003.

Competing at the 2004 Athens Olympics, Roberts won a gold medal in the 4000m team pursuit when Australia set a new world record of 3mins, 56.610secs, breaking their previous 2003 world record set in Stuttgart. In an interview with veloVeritas (UK) in 2014 he said the team pursuit was becoming a race for "endurance sprinters and that the best teams can start fast in the first kilo but don't overcook it".

From 2002 Roberts competed in road racing winning the Tour of Tasmania and later rode for professional teams. He won many race stages, European road races, posted a GC second at the Sun Tour and GC thirds at the Tour of Britain and the Tour of Bavaria. In 2016, Roberts joined world tour road cycling team Sunweb in a coaching role.

Brett Lancaster

Brett Lancaster (born 1979) hailed from Shepparton in Victoria. In 1996-97 he was a junior national champion in the criterium, track individual pursuit and time trial, won the team pursuit in the junior track world junior championships in 1999 and an AIS scholarship holder.

In 1998 at the Commonwealth Games at Kuala Lumpur, he won gold in the team pursuit with Michael Rogers, Brad McGee, Luke Roberts, and Tim Lyons.

Competing at the UCI track world cycling championships: at Ballerup in 2002 Lancaster won gold in the team pursuit with Peter Dawson, Stephen Wooldridge, and Roberts. At Stuttgart in 2003 he won gold in the team pursuit when Graeme Brown replaced Wooldridge in the Australian team.

Lancaster, one of our top track champions in the demanding 4000m team pursuit, had his biggest win in 2004 at the Athens Olympic Games, taking gold in the team pursuit with Brown, Dawson, Roberts, Wooldridge, and Brad McGee in world record time. It was Australia's first team pursuit gold since Los Angeles in 1984.

Lancaster was a successful road cyclist from 2003 to 2015, posting around 10 wins in major tour stages and classics and was part of the Orica GreenEDGE team that won the team time trial at the 2013 Tour De France setting a race record of 57.841kph.

In 2015 he won the prologue at the Giro d'Italia and later that year at age 36, he signed with Team Sky in the UK as a sports director.

Jack Bobridge

Jack Bobridge (born 1989) came from Adelaide and in 2006-2007 won the team pursuit at the UCI world junior track titles. Bobridge won eight national track titles including three in the individual pursuit and team pursuit. One of our most successful endurance cyclists, at the UCI track world championships he won gold in the team pursuit and bronze in the individual pursuit at Ballerup in 2010; gold in the team pursuit and individual pursuit at Apeldoorn in 2011; silver in the team and individual pursuit at Melbourne in 2012; and individual pursuit silver at Yvelines in 2015.

At the Commonwealth Games at Delhi in 2010 he won gold in the 4000m individual pursuit and team pursuit and at Glasgow in 2014, he again claimed gold medals in the individual pursuit and in the team pursuit, setting a Commonwealth record of 3mins, 35.851secs riding with Alex Edmondson, Glen O'Shea and Luke Davison.

At the Olympic Games, Bobridge won a silver medal in the team pursuit in 2012 at London and won silver in the team pursuit in 2018 at Rio De Janeiro. He rode with O'Shea, Rohan Dennis and Michael Hepburn in the team pursuit at the 2012 London Olympics winning silver.

Bobridge competed successfully on the road but retired due to rheumatoid arthritis in 2016. He was charged in court for selling trafficable quantities of recreational drugs in 2017. In 2019 he admitted in court to using drugs such as cocaine days before competing in Europe, knowing the drug would likely have left his system.

Leigh Howard

Leigh Howard (born 1989) came from Geelong, Victoria and began cycling at the age of 9 at the Geelong Cycling Club. He held an AIS scholarship and from 2008 won a team pursuit and three madison titles at the TrackNats.

At the UCI track cycling world championships from 2008 to 2012, Howard showed he was one of Australia's best all-round track endurance cyclists winning eight medals: at Manchester in 2008 he won silver in the omnium; in 2009 he won three medals at Pruszkow with gold in the tough omnium event, silver medals in the team pursuit and in the madison teaming with Cameron Meyer; and in 2010 at Ballerup won silver in the omnium, and gold in the madison with Cameron Meyer. With Meyer in 2011 at Apeldoorn he won another gold in the madison. At Melbourne in 2012 he won bronze in the madison.

Returning to international track cycling in 2018 at the Commonwealth Games he rode in the 4000m team pursuit with Alex Porter, Sam Welsford and Kelland O'Brien, to win gold in Commonwealth and world record time, becoming the first team pursuit team in history to break the three-minute (3:49.804) fifty-second barrier.

Howard claimed his ninth medal at the track world's in 2019 at Pruszkow with gold in the 4000m team pursuit. Cycling Australia said Howard was part of the quartet of Porter, Welsford and O'Brien which smashed their team pursuit world record posting 3min, 48.012secs.

At the 2020 track world's in Berlin, Porter, Welsford, Howard, Scott and Luke Plapp were just two-hundredths of a second off the podium when they finished fourth clocking 3mins, 50.015secs for the 4000m distance.

Howard has a great record in Europe and Australia competing on the road from 2007 posting around eight one-day race and 15 tour stage wins and rode in the grand tours. In 2018 he rode with the ACA Pro Racing Sunshine Coast team and was second at the London Six Days race.

Stephen Wooldridge

Stephen Wooldridge (born 1977) started cycling at a young age. He joined Sydney's St George cycling club in and was guided by New South Wales track coach Gary Sutton. He missed the world junior championships and completed a degree in technology management.

Wooldridge made the nine-man squad for the 2000 Olympic Games in Sydney but wasn't selected to ride. He won an individual pursuit and three team pursuit titles at the TrackNats and became a top track endurance cyclist.

Competing at the UCI track world cycling championships in the team pursuit, Wooldridge won three gold medals: at Ballerup in 2002; at Melbourne in 2004; and at Bordeaux in 2006, when he teamed with Matt Goss, Peter Dawson and Mark Jamieson. He also won bronze in the team pursuit at Los Angeles in 2005.

Representing Australia at the Commonwealth Games, Wooldridge won gold in the team pursuit at Manchester in 2002 and silver in the team pursuit at Melbourne in 2006. He won gold as part of the Australian team pursuit at the 2004 Olympic Games at Athens. Not in the winning quartet of Brown, Lancaster, McGee and Roberts, he was awarded gold due to his preliminary round participation. Australian newspapers reported on August 15, 2017 that Australian Olympic track cycling champion Stephen Wooldridge had taken his own life at the age of 39.

Wooldridge was inducted into the NSW Hall of Champions in 2015 and sat on Cycling Australia's board from 2007 to 2013. "Steve will be remembered by so many for not only his success in competition, but also for the contributions he made across so many roles in the sport," CA chief executive Nick Green said.

Peter Dawson

Peter Dawson (born 1982) came from Pinjarra, Western Australia. His cycling career took off when a junior, following good results winning national and world championships on the track in 1999-2000. He was an AIS scholarship holder and won the elite individual pursuit title at the 2002 national track championships and the Sydney World Cup.

At the 2002 UCI track world championships at Ballerup, Dawson won gold in the 4000m team pursuit with Brett Lancaster, Stephen Wooldridge and Luke Roberts in world record time. He became one of our top track endurance cyclists claiming three more gold medals in the 4000m team pursuit at the track worlds at Stuttgart in 2003, Melbourne in 2004, and Bordeaux in 2006.

Dawson won a gold medal at the Commonwealth Games in the 4000m team pursuit in 2002 at Manchester when the

Australian team set a world record time and in 2006 at Melbourne he won a silver medal in the same event.

In 2004 he won gold for his qualifying rounds of the 4000m team pursuit at the Athens Olympics, Australia's first team pursuit gold since Los Angeles in 1984.

Between 2004-2008, Dawson competed on the road internationally, including with the USA's Rock Racing Team, winning road races and stages. WAIS head cycling coach Daryl Benson said: "Peter has been an outstanding member of the WAIS Cycling program representing his state and country with distinction."

Cameron Meyer

Cameron (Cam) Meyer (born 1988) comes from Western Australia and took up cycling at age 13. Meyer was an AIS scholarship holder and won the madison race at the national junior track championships in 2005 and 2006, and three titles at the UCI junior world championships, in the individual pursuit, madison and team pursuit.

He had a breakthrough year in 2009 winning gold in the points race at the UCI track world cycling championships in Pruszkow, when he also won silver in the madison with Leigh Howard and silver in the team pursuit. Meyer went on to win nine gold medals and 18 medals overall to 2018 at the UCI track world championships: three gold medals in 2010 at Ballerup, including in the madison with Leigh Howard, in the points race and team pursuit; in 2011 at Apeldoorn, gold in the madison with Howard and points silver; and gold in the points race at Melbourne in 2012.

Cycling Australia said Meyer returned to the track in 2017 in the UCI track worlds at Hong Kong, winning dual gold in the points race and team pursuit. He added a fifth gold in the points race in 2018 becoming Australia's most successful male track cyclist at the world titles. In 2017, Meyer won his fourth national madison title at Melbourne in a brilliant performance riding with Sam Welsford.

At the Commonwealth Games, in Delhi, India, in 2010 Meyer won three gold medals on the track in the 4000m team pursuit, the points race, and the 25km scratch race when Australia's men won 18 gold medals on the track.

In 2018 at the Gold Coast he won the individual road time trial in a time of 48mins, 13.04secs over the 38.5km course, 30 seconds ahead of England's Harry Tanfield. "Meyer, a nine-time world champion in track cycling, added Commonwealth Games gold on the road to his lengthy list of accomplishments," ABC News said. Meyer competed successfully on the road (see road cycling).

Sam Welsford

Sam Welsford (born 1996) came from Perth, Western Australia and rode for Northern Beaches Cycling Club. He started cycling when quite young and at the UCI junior track world championships in 2013-14, Welsford won back-to-back gold medals in the team pursuit. In 2016 at the elite UCI track world championships in London, he won gold in the 4000m team pursuit with Michael Hepburn, Callum Scotson, Miles Scotson, Alexander Porter, and Luke Davison. In the team pursuit at the 2016

Rio Olympics, Welsford won silver after the Australian team were beaten by a record-breaking British team.

He won five TrackNats titles to 2019 and in 2017 teamed with Cameron Meyer at the madison titles at Melbourne, winning gold with 97 points in a dominating performance. At the 2018 Commonwealth Games on the Gold Coast, Welsford won gold in the 15km scratch race and teamed with Porter, Leigh Howard and Kelland O'Brien to win the gold medal in the 4000m team pursuit, becoming the first team in history to break the three-minute and fifty-second barrier (3:49.804).

"The quartet smashed this at the 2019 Worlds Championships in 3min, 48.012sec, with Welsford winning two golds in 30 minutes after taking top honours in the men's scratch," Cycling Australia said.

Described as a "freight-train" in the fast and precision cycling of the team pursuit, Welsford won gold in the team pursuit at the 2017 UCI track world championships in Hong Kong. In February 2019 at the Pruszkow track worlds he rode with Porter, Howard and O'Brien to outclass Great Britain in the team pursuit in world record time, then won gold in the scratch race. In the 2020 Berlin track world's team pursuit, Welsford, Porter, Howard, Cam Scott and Luke Plapp just missed the bronze.

Welsford is part of the Australian track cycling team for the Tokyo 2021 Olympic Games. On the road, he placed second in the Melbourne to Warrnambool in 2017 and in 2020 won the national road criterium championship and the GC at the Lexus of Blackburn Bay Crits series.

Michael Hepburn

Michael Hepburn (born 1991) came from Brisbane and initially competed in triathlons. He switched to cycling when 14 and in 2009, won the UCI world junior track championships in the individual pursuit, and two UCI World Cup races in the team pursuit. At the TrackNats championships in 2010 he won the omnium race and in 2012-2013, claimed the individual pursuit title.

In 2010, Hepburn won gold in the team pursuit at the UCI track world championships at Ballerup and at the Commonwealth Games at Delhi, won a gold medal in the team pursuit and bronze in the individual pursuit.

Hepburn won another track worlds' gold in the 4000m team pursuit in 2011 at Apeldoorn, riding with Jack Bobridge, Rohan Dennis, and Luke Durbridge, and took bronze in the 4000m individual pursuit. He claimed his third UCI track world gold in Melbourne in 2012 in the individual pursuit clocking 4mins, 15.839secs, then won silver in the team pursuit when Great Britain defeated the Australians by just 0.206 seconds.

At the 2012 Olympic Games in London he won silver in the 4000m team pursuit. "Hepburn and his team could not match it with the home team in the final as the British again broke their own world record (3:51.659) with the Australians going home with the silver," the AOC said.

Hepburn became one of our best track pursuit and endurance cyclists winning two gold medals in the individual pursuit and team pursuit at the 2013 UCI track world championships in Minsk. He returned to the UCI track worlds in 2016 in London winning his sixth world's gold in the team pursuit. At the 2016 Rio Olympics he won a silver medal in the team pursuit.

Competing at the UCI road world championships, he won two silver and one bronze in the team time trial from 2013 to 2016. Hepburn became a European grand tour rider after he joined the Mitchelton-Scott cycling team in 2012.

Rohan Dennis

Better known as the 2018-2019 world road time trial champion, Rohan Dennis (born 1990) came from South Australia and won junior national track championships titles in 2007 and in 2008 and at the UCI 2008 junior track world championships, won gold in the team pursuit.

Dennis was also a top track endurance rider. At the UCI elite track world championships, at Pruszkow in 2009 he won silver in the 4000m team pursuit and won gold at Ballerup in 2010 in the 4000m team pursuit riding with Jack Bobridge, Michael Hepburn and Cameron Meyer. He backed up in the 2011 track worlds at Apeldoorn, winning gold in the team pursuit and in 2012 at Melbourne won silver in the 4000m individual pursuit.

Competing in the track World Cup Dennis won gold at Melbourne in the team pursuit in 2010 and was the overall winner of the individual pursuit World Cup in 2010-11.

Dennis won a silver medal at the 2012 Olympic Games in London in the 4000m team pursuit, when the British again broke their own world record with the Australians going home with the silver medal.

In February 2015 Dennis set a world hour track record at Grenchen, Switzerland, clocking 52.491 kilometres per hour. He signed with leading Tour De France winning team the UK's Team Ineos Grenadiers in late 2019 and is in Cycling Australia's road team for the Tokyo Olympics 2021 (see road cycling).

Glenn O'Shea

Glenn O'Shea (born 1989) grew up in Bendigo and started cycling when he was eight. In 2007 he started a 10-year career at the top of international track cycling winning the junior omnium and the team pursuit at the UCI track world championships. He also won the omnium and the scratch race at the Oceania championships.

Competing at the TrackNats championships from 2007 to 2015, O'Shea posted wins in the omnium (3), madison (3), points race (3), and team pursuit (5) for 14 national track titles. He won the points race at the Melbourne World Cup and won under 23 European Cup races.

Representing Australia at the 2012 Olympic Games at London, O'Shea won a silver medal in the team pursuit. When the Commonwealth Games came to Glasgow in 2014, he won gold in the team pursuit and silver in the scratch race.

Adelaide's The Advertiser said: "Aussies smash Bradley Wiggins-led Poms in team pursuit cycling at Commonwealth Games 2014." In the 4000m team pursuit at Glasgow, O'Shea, riding with Jack Bobridge, Luke Davison and Alex Edmondson rode to their race plan and clocked a sizzling time of 3mins, 54.851secs, almost catching the England team. Australia's time was a Commonwealth Games record.

At the UCI track world championships, O'Shea won gold in the omnium event and silver in the team pursuit at Melbourne in 2012; gold in the team pursuit and bronze in the omnium at Minsk in 2013; gold in the team pursuit at Cali in 2014; silver in the omnium at Yvelines in 2015; and bronze in the omnium at London in 2016 to become one of our most successful track cyclists. The AOC said at the 2012 world championships, "O'Shea showed consistency is needed across the six-discipline omnium. Although he didn't win an individual race, he never finished lower than sixth to be crowned world champion."

He was appointed as a Cycling Australia women's track endurance coach in 2020. O'Shea also competed in road racing from 2008 to 2016, placing in and winning stages at tours in Australia and internationally.

Alex Edmondson

Alex Edmondson was born in Borneo, Malaysia (1993) and lived in South Australia from 1998. He started in downhill mountain bike racing. In 2011 he won the UCI junior track world championships in the madison and the team pursuit and the UCI World Cup in the madison.

Edmondson, the brother of world track champion Annette Edmondson, won 12 TrackNats championship titles between 2011 and 2016 in the madison, individual pursuit, omnium, points and team pursuit (6). He became one of our top track endurance cyclists and at the UCI track world cycling championships, Edmondson won gold in the 4000m team pursuit in 2013 at Minsk, gold in the team pursuit and in the individual pursuit in 2014 at Cali, and bronze in the team pursuit in 2015 at Yvelines.

At the Rio Olympic Games in 2018, he won silver in the 4000m team pursuit with Jack Bobridge, Michael Hepburn and Sam Welsford in 3mins, 51.008secs, when the Bradley Wiggins-led Great Britain broke the world record in the first round and bettered it in the final against Australia clocking 3mins, 50.265secs.

Edmondson had more success competing in the 2014 Commonwealth Games at Glasgow, winning a gold medal in the team pursuit and silver in the individual pursuit. He moved to road cycling, winning the under 23 GC at the 2015 Tour of Flanders for WorldTour team GreenEDGE. He won the 2018 national road championship and in 2019 rode for Mitchelton-Scott in their Chase road race win at the Hammer Limburg series.

Chris Scott

From Gympie, Queensland (born 1968), Chris Scott was born with cerebral palsy and moved to Brisbane when two years old. He played school soccer and became involved the Sporting Wheelies and Disabled Association. At the Seoul paralympics in 1988 he competed in seven-a-side football and athletics at the 1992 Barcelona Paralympics. Scott switched to cycling when he broke his ankle and first competed at the 1996 Atlanta Olympics.

He represented Australia in cycling at four consecutive Paralympic Games. His record at the Paralympic Games includes gold at the 1996 Atlanta Mixed 5,000m Time Trial Bicycle CP Div 4; gold at Sydney 2000, Mixed Bicycle Time Trial CP4; gold at Athens 2004 Men's Road Race/ Time Trial Bicycle CP4; gold Athens Men's Individual Pursuit Bicycle CP4 and gold Athens Men's Team Sprint in LC14/CP ¾.

He won a gold medal at Beijing in 2008 in the Men's Individual Pursuit CP4; a silver medal at Atlanta in 1996 in the Mixed 20k Bicycle CP4; a silver at Beijing in 2008 in the Men's Individual Time Trial CP4; bronze medals at Sydney in 2000 in the Mixed Bicycle Road Race CP4 and at Beijing in 2008 in the Men's 1km time trial in CP4.

The Cycling Australia Hall of Fame said Queensland's Chris Scott was the first para-cyclist inducted into the Hall of Fame and represented Australia in cycling at four consecutive Paralympic Games, claiming 10 Paralympic cycling medals including six gold medals and was named captain of the 2004 Australian Paralympic team. "It feels surreal to be inducted into the Hall of Fame," Scott said.

"I grew up idolising people like Sir Hubert Opperman and Sid Patterson who are not just legends of Australian cycling but for cycling worldwide.

"To be the first para-cyclist to be inducted represents recognition for the years of dedication I have given to the sport and, to honour someone who has achieved in this arena, represents the respect Cycling Australia gives to para-cycling events."

Alex Porter

Alexander (Alex) Porter (born 1996) is from Adelaide. In 2014 he won the junior team pursuit world championship and elite World Cup gold in the points race. At the TrackNats championships he won nine medals including the team pursuit (2015-16), the omnium in 2017 and the madison with Rohan Wright in 2018.

Representing Australia at the 2018 Commonwealth Games at Brisbane in the 4000m team pursuit, he won the gold medal with Leigh Howard, Kelland O'Brien and Sam Welsford becoming the first team to break the three-minute and fifty-second barrier (3mins, 49.804secs).

At the UCI track world cycling championships, Porter won three gold medals: in the team pursuit at London in 2016, at Hong Kong in 2017, and at Pruszkow in 2019 with Howard, O'Brien and Welsford, when the Australians broke their own record clocking 3mins, 48.012secs. In 2020 at the track worlds at Berlin, Porter, Welsford, Howard, Scott and Luke Plapp (3:50.015) were just two-hundredths of a second off the podium when they finished fourth. He was named in the Australian Cycling Team for the 2021 Tokyo Olympics.

Kelland O'Brien

Kelland O'Brien (born 1998) rode for St Kilda cycling club and won gold medals in the under 19 madison and team pursuit at the 2015 track world championships. From 2018, he won five elite titles at the TrackNats in the points, madison (2), team pursuit (2), and scratch race.

At the UCI track world championships O'Brien claimed a gold medal in the team pursuit and bronze in the individual pursuit at Hong Kong in 2017 and at Pruszkow in 2019, won a gold medal in the 4000m team pursuit when the team broke the world record. He missed the 2020 track worlds at Berlin when he broke his collarbone.

In 2018 in the Commonwealth Games at Brisbane O'Brien won gold in the team pursuit with Sam Welsford, Leigh Howard and Alex Porter, the first team to break the three-minute, fifty-seconds barrier.

On the road, O'Brien won the GC at the Tour of the Great South Coast in 2019 and at the RoadNats won the under 23 criterium in 2020 and silver in the road race in 2021. He is in Australia's Tokyo Olympics track team.

Also included are other top track cycling champions who have won medals at the world championships, World Cup, Olympic and Commonwealth Games: Ashley Hutchinson, Michael Freiburg, Alex Morgan, Luke Davison, Mitchell Mulhern, Cameron Scott, Callum Scotson, Miles Scotson, Luke Plapp, Nathan Hart, Matt Richardson, and Tom Cornish.

Ashley Hutchison

Hutchison was a top pursuit rider who won a gold medal at the 2004 UCI track world championships in Melbourne and bronze in 2005 at the Los Angeles track world championships in the team pursuit.

At the Commonwealth Games in Melbourne in 2006 he claimed the silver medal in the 29km scratch race and a silver medal in the team pursuit. Hutchison also won World Cup and Oceania track titles.

Michael Freiberg

Michael Freiberg won gold in the omnium at the 2011 track world cycling championships at Apeldoorn but was overlooked for the 2012 Olympics. At the 2010 Commonwealth Games in Delhi, Freiburg won gold in the team pursuit and silver in the scratch race.

On the road he placed in Oceania road championships, European one-day races and tours and won the national road championship in 2019. He rode for ACA Pro Racing Sunshine Coast.

Alexander Morgan

Alexander Morgan was a top individual pursuit rider who was in the winning team pursuit at the junior track world track championship in 2011-12 and at the UCI elite track world championships at Minsk in 2013. In 2016 he won the Oceania road time trial championship.

Luke Davison

Luke Davison was a junior track world champion in the madison and team pursuit in 2008 and at the TrackNats championships, won a madison, kilo time trial and two team pursuit titles.

Davison won gold medals in the team pursuit at the elite track world cycling championships at Cali, Colombia in 2014 and at London in 2016. At the 2014 Commonwealth

Games at Glasgow, Davison won gold in the team pursuit riding with Edmondson, O'Shea and Bobridge, clocking a Games record time of 3mins, 54.851secs.

Mitchell Mulhern

Mitchell Mulhern, competing in the team pursuit, won a gold medal at the track world cycling championships at Cali, Colombia in 2014 and a bronze medal at Yvelines, Paris in 2015 when the team pursuit team was hit by a mechanical and a puncture and missed a ride off for the gold. Mulhern was also placed several times in the team and individual pursuit at the TrackNats championships.

Callum Scotson

Callum Scotson won a silver medal in the 4000m team pursuit at the 2016 Olympic Games in Rio De Janeiro. At the track world championships, he won a gold medal in the team pursuit at London in 2016, silver in the madison in 2017 at Hong Kong, and bronze medals in the madison and the scratch race in 2018 at Apeldoorn.

At the TrackNats Scotson won two team pursuit titles and one madison title and he was also a triple under 23 national road time trial champion.

Miles Scotson

Miles Scotson claimed two gold medals at the UCI track world championships at Cali in 2014 and London in 2016, and a bronze at Yvelines, Paris in 2015 in the team pursuit. He also won four TrackNats titles and under 23 national road race and road individual time trial championships.

Scotson switched to road racing and in 2016 won bronze at the under 23 road world time trial championship at Doha.

Cameron Scott

Cameron Scott was the 2018 under 23 national criterium champion. He won gold in the team pursuit at the track world cycling championships in 2019 at Pruszkow. In 2020 he placed fourth in the team pursuit at the track world championships at Berlin and competed on the road.

Luke Plapp

Lucas (Luke) Plapp was a dual junior world track champion in 2018 in the points race and madison. At the 2019-20 TrackNats, Plapp won individual pursuit and team pursuit titles, and in 2020 the under 23 road time trial.

Plapp was fourth in the team pursuit at the 2020 track worlds at Berlin and is in the Australian Cycling Team for the 2021 Tokyo Olympics. In 2021 he won the RoadNats elite road national championships time trial at Ballarat.

Nathan Hart

Nathan Hart is from Canberra and at the Commonwealth Games in 2014 at Glasgow he won bronze in the team sprint with Shane Perkins and Matthew Glaetzer and in 2018 at Brisbane, team sprint bronze with Glaetzer, Jacob Schmid and Patrick Constable.

From 2013 to 2019 Hart won six medals at the TrackNats in the sprint/team sprint. He placed fourth at the 2016 Rio

Olympics in the team sprint and won team sprint bronze riding with Richardson and Cornish at the Berlin track world championships in 2020.

Matt Richardson

From Western Australia, he rode for Midlands CC and won dual under 19 national titles in the sprint and team sprint in 2017 and two elite medals at the TrackNats. In 2019 he won UCI World Cup gold in the team sprint. At the 2020 Berlin track worlds, Richardson won bronze in the team sprint with Cornish and Hart, and with Hart is in Australia's track team for the Tokyo Olympics.

Thomas Cornish

Thomas Cornish rides for Sutherland/Southern Cross cycling clubs in Sydney. He won the 2019 kilo time trial at the national track championships and in 2018 at the UCI junior track world championships in Switzerland won the one kilo time trial title in world record time and silver in the sprint.

Cornish won a bronze medal in the team sprint at the 2020 UCI track world championships in Berlin riding with Hart and Richardson.

From the 1990s, more of our top men's road cyclists headed for Europe to join amateur or professional cycling teams and rode on the tough European circuit, its classic road races and gruelling grand tours.

They were inspired by the performances at the grand tours of the Tour de France, Giro d'Italia, Vuelta a Espana and Europe's classic road races of our trailblazing cyclists from the 1970s-1990s such as Don Allan, Michael Wilson, Phil Anderson, Neil Stephens, Allan Pieper, Stuart O'Grady and Robbie McEwen.

In 1981, Phil Anderson was the first Australian to wear the leader's Yellow Jersey at the Tour de France and finished fifth in 1982, Australia's best Tour result. At the Giro d'Italia, Michael Wilson won a stage in 1982 and Allan Pieper won a stage in 1990, while Neil Stephens won a stage of the Tour De France in 1997.

Leading the third wave of Australians from around 2000 was Cadel Evans with his Tour de France win in 2011 and two second places. And Ritchie Porte (GC third in 2020) was seventh in the 2020 UCI men's road rankings, while Australia was the fifth ranked road cycling nation.

The Tour Down Under stage race joined the UCI WorldTour in 2008 and became a welcome season opener for Australia's top road cyclists, along with the Cadel Evans Great Ocean Road Race and the Herald Sun Tour.

National Road Championships, NRS

The National Road Series road competition included the national road championships and was started in 1991 by the

Australian Cycling Federation and its state bodies and was run by Cycling Australia from 1999. Races were declared open to amateurs and professionals from 1993. The NRS includes major state and national road classics and tours and offers pathways for top road cyclists to compete on the international circuit with automatic invites for men and women to UCI events, including the Tour Down Under and the Cadel Evans Road Race.

Among the two-time winners of the national men's road championships (RoadNats) since the 1990s were Neil Stephens, Robbie McEwen, Simon Gerrans, and Jack Bobridge.

From 2000, under 23 RoadNats national road champions who performed well internationally include Chris Sutton, Simon Clarke, Michael Hepburn, Rohan Dennis, Caleb Ewan, and Chris Hamilton.

Since 1994, multiple winners of the RoadNats national time trial championships include Rohan Dennis, Luke Durbridge, Jonathan Hall, and Cameron Meyer. Other winners were Adam Hansen, Michael Rogers, Michael Hepburn, and Ritchie Porte.

Multiple winners of the RoadNats criterium championship include Robbie McEwen (4), Caleb Ewan (2), and Steel Von Hoff (2). Von Hoff also won the road race gold medal at the 2018 Commonwealth Games.

The Tour Down Under

South Australia's Santos Tour Down Under started in 1999 and quickly became the leading elite men's road stage race in Australia, and later the top women's road stage race in 2016. Originally a UCI 2.4 class race, the TDU has six road stages and is held in January.

The Tour Down Under joined the prestigious UCI WorldTour in 2008, the first event and stage tour outside cycling's European base, guaranteeing the appearance of around 18 of the world's top cycling teams and an Australian team.

Many of Australia's European-based professional cyclists returned to try to add the TDU to their cycling record or palmares and some of our best ever road cyclists were successful.

At the first ever Tour Down Under in 1999, Australia's Stuart O'Grady won the General Classification for the race and he became the first cyclist to secure two Santos Tour Down Under wins in 2001.

In 2006, the Tour Down Under introduced the iconic Ochre Leader's Jersey. The GC winner was Australia's Tour De France and road classics rider Simon Gerrans. The Tour Down Under was awarded ProTour status in 2009 and became the first event on the UCI World Ranking calendar.

Australia's Allan Davis became the only rider in 2009 to have competed in every edition of the TDU and won the 2009 GC for the race.

Australian cyclists won seven out of the last ten Tour Down Under General Classifications between 2011-2020: Cameron Meyer in 2011; Simon Gerrans in 2006, 2012 and 2014; Rohan Dennis in 2015; Simon Gerrans again in 2016; and Richie Porte in 2017 and 2020.

Australia's first professional WorldTour cycling team Orica-GreenEDGE made its debut at the Tour Down Under in 2014 and team member Simon Gerrans claimed the overall victory one second ahead of Cadel Evans. Gerrans became the first person to win three editions of the Tour. Australia's Richie Porte (BMC Racing) won the Tour Down Under and the Ochre Jersey in 2017 for the first time, with Caleb Ewan (Orica-Scott) taking the sprint points jersey. While Porte, the 'King of Willunga Hill' has won six Willunga Hill final stages, when he won his second GC at the Tour Down Under in 2020, he had to settle for second place on the Willunga Hill stage.

The Cadel Evans Great Ocean Road classic

The Cadel Evans Great Ocean Road Race launched in January 2015 as annual one-day elite professional road race backed by a Victorian Government tourism department (Visit Victoria). It is one of the first events on the UCI WorldTour road racing calendar. The first Cadel Evans Great Ocean Road Race was inspired by Europe's one-day classic races and race director Scott Sunderland designed the course in consultation with Evans.

In 2015 it acted as a tribute to Australia's only Tour De France winner (2011) and UCI world road race champion Cadel Evans, who comes from Barwon Heads near the Great Ocean Road. The 2015 event marked Evans' final professional race, when he finished a courageous fifth.

The January long weekend of events attract many spectators on the road and at the finish line at Geelong and includes the elite Deakin University Women's (Great Ocean Road) Road Race, which was added as a UCI WorldTour event in 2020, and the Towards Zero Race Torquay criteriums.

The 172-kilometre Cadel Evans Great Ocean Road Race runs from Geelong to the Great Ocean Road and passes Barwon Heads, Torquay and Bells Beach before returning to Geelong, where it features four circuits of the challenging climb of Challambra Crescent.

In 2019, Italian superstar Elia Viviani sprinted home to claim victory in a thrilling finish to the elite men's race from Australia's Caleb Ewan (Lotto Soudal) and Daryl Impey (Mitchelton-Scott). Viviani sought redemption after finishing second to 29-year-old Australian Jay McCarthy in 2018, Australia's only winner of the race.

In 2020, 16 men's teams including 15 of the top 18-20 world professional teams lined up for the 172km road race at Geelong, among them Mitchelton-Scott and the KordaMentha Australian teams.

Dries Devenyns (Deceuninck-QuickStep), won in a sprint finish from Pavel Siakov (Ineos), while Jay McCarthy (fifth) was the best placed Australian.

Another factor driving the success of Australia's world men internationally was the formation of the GreenEDGE and Mitchelton-Scott (from 2018) cycling teams, with Simon Gerrans winning the Milan-San Remo road classic in 2012 and Matt Hayman winning the Paris-Roubaix 'Hell of the North' cobblestone classic in 2016, among highlights for the two cycling teams.

Drug taking accusations and scandals were common at grand tours and major races. Australia's road cyclists were not immune and included: Neil Stephens (never proved); Michael Rogers (dismissed); in 2012 Tour de France cyclist Stephen Hodge admitted to doping during the last six years of his career; Stuart O'Grady voluntarily admitted to EPO doping two weeks before the start of the 1988 Tour de France; while Nathan O'Neill copped a 15-month ban in 2008 for a 2007 USA tour doping violation.

Australia's team of the century

Cycling Australia announced its Tour de France team of the century in November 2014, which was chosen by a panel of judges. Cadel Evans topped the list of the nine cyclists as the General Classification rider, followed by Phil Anderson as another GC rider, with Richie Porte and Michael Rogers named as the two 'super domestiques'. Robbie McEwen was selected as the team's sprinter, while Mark Renshaw and Brad McGee were chosen as the two lead out cyclists for McEwen in the sprints. Simon Gerrans was picked as the team's all-rounder, while the final spot as team captain went to Sir Hubert Opperman.

In this chapter Australia's road cycling champions 1990-2020 were selected from the most successful at the highest level, including the UCI road world championships, UCI WorldTour races, Olympic Games and Commonwealth Games, Australia's major road races and tours, the grand tours of the Tour de France, Giro d'Italia and Vuelta a Espana, and Europe's classic road races.

Cadel Evans

Cadel Evans (born 1977) grew up in the Northern Territory and country New South Wales and later at Plenty near Melbourne. Taking up mountain biking, from 1992 to 1997 he won four Australian junior/elite MTB Championships and silver medals at the under-23 world MTB championships. He won a scholarship in the MTB squad at the Australian Institute of Sport from 1995.

Evans joined the Australian Under-23 road squad in Italy in 1997, later basing himself in the Swiss village of Lugnorre, when Switzerland became his home base.

In his first year competing as a professional cyclist in 1999, when Evans stormed to victory at the Tour of Tasmania on the last stage up Mt Wellington (1271 metres), commentator Phil Liggett announced that Evans would win the Tour de France one day.

At the 2000 Sydney Olympics he was seventh in the MTB XC. Evans focused on elite road cycling in 2001 and won the GC at the Tour of Austria. He rode for Mapei-Quick Step in 2002, thriving under the coaching of Mapei's Aldo Sassi in Switzerland.

Selected for the road events at the 2002 Commonwealth Games in Manchester, Evans won gold in the road time trial and silver in the road race. He was third in the GC at the Coppi e Bartali stage race and the Tour of Romandie. When Evans rode in his first grand tour at the Giro d'Italia in 2002, he led the race after stage 16 and became the first Australian to wear the leader's pink jersey, while he finished fourteenth overall.

Described as being very mentally strong, Evans also had the qualities of endurance, time trial and all-round ability needed to succeed as a road champion on the tough European road circuit. He rode for Team Telekom from 2003 and in 2004 won the Tour of Austria again, was third in the GC at the Vuelta a Murcia and fourth in Italy's Il Lombardia one-day classic.

From 2005-09 he joined the Davitamon-Lotto teams and was fifth in Belgium's Leige-Bastogne-Liege classic in 2005. Evans made his debut at the Tour de France in 2005 and placed eighth in the GC, the first Australian to finish in the top ten since Phil Anderson.

When Evans won the Tour of Romandie in Switzerland in 2006 from Contador and Valverde, he claimed it on the final 20km time trial stage. He was fourth at the Tour de France after winner Floyd Landis failed a drug test. Evans was named Australian Cyclist of the Year. In 2007, he claimed a GC second at the Criterium du Dauphine Libre, GC fourth at the Vuelta a Espana and the Tour de Romandie, and fifth in the UCI road world championship.

At the 2007 Tour de France, when Vinokourov and Rasmussen were thrown out for doping, Evans won the two individual time trial stages riding inferior bikes then lost the GC to Alberto Contador by 23 seconds. He finished second and was the first Australian to stand on the podium in Paris. Evans later told ABC Radio about his frustrations over the dopers in the Tour de France. He was named the 2007 UCI ProTour points winner, the first Australian road cyclist to win the award.

He was in solid form in 2008 winning the Coppi e Bartali stage race, was second in the La Flech Wallone classic and fifth in the Olympic Games road time trial in Beijing. At the 2008 Tour de France won by Carlos Sastre, he held the Yellow Jersey from stage 10 to 14 and crashed into another cyclist. Later his team told Evans to chase down Sastre on the Alpe d'Huez climb with no support, emptying his tank. He won the final time trial but fell 51 seconds short to claim another GC second place.

When Evans placed third in the GC at the Vuelta a Espana grand tour in 2009 he was the first Australian to stand on the podium. Evans went on to win Australia's first gold medal in the UCI road world championship at Mendrisio, Switzerland in September 2009 aged 32, winning his third Australian Cyclist of the Year Award.

He signed with the BMC Racing Team for 2010 and won the Flech Wallone road classic, was third in the GC at the Tirreno-Adriatico, fifth in the GC at the Giro d'Italia, fourth in the Liege-Bastogne-Liege classic and finished 26th at the Tour de France after riding with a hairline fracture in his left elbow. In 2011, Evans won the Tirreno-Adriatico tour and the Tour de Romandie.

Our first Tour de France champion

At the 2011 Tour de France, Evans finished second on stage 1, won stage 4, maintained his GC fifth position and was third in the GC on the second last mountain stage. On the last, short 109km mountain stage from Modane to the Alpe d'Huez, Evans had a mechanical with his bike.

But Evans was brought back to the leading bunch by George Hincapie and the BMC team. Evans joined the leading group containing Andy and Frank Schleck, Pierre Rolland and Contador and finished the stage in fourth place behind Rolland with a deficit to Andy Schleck of only 57 seconds going into the last stage.

He rode a strong time trial on the penultimate 42.5 km individual time trial stage at Grenoble to place second, seven seconds adrift of stage winner Tony Martin, beating Andy Schleck by two and a half minutes.

Evans now led Schleck by 1min, 34secs going into the final stage into Paris. Evans, now 34, barring an accident on the road into the Champs-Elysees would become the first Australian to win the Tour de France GC and wear the Yellow Jersey on the Champs-Elysees at Paris.

The Herald Sun (Melbourne) reported on July 25, 2011 that, "Cadel Evans becomes first Australian to win the Tour de France, joining the greats of Australian sport." Evans stood on the podium on the Champs-Elysees wrapped in Australia's national flag and had tears in his eyes, while Australian pop music star Tina Arena sang the national anthem in his honour. Evans was also the oldest rider since World War II to win the Tour de France.

In his book, Cadel Evans The Art of Cycling, Evans paid tribute to his Italian coach and mentor in Switzerland, Aldo Sassi, his vision and cycling philosophies and said that Sassi had inspired him to go on and claim the Yellow Jersey at the Tour.

In 2012, Evans won the Criterium International but was

a GC seventh at the Tour de France when Chris Froome won the race. He was third in the GC at the 2013 Giro d'Italia after being second before the last mountain stage. But he battled freezing conditions and bike equipment issues and said later he felt wiped out after the Giro.

Six weeks later at the 2013 Tour de France Evans finished 39th. He was not selected by BMC for the 2014 Tour de France. Evans started 2014 well with a GC second at the Tour Down Under and won the Giro del Trentino. He finished eighth in the GC at the Giro d'Italia, wearing the leader's jersey after stages 8-11. However, Evans was cut from the BMC team for 2015 and he announced his retirement from February 2015.

In early 2015 he was third in the GC at the Tour Down Under when 37 years old and at the inaugural Cadel Evans Great Ocean Road Race, placed fifth overall to end his brilliant career. His awards include the 2007 Australian Sports Awards Male Athlete of the Year, the Order of Australia Medal in 2013, and in December 2020 he was inducted into the Sport Australia Hall of Fame.

In 2015, Greg LeMond described Cadel Evans as one of the "biggest talents" cycling has ever seen and said he believes that Evans was "hard done by early in his career by a doped-up peloton".

ABC News reported that many believe that Evan's consistency is proof he raced clean during his brilliant career. Asked if his Tour win was a bright light after years of doping darkness, he said: "I hope so. I can only speak about my own credibility."

Michael Rogers

Michael Rogers (born 1979) grew up in Canberra and rode for the Canberra Cycling Club. He won the national junior individual time trial in 1996 and started a scholarship at the Australian Institute of Sport.

From 1996, Rogers won silver medals at the UCI junior road time trial championships and under 23 silver in the time trial and two silvers in the road championships. At the 1998 Commonwealth Games in Kuala Lumpur he won two gold medals on the track and silver in the road time trial and in 2009, won his first national road time trial championship. In 2000 he raced for Mapei-Quick-Step amateur cycling team and joined its pro team for 2001-02.

Teaming with Fabian Cancellara in 2001, he was second in the Grand Prix Eddy Merck and Duo Normand team time trials.

In 2002 Rogers claimed GC wins at the Tour Down Under and at Canada's Tour de Beauce, and silver in the 2002 Commonwealth Games road time trial. He was in superb form in 2003 winning the GC at three tours: the Deutschland Tour, Route du Sud and Tour of Belgium.

After he won the silver medal at the 2003 UCI road world championships time trial, Rogers was awarded gold when winner David Millar tested positive for drugs.

Rogers won his second gold medal in the time trial 'race of truth' at the 2004 UCI road world championships. He competed at every Olympic Games from 2000 to 2012 and won a bronze medal in the road time trial at the 2004 Athens Olympics.

In 2005 Rogers won his third gold medal in the individual time trial at the road world championships, the first cyclist to win three in a row. Riding for T-Mobile in 2006 he was ninth in the GC at the Tour de France and in 2007 was positioned to wear the Yellow Jersey on stage 8 but crashed out and broke his shoulder. In 2008 he placed fifth in the Olympic road race in Beijing.

The leader of Team Columbia-High Road in 2009 he posted a third in the Tour of California and GC sixth at the Giro d'Italia. In 2010 Rogers was in top form with GC wins at the Tour of California and Vuelta a Andalucia, and a GC third in the Tour de Romandie.

Rogers rode for Team Sky from 2011 but early on was hit by glandular fever. In 2012 he claimed the GC at the Tour of Bavaria and GC second at the Criterium du Dauphine. He rode in the Tour de France as a 'super domestique' for eventual winner Bradley Wiggins and at the London Olympics was sixth in the road time trial.

Rogers signed with Saxo-Tinkoff in 2013 and rode in the Tour de France to support Alberto Contador and finished sixteenth. After he won the Japan Cup one-day race and tested positive for clenbuterol he was suspended. He was cleared in April 2014 on the probability he ate contaminated meat competing in China.

In 2014 Rogers was third in the Route du Sud tour, won two stages at the Giro d'Italia, and won his first stage at the Tour de France on his 10th attempt. After 16 years at the top of road cycling Rogers announced his retirement in April 2016 due to a worsening congenital heart defect.

Publisher of Ride Media and Ride Cycling Review Rob Arnold said of Rogers in April 2016: "It was his tactical mind as much as his physical prowess that made him such a valuable ally for the likes of Bradley Wiggins, Chris Froome, Mark Cavendish, Alberto Contador and Peter Sagan. Rogers has helped all these riders win races."

Robbie McEwen

Robbie McEwen (born 1972) was a former Australian BMX champion from Brisbane who took up road racing in 1990 aged 18. He later joined the Australian Institute of Sport in Canberra under road cycling coach Heiko Salzwedel. In 1994, McEwen rode in the Czech Republic's Peace Race and won three stages.

In Australia he won three stages of the Herald Sun Tour in 1996 and at the 1996 Atlanta Olympic Games, finished 23rd. He posted wins in 1997, 1999 and 2005 in the Geelong Bay Classic Series and in the national road championship in 2002 and 2005.

From 1996 he rode for European cycling teams such as Rabobank, Lotto-Adecco and RadioShack and showed his incredible road sprinting and tactical ability by winning many stages of major tours and grand tours.

In the road race at the 2000 Olympic Games in Sydney he finished 19th. He won the sprint points classification at the Tour Down Under in 2002 and 2004 and claimed the GC at the Tour Down Under in 2009.

McEwen rode in the Tour de France 12 times beginning in 1997. He claimed his first stage win at the Tour de

France in 1999 on the final sprint up the cobblestones of the Champs-Elysees and went on to post 12 stage wins at the Tour and three sprinter's Green Jersey classifications.

He lived for many years in the Belgian town of Everbeek and between 2002 and 2011 won major road races and one-day classics, including the Dwars door Vlaanderen, a race record five times in the Paris-Brussels, the Vattenfall Cyclassics, and two GC wins at the Tour de Wallonie-Picardie.

When McEwen claimed the silver medal at the road world championships in 2002, he was only the second Australian to stand on a world road podium. He also won two stages at the Giro d'Italia and the Tour de France and his big breakthrough came at the 2002 Tour de France when he won his first Green Jersey in the sprint points classification, the first by an Australian.

At the Tour de France in 2004 McEwen held the Yellow Jersey on stage 3, won two stages and his second Tour de France sprint points Green Jersey, defeating Thor Hushovd and Erik Zabel. He won the Green Jersey despite fracturing two vertebrae during a mass crash on stage 6. He was eleventh in the road race at the Athens Olympics.

Riding in the grand tours in 2005 he won three stages at the Tour de France and three stages at the Giro d'Italia, where he held the leader's jersey after stages 2-3. McEwen was the Australian Cyclist of the Year in 2002 and 2005.

McEwen won three stages at the Giro d'Italia in 2006 and competing at the Tour de France in 2006, won another three stages and claimed his third sprint points Green

Jersey classification beating Erik Zabel and Thor Hushovd to become Australia's greatest sprinter in road cycling at the Tour de France.

McEwen won his Tour De France Green Jerseys usually without lead-out trains against the best sprinters in the world, including Erik Zabel, Tom Boonen, Thor Hushovd, Stuart O'Grady and Baden Cooke.

Peloton magazine (USA) said in 2020 that McEwen's big breakthrough came at the age of 27 in 1999 when he won the final Tour de France stage on the Champs-Élysées: "Robbie McEwen wasn't the most powerful sprinter, but what he may have given up in watts he more than made up in tactical positioning and acceleration."

He joined the new Australian team Orica-GreenEDGE for the 2012 season, later becoming a technical advisor to the team and rode in his last race, the Tour of California. McEwen was an inaugural inductee into the Cycling Australia Hall of Fame in 2015 and was inducted into the Sport Australia Hall of Fame in 2019.

In 2012 McEwen's autobiography titled One Way Road was published.

Simon Gerrans

Simon Gerrans (born 1980) grew up in Mansfield, Victoria and was introduced to cycling by his neighbor Phil Anderson. Gerrans won a scholarship to the AIS and from 2000 won the under-23 national road championship and two elite road championships. In Australia, Gerrans won major races: the GC at the Tour of Tasmania in 2002, the

Melbourne to Warrnambool road classic in 2003, and two GCs at the Herald Sun Tour in 2005-06. Heading to Europe, he rode for amateur teams from 2003. From 2005 he rode as a professional for AG2R, Credit Agricole, Cervello, Team Sky, GreenEDGE, and BMC Racing.

Gerrans had great sprinting ability and won a lot of close finishes against the best cyclists in the world. Cyclingnews said that Gerrans, "was known as one of the most tactically astute riders in the peleton."

Riding from 2002-2018 in major road races and tours, Gerrans claimed 33 career race wins and was placed 13 times, including winning the silver medal at the UCI road world championships at Ponferrada, Spain in 2014. Among his best results were his first GC victory at the Tour Down Under in 2006, his second in 2012 for Orica-GreenEDGE in its first WorldTour event, his third in 2014 and fourth in 2016; and the Tour of Denmark GC in 2011. At the Tour de France he won stage 15 in 2008 and stage 3 in 2013 beating Peter Sagan on the line when he also held the Yellow Jersey after stages 4-5 in 2013 and was in winning team time trial stages with Orica GreenEDGE.

He also won a stage of the Giro d'Italia in 2009 and was in the winning team time trial in 2015. At the Vuelta a Espana, Gerrans won stage 10 in 2009 to become the first Australian to win a stage in each of the three grand tours. Among his greatest achievements is his record of success riding in Europe's spring classic one-day races, semi-classics and the older five 'monument' classic races.

Gerrans is the only Australian cyclist to have won two

monument classics: the Milan-San Remo in Italy in 2012 in a three-man sprint finish with Fabian Cancellara and Vincenzo Nibali; and Belgium's Liege-Bastogne-Liege in 2014 in a sprint finish with Valverde, Kwiatkowski, and Caruso. He placed sixth in 2009.

In 2009 he placed eighth in the La Fleche Wallone, won the GP Ouest France-Plouay and placed second in 2011, and placed three times in the Netherlands' Amstel Gold Race in 2011 and 2013-14. In Canada, he won the Grand Prix Cycliste de Quebec in 2012 and in 2014, and the Grand Prix Cycliste de Montreal in 2014.

In late 2018 when 38, Gerrans announced his retirement from competition and said he enjoyed working in a team environment and the tactics of cycling: "The times I was able to outsmart an opponent in a high-pressure situation and beat someone stronger was satisfying."

Stuart O'Grady

Stuart O'Grady (born 1973) came from a cycling family in South Australia. He represented Australia in track cycling at every Olympic Games between 1992-2012 (see track cycling).

In road cycling, O'Grady posted GC wins at the Herald Sun Tour in 2008, at the Tour Down Under in 1999 and 2001 and won the elite national road championship in 2003. Earlier in 1995 he joined the GAN professional team in Europe and later Credit Agricole, CSC/Saxo Bank, Leopard Trek and Orica-GreenEDGE. O'Grady's race wins included the UK Prudential Tour in 1998 and in 1999

France's Classic Haribo, and a GC second at the Tour of Sweden in 2001. In 2002 at the Manchester Commonwealth Games, O'Grady won gold in the road race and was also second in the GP Ouest-France Plouay classic. In 2003 he claimed third places in the Paris-Tours one-day race, the Tour of Flanders classic and Deutschland Tour and became known for his sprinting ability and one-day classic performances.

Other top results include wins at Germany's HEW Cyclassics and GP deVilliers-Cotteretts, GC third at the Tour Down Under, second and third in Portugal's Volta Algarve, fourth and fifth places in the Milan-San Remo classic, third in the Dwars door Vlaanderen, second and third at the Tour of Denmark; fourth and sixth in the road world championships in 2004 and 2006; second at the 2009 Tour Down Under and the 2011 GP d'Iserbergues.

O'Grady claimed one of his greatest victories by winning the gruelling 'Hell of the North' Paris-Roubaix cobblestone classic in 2007, also claiming fifth in 2008.

The Australian Olympic Committee said of O'Grady's 2012 Olympic Games road race at London when the 39-year-old was sixth: "He produced a brave and incredible ride as captain of the men's team spending nearly six hours in the saddle, setting the pace for the world's best riders for almost the entire 250km, missing gold by just eight seconds and bronze by a couple of metres."

At the Tour de France in 2003, he won the Centenaire Classification for the best placed rider over six stages for the centenary of the 1903 tour. O'Grady raced at the Tour de France 17 times for 15 completed tours to almost equal the record. He was a four-time runner up in the competition for the Tour de France's sprint points Green Jersey in 1998-99, 2001 and 2005. O'Grady won stages of the Tour de France in 1998 and 2004, and in 2001 held the leader's Yellow Jersey for six days.

He rode for Orica-GreeEDGE in 2012-13 and retired after his 17th Tour de France. O'Grady's awards include the Order of Australia Medal. In 2020, he was appointed as the Race Director of the Tour Down Under - South Australia beginning with the 2021 Tour.

Allan Davis

Allan 'Alby' Davis (born 1980) came from a cycling family in Bundaberg. He started cycling at age 10 and represented Australia as a junior. He arrived in Europe in 1997 when 17 and lived and raced mainly in Italy in the junior and under 23 ranks. After five years in 2002 he realised his ambition and turned professional, riding for Italian team Mapei-Quick-Step.

Known for his road sprinting ability, Davis later rode for teams such as ONCE-Eroski, Quick-Step, Astana (with brother Scott Davis) and Green-EDGE.

In 1999 he won the Tour di Basilicata in Italy and in 2000, was seventh in the UCI under 23 road championships then sixth in 2001 and placed in road races in Italy and Slovenia. He was second in the 2003 elite national road championship and won the Trofero Manacor (Mallorca) road race in Spain.

In 2004 Davis posted top results winning the Giro del Piemonte and two road races in Mallorca and was fifth in the UCI world road championship. In 2005 he claimed a GC second at the Tour Down Under and third in the Paris-Tours classic. He rode in the Tour de France in 2005-06 placing fifth in the sprint points classification in 2005.

At the Tour Down Under in 2006 he won two stages and the sprint classification. He later won the bronze medal in the Commonwealth Games road race at Melbourne.

Davis placed second in the Milan-San Remo classic in 2007 and top results in 2008 include second places in the GC at the Tour Down Under, the Geelong Bay Classic Series, and GC second in France's Tour of Limousin. In 2009 he was in brilliant form, winning the GC at the Tour Down Under and in one-day races, was second in the Paris-Brussels semi-classic and the GP de Wallonie, and placed fourth in the Milan-San Remo classic.

In 2010 Davis's stellar form continued winning gold in the Commonwealth Games road race at Delhi, the bronze medal at the UCI road world championships and a GC third in the Tour de Picardie. Riding for the Orica GreenEDGE team in 2012, he won the Geelong Bay Classic Series and placed sixth at the UCI road world championships. His contract with GreenEDGE was not renewed for 2013 and he retired in February 2014.

Davis told Bikeexchange.com that the team aspect of road cycling is getting proper attention: "The riders are being applauded as much for emptying their tanks to help a teammate as if they were to win the race itself." Davis runs Allan Davis Cycling from San Sebastian, organising cycling and cultural tours including at the Tour de France.

Michael Matthews

Michael Matthews (born 1990) grew up in Canberra and started cycling as a teenager with the local Vikings Cycling Club and was an AIS scholarship holder. In 2013 he placed second in elite national road championship.

He won the Oceania road race and time trial championships in 2009. At the UCI under 23 road world championship at Geelong in September 2010 Matthews won in a sprint finish with John Degenkolb and Taylor Phinney, the fifth Australian to win a road world title. From 2010 he rode for professional teams Team Jayco-Skins, Rabobank, Orica-GreenEDGE and Team Sunweb.

Matthews posted many wins and places internationally between 2008-2017 including second at the under 23 Tour of Flanders in 2010, a GC win at Germany's Tour of Cologne classic and third in the Eschborn-Frankfurt race in 2011, and won Spain's Classica de Almeria road race in 2012. Matthews was second in the Vuetla a La Roja tour in 2013 and won the tour in 2014.

In 2015 he was third in the Milan-San Remo and Amstel Gold road classics and second in Canada's GP Cycliste de Quebec classic.

Matthews capped his year by winning the silver medal in the UCI road world championship at Richmond, USA.

In 2016 Matthews won another Vuelta a La Roja and was fifth in the Amstel Gold classic and at the 2016 UCI road world championships finished fourth and won bronze in the road worlds team time trial. Riding for Team Sunweb in 2017 he placed third in the GP Cycliste de Quebec and fourth in the Liege-Bastogne-Liege classic.

Matthews results at the UCI road world championship continued, winning bronze in 2017 at Bergen and gold in the winning team time trial. Competing in his first Vuelta a Espana grand tour in 2013 he won stages 5 and 21 and held the leader's pink jersey after stages 6 and 7. In 2014 he won stage 3 and held the leader's jersey after stage 4. Matthews, known as a perfectionist and for his sprinting prowess, was outsprinting the world's best road sprinters.

At his first Giro d'Italia in 2014 he won a hilltop finish on stage 6 and the team time trial with Orica-Green EDGE, holding the leader's jersey after stages 2-7 before crashing out. Competing at his first Tour de France in 2016 Matthews won stage 10 and was third in the Green Jersey sprint classification. At the UCI road world championships in 2016 he was fourth in the road race and won bronze in the team time trial and in 2017, won bronze in the road race and gold in the team time trial.

Matthews rode at his second Tour de France in 2017 and won stages 14 and 16. Following a team plan he won his first sprint Green Jersey classification from Greipel and Boasson Hagen, after Sagan was disqualified and Kittel crashed. Phil Anderson told the Sydney Morning Herald on July 21, 2017: "It's a huge achievement and something which he's been earmarked to do for a while now. He's worked really hard and deserves everything he's got."

In 2017 Matthews won the 'Oppy' Award for Cyclist of the Year. Riding for Team Sunweb from 2018 he performed well in the road classics, winning the GP Cycliste de Quebec and GP Cycliste de Montreal, was second in the Eschborn-Frankfurt and fifth in La Fleche Wallonne. Matthews won the GP Cycliste de Quebec and was sixth in the Tour of Flanders in 2019. At the Tour de France he was fifth in the Green Jersey sprint points after a mechanical on the final stage on the Champs-Elysees.

In August 2020 at the Milan-San Remo road classic he was well positioned for first or second but was pushed into a wall. He recovered to take third place in the bunch sprint. In late August, he won the one-day Bretagne Classic-Ouest-France and at the 2020 Tour de France, Mitchelton-Scott announced that Matthews would join the team for 2021-22. In September he placed seventh with a strong ride at the UCI road world championships.

Richie Porte

Richard 'Richie' Porte (born 1985) came from Launceston, Tasmania and competed in the triathlon. He took up road cycling when 21 riding for amateur teams including Team UniSA and in 2007-08 won the Tour of Bright, the Tour of Perth, and Tour of Tasmania. From 2007 he rode as an amateur in Europe and won the GP Citta di Felino. Porte, a great climber helped by his power to weight ratio and a top time triallist, in 2010 signed as a professional with Team Saxo-Bank.

Riding in his first grand tour at the Giro d'Italia in 2010,

Porte was seventh in the GC and held the leader's pink jersey for three days after stages 11-13. Porte's best results in 2011 were third places in the GC in the Paris-Nice tour, the Tour de Romandie and the time trial at the UCI road world championships.

He joined Team Sky in 2012 and won the GC at the Volta ao Algarve and was a key domestique when Bradley Wiggins won the 2012 Tour de France. Porte had a strong season in 2013 posting a win at the Paris-Tours race and second places at the Criterium International, Tour of the Basque Country and Criterium du Dauphine. Porte rode in the Tour de France as a domestique to eventual winner Chris Froome and helped the Briton through the difficult stage 18 up the Alpe d'Huez.

In 2014 he was second in the Vuelta a Andalucia but missed the Giro d'Italia due to illness. At the Tour de France Porte took leadership of Team Sky in the first week after Froome retired injured. Porte was hit by illness in the mountains and finished twenty-third and was later diagnosed with pneumonia.

Porte bounced back in 2015 with a GC second at the Tour Down Under and won the national time trial championship. In the spring, he won the GC at three tours: Paris-Nice, the Volta a Catalunya, and the Giro del Trentino, the first cyclist to win all three in one season. He led Team Sky at the Giro d'Italia but abandoned the race due to crashes and a leg injury.

At the Tour de France he rode as a super domestique to Chris Froome and played a key role helping Froome to win his second Tour. Porte announced he would join the BMC Racing team for 2016 and posted top GC results, coming second in the Tour Down Under, third in Paris-Nice and fourth at the Criterium du Dauphine. He placed fifth in the GC at the Tour de France, his best result.

In 2017 Porte claimed his first Tour Down Under GC win, a GC win at the Tour de Romandie and GC second at the Criterium du Dauphine. He lined up at the 2017 Tour de France as BMC's lead rider for the Yellow Jersey but crashed out on stage 9 on a wet downhill descent suffering a fractured collarbone and hip.

He was second in the Tour Down Under in 2018 and an impressive GC winner at the Tour de Swisse and third in the Tour de Romandie. Now 34, Porte said his big goal was to be on the podium at the Tour de France. But after his BMC Racing team won the team time trial on stage 3 at the Tour de France, Porte crashed on stage 9 with a broken collarbone.

Riding for Trek-Segafredo in 2019, he was a GC second at the Tour Down Under and took his sixth 'King of Willunga Hill' title. But Porte had a disappointing season and finished eleventh at the Tour de France. Porte, who resides in Monaco, started 2020 well taking his second GC win at the Tour Down Under and a GC third in the Tour des Alpes-Maritimes in France.

At the delayed 2020 Tour de France, 35-year-old Porte climbed strongly in the mountain stages during the race and rode a great individual time trial on the second last stage to jump from fourth into third in the GC at 3:30

minutes behind Slovenians Tadej Pogacar and Primoz Roglic. Porte rode into Paris to claim a GC third place, becoming Australia's second cyclist to stand on the Tour de France podium. Porte said on Trek-Segafredo's website: "It's a great feeling, a dream come true, to be honest to stand on the podium in Paris is just unbelievable. It was so nice to be up there with two champions. It's a moment I will savour for the rest of my life."

He told SBS Cycling Central on September 21, 2020: "This stage is not a procession as they say. The pave here is not the nicest to ride on. Just such a great moment and I got to savour that today." Porte signed with Team Ineos Grenadiers for the 2021 season.

Matt Goss

Matthew (Matt) Goss (born 1986) is also from Launceston and was a top junior track cyclist, winning the UCI junior track world championships in the team pursuit and madison in 2004. At the elite track world championships, he won gold in 2006 in the team pursuit. Goss started his road career with the South Australia AIS team in 2006 and in Italy, won the GP della Liberazione and placed second in two one-day races in Italy. He also won a silver medal in the team pursuit at the 2006 Commonwealth Games in Melbourne.

Known for his road sprinting prowess, he rode for Team CSC in 2007-08, winning stages at the Tour of Britain, its sprint points classification in 2008 and placed third in the Kuurne-Brussels-Kuurne semi-classic.

Goss was in top form in 2009 winning the Paris-Brussels classic and claimed third place in the Gent-Wevelgem classic and a stage at the Tour de Wallonie. In 2010-11 he rode for HTC-Colombia and in 2010 he won the GP Ouest France-Plouay classic, the Philadelphia International Championship, and won stage 9 at the Giro d'Italia, but retired from the tour due to illness.

In 2011 he won the Jayco Bay Classic Series, was second in the national road championship, and at the Tour Down Under claimed a GC second and the points classification. Goss posted the biggest win of his career in the Milan-San Remo, beating Fabian Cancellara in a sprint finish, becoming the first Australian to win the Italian one-day classic.

At the 2011 UCI road world championships in Copenhagen, Goss won silver in the road race, losing by less than a wheel in a sprint finish with British great Mark Cavendish, with Greipel third and Cancellara fourth. Goss said in 1986: "Still hate that I lost the worlds by this much in 2011 but, I was beaten by a class act and the best sprinter of our time."

Goss joined GreenEDGE cycling for 2012-14 and at the 2012 Giro d'Italia, won stage 3. He competed in the Tour de France from 2011 to 2013 and in 2012, finished third in the Green Jersey sprint points classification after losing 30 points for dangerous riding in a sprint with Peter Sagan. Goss rode for Team MTN-Qhubeka in 2015 and he switched to ONE Pro Cycling in 2016. He announced his retirement from competition from the end of 2016.

Rohan Dennis

Rohan Dennis (born 1990) came from Adelaide. He was a top junior track cyclist winning silver at the 2012 Olympic Games (see track cycling). Dennis showed his talent in the individual time trial time winning the under 23 national road championship time trial in 2010 and 2012, the elite road time trial in 2016-18, and the elite road championship in 2012. From 2009 Dennis rode for amateur road teams Rabobank and Team Jayco-AIS.

In 2012 he won the under 23 Thuringen tour in Germany and France's Chronos Champenois time trial. At the UCI under 23 road world championships he won silver in the individual time trial. Dennis turned professional in 2013, winning the GC at the Tour of Alberta in Canada and rode for professional teams including Garmin-Sharp, BMC Racing, and Bahrain-Merida.

Dennis demonstrated his ability in the 'race of truth' against the clock at the Glasgow Commonwealth Games in 2014 winning silver in the individual road time trial then gold in the team time trial at the UCI road world championships. He posted second places in the GC at the Tour of California and Circuit de la Sarthe tour in France.

In 2015 Dennis claimed GC wins at the Tour Down Under and the Tour of Colorado. At the Tour de France in July 2015 he won the two individual time trial stages, holding the Yellow Jersey after the first stage time trial, when he broke the race record with an average speed of 55.446km/hr. At the 2015 UCI road world championships in the USA, Dennis won gold in Australia's winning team time trial and placed sixth in the individual time trial.

In 2016 he posted second places in the GC at the Tour of California and at the Tour of Britain and was fifth in the individual time trial at the Rio Olympic Games. In 2017, Dennis won the GC at the Tour La Provence and was second at the Tirreno-Adriatico tour.

At the Giro d'Italia in 2018, Dennis won the stage 16 individual time trial and held the leader's jersey after stages 2-5, only the third Australian to wear the leader's jersey at all three grand tours. He later won the two individual time trial stages at the Vuelta a Espana.

Heading to Innsbruck, Austria, he won the 2018 UCI road world championship individual time trial, beating defending champion Tom Dumoulin by one minute and 21 seconds, the second Australian to wear the Rainbow Jersey. "I've been chasing this since I was a junior. I've never won it in any age group so to win my first one in the seniors is really special," Dennis said. He won Cycling Australia's 'Oppy' medal, which he also won in 2015.

Riding for Bahrain-Merida in 2019, Dennis was second at the Tour de Swisse but abandoned the Tour de France on stage 12 citing team equipment issues. He defended his UCI world time trial title at Yorkshire in September 2019, winning the 54km race by 68 seconds ahead of Belgian teenager Remco Evenpoel. Dennis, who resides in Andorra, Spain, signed with Team Ineos for the 2020 season and led the team at the Tour Down Under. He finished fifth (at 39.76secs) in September at the UCI world individual time trial championships in Italy.

Matthew Hayman

Matthew Hayman (born 1978) came from the Goulburn area and rode for the Canberra Cycling Club and in 1996 won the UCI junior time trial at the road world championships. Moving to Europe in 1997 he rode as an amateur. In 1999 he posted a GC win at Belgium's Triptyque des Monts et Chateux, was second in the Olympia's Tour and third in the Omloop der Kempen.

He turned professional in 2000 and rode for Rabobank. In 2001 he claimed the GC at the Challenge Vuelta Mallorca series and the GC at the Sachsen Tour in 2005. At the Melbourne Commonwealth Games in 2006 Hayman won the gold medal in the road race. In the road classics he was fourth at Dwars door Vlaanderen in 2007, fifth in 2010 and fourth at the Gent-Wevelgem in 2009.

Hayman rode for Team Sky in his 'super domestique' role from 2010. He won the Paris-Bourges road race in 2011 and continued his top form in the one-day classics with third in the Omloop Het Nieuwsblad, tenth at the Paris-Roubaix cobblestone classic, eighth in Paris-Roubaix in 2012 and third in the 2013 Dwars door Vlaanderen. He rode for GreenEDGE from 2014 then Mitchelton-Scott from 2018 as the road captain.

In 2016 at his 17th Paris-Roubaix 'Hell of the North', Hayman was in the top five riders in the last five kilometres and outsprinted Tom Boonen and Ian Stannard on the Roubaix velodrome to win the classic and said: "It was the single proudest moment in my sporting career, a culmination of all the trying, learning, and never quitting."

At the grand tours, Hayman made four appearances at the Giro d'Italia from 2002, four at the Tour de France from 2014, and three at the Vuelta a Espana from 2003. He retired after the Tour Down Under in 2019 and took up a part-time role with Mitchelton-Scott.

Brad McGee

Brad McGee came from Sydney (born 1976) and was a champion junior track cyclist in the team pursuit and individual pursuit winning a gold medal on the track at the Athens Olympic Games in 2004 (see track cycling).

Turning to road racing from 1999, McGee rode for French professional team FDJ and later CSC. He won the Route du Sud (Occitane) tour in 2004, was second in the Tour of the Netherlands in 2003 and won the GP de Villiers-Cotterets in 2005.

McGee's road time trial prowess put him in the record books. The Cycling Australia Hall of Fame said McGee, "became the first Australian to wear the leader's jersey in all three grand tours of the Tour de France, Giro d'Italia and the Vuelta a Espana."

At the Tour de France McGee competed in five tours, won stages in 2002 and 2003 and held the Yellow Jersey for three days in 2003. He rode in four Giro d'Italias and was eighth in the GC in 2004 when he won the prologue stage and held the leader's jersey for two stages. At the Vuelta a Espana in 2005, McGee held the leader's jersey for four days after stages 1-4.

McGee retired and became a director of sport in the

WorldTour, a coach with the NSW Institute of Sport and more recently the road director with Cycling Australia.

Heinrich Haussler

Heinrich Haussler grew up in Inverell, NSW (born 1984) and had dual German-Australian citizenship. Haussler left Australia aged 14 and competed in junior road races in Germany. In 2002 he won the junior individual time trial at Germany's road championships. Turning professional in 2005 he rode for teams such as Gerolsteiner, Cervello, Garmin-Sharp, and current team Bahrain-Merida.

Haussler was third in the Saschen Tour in 2005. He won the GP Triberg-Schwarzwald and was second at the Tour of Flanders classic and the Tour of Qatar in 2009. A good sprinter, he became known for his performances in the European 'monument' and classic one-day races.

His best results in the classics were second place in Milan-San Remo in 2009 and seventh in 2016; fourth in the Dwars door Vlaanderen in 2009 and tenth in 2019; eighth in the Omloop Het Nieuwsblad in 2009, second in 2010 and fourth in 2012; third in the GP Ouest-France Plouay in 2012; fourth in the Gent-Wevelgem in 2013; sixth in the Paris-Roubaix cobblestone classic in 2009 and sixth in 2016. Haussler was also second in the GC at the Tour of Qatar in 2011 and won the elite national road championship in 2015.

Haussler competed in the Tour de France four times from 2007 and won stage 13 in 2009. He rode in the Vuelta a Espana five times from 2005 winning stage 18 in 2005 and rode in the Giro d'Italia in 2015-16. Haussler was the classics road captain for his team Bahrain-Merida in 2019 and in 2020 was fifth in the GC at the Saudi Tour.

Scott G. Sunderland

Scott G. Sunderland (born 1966) came from Inverell NSW and was a junior road and track cycling champion and aged 19, won the 1986 Australian amateur road championship. He rode for professional teams in Europe including TVM, Lotto, GAN, and Alessio-Bianchi.

In 1987-88 he won the Vuelta a Bidasoa twice, the Giro del Mendrisio and the GP des Marroniers. From 1991 he won six European one-day races including Belgium's GP Nokere semi-classic in 1998.

In 1992 Sunderland won Australia's Mazda Alpine Tour, was fifth in the Milan-San Remo road classic and won the 'Oppy' medal as Australian Cyclist of the Year.

He was hit by his team car in May 1998 during the Amstel Gold race and injuries put him out of action until July 1999. He was fourth in the GC at Australia's tough Commonwealth Bank Classic stage race in 1999.

In 2000 Sunderland won the Noosa Criterium, was second in the national road championship and seventh in the UCI road world championships and in 2001 won the GP Pino Cerami and the GP de Fourmies classic.

He rode in the Tour de France in 1996 and 2004, the Vuelta a Espana in 1993, and the Giro d'Italia in 1990 and in 2003 when he placed 23rd.

Sunderland was a road director for cycling teams and he

was appointed general race director for the Flanders Classics in Belgium in 2019.

Simon Clarke

Simon Clarke is from Melbourne (born 1986) and was a top junior track cyclist, winning the UCI junior team pursuit at the world championships in 2004. He rode for South Australia-AIS from 2006 and in 2007 was a GC third at the Tour Down Under, third in the GP Liberazione and won the under 23 national road championship. In 2008 Clarke won the Trofero Citti San Vendemiano race.

A good climber and sprinter, from 2009 Clarke rode for professional teams including Astana, Orica GreenEDGE, Cannondale and more recently for EF Education First.

Clarke's best performances include in 2012, winning a stage at the Vuelta Espana and the mountains classification jersey and two GC seconds places at the Tour of Norway and the Rogaland GP in Norway. He came seventh in the UCI road world championship in 2013 and was in the team time trial win at the Tour de France. In 2014 Clarke won the GC at the Herald Sun Tour, in 2015 was second in the Cadel Evans Great Ocean Road Race and held the leader's jersey after stage 4 at the Giro d'Italia. In 2016 he won the GP Industria & Artigianato road race.

Up to 2019 he rode in five Tour de France tours, two Giro d'Italias, and six Vuelta a Espanas, winning stage 5 at the Vuelta a Espana in 2018. Clarke was second in the GC at the Tour de la Provence in 2019. In the one-day road classics he claimed second in the Amstel Gold, eighth in the Strade Bianchi and ninth in the Milan-San Remo. In March 2020 he raced in two new Ardenne 'classics' one weekend. Clarke told Cyclingtips that at the Royal Bernard Drome Classic he "put all his eggs in one basket" when he won the race from Warren Barguil and Vincenzo Nibali. In November he signed with a new team Qhubeka-Assos.

Baden Cooke

Baden Cooke came from Benalla, Victoria (born 1978). He won the 1999 national junior track title in the points race and the elite madison in 2000 and was an AIS scholarship holder. Riding in Europe he won the Prix de Bles d'Or in 2000 and joined professional team Mercury.

One of Australia's best road sprinters, Cooke won the sprint classification at the Tour de l'Avenir in 2001. Signing for FDJ in 2002 he claimed GC wins at the Herald Sun Tour and Paris-Correze tour, won the Dwars door Vlaanderen classic and Brittany's Tro-Bro Leon race.

Other top results in 2002-2003 were a bronze medal in the 2002 Commonwealth Games road race at Manchester, ninth in the UCI road world championships, and third in the GP Ouest France-Plouay classic; in 2003 wins at the GP de Fourmies classic, the Kampioenschap van Vlaanderen and the La Voix du Nord races, and second at the Dwars door Vlaanderen. At the 2003 Tour de France he won stage 2 and claimed the Green Jersey in the sprint classification in a close contest with Robbie McEwen.

Major results in 2004 were wins in the Bay Classic Series and the GP d'Ouverture La Marseillaise, and a GC third at the Tour Down Under. In 2005 he was fifth in the Dwars door Vlaanderen and sixth in the Gent-Wevelgem classics. In 2006 he won the GP d'Ouverture La Marseillaise and the Halle-Ingooigem, won the Kampioenschap van Vlaanderen in 2007, was fourth in Paris-Brussels and eighth in Gent Wevelgem classics. Riding for Saxo Bank from in 2011 he claimed second in the Paris-Bourges and fifth in the Dwars door Vlaanderen.

Cooke rode in the three grand tours from 2002 including six Tour de France tours and joined Green-EDGE cycling for 2012-13. After 14 years as a pro cyclist he retired in 2013 and became a cyclist's agent based in Monaco.

Mark Renshaw

Mark Renshaw (born 1982) came from Bathurst NSW and was a top junior track cyclist and won nine TrackNats track titles from 2001 in the kilo time trial, points, scratch, team pursuit and madison. Riding in the team pursuit in 2002 and 2004 he won gold at the UCI track world championships and gold at the 2002 Commonwealth Games. He won the under 23 road time trial national title in 2000. Renshaw rode in France as an amateur from 2002 and for the FDJ professional team in 2004.

He won the Be Active criterium series and placed second in the Trofero Citta di Brescia road race in 2003. From 2006-08 he joined Credit Agricole where he became a lead-out rider for Thor Hushovd and showed his sprinting ability. Renshaw won Brittany's Tro-Bro Leon race in 2006, the Bay Classic Series in 2007 and claimed second places in the GP de Denain and Tour de Vendee. In 2008 he was second in the Vattenfall Cyclassics and won the Bay Classic Series. In 2011 he won the GC at the Tour of Qatar and was controversially omitted from the Australian men's team for the road world championships.

Riding for Rabobank he was second in the Paris-Brussels classic and won Spain's Clasica de Almeria race in 2013. Renshaw placed fifth in the road race at the 2014 Commonwealth Games in Glasgow, third in the Clasica de Almeria in 2015 and second in the 2016 London-Surrey Classic riding for Team Dimension Data.

Renshaw gained many accolades as cycling's best lead-out man supporting British sprinter Mark Cavendish after joining Team Columbia-High Road in 2009. He helped Cavendish to a successful Tour de France in 2009 placing second to Cavendish on the Champs-Elysees' final stage. At the Tour de France, Renshaw supported the Brit in 2011 when he won seven stages and the Green Jersey, in 2014 to five top five finishes and three stage wins in 2016.

Renshaw rode in 10 Tour de France, five Giro d'Italia and two Vuelta a Espana tours. He retired at the end of the 2019 season. Renshaw told Ride Media on April 29, 2020 that a personal highlight was in 2011 winning the Tour of Qatar GC: "It was super-hard, it was one of the toughest races of the year to win. For team success working with Cavendish with a special 2009 Tour de France victory on the Champs-Elysees when we were first and second for HTC." He opened Renshaw's Pedal Project bike shop in Bathurst in May 2020.

Caleb Ewan

Caleb Ewan comes from Sydney (born 1994) and started cycling at age 10. He was a junior national road champion in 2010 and won the omnium at the 2012 UCI junior track world championships.

Competing in Europe in 2012, Ewan won the silver medal in the UCI junior road world championships in The Netherlands. He won the Bay Classic Series in 2013 and in Europe, won the GP Premio Palio Recioto and the La Cote Picardie road races.

Ewan rode for Jayco-AIS World Tour Academy Team in 2014. He won the under 23 national road championship, was second in the Trofero Citta San Vendenmiano and won the silver medal at the under 23 UCI road world championship in Spain. He signed with GreenEDGE cycling as a professional in 2014.

Ewan showed his versatility and sprinting ability in 2015 winning the Bay Classic Series, the GC at the Tour of Korea and Vuelta la Roja, and the sprint classification at the Tour of Langkawi. At his first grand tour, he won stage 5 at the Vuelta a Espana. Ewan won the national criterium championships in 2016, the Bay Classic Series and the EuroEyes Cyclassics.

In 2017 his wins included the national criterium championship, the sprint classification and four stages at the Tour Down Under, the sprint classification and three stages at the Tour de Yorkshire, while he claimed tenth in the Milan-San Remo classic. At the Giro d'Italia, Ewan won stage 7 in a sprint finish. He won his third national criterium championship in 2018, Spain's Clasica de Almeria and was second in the Milan-San Remo classic. The 23-year-old 'pocket rocket' was one of the world's fastest road sprinters but was not selected by Mitchelton-Scott for the Tour de France.

Joining Lotto-Soudal in 2019 as sprint marquee to replace Andre Greipel, he was second at the Cadel Evans Great Ocean Road Race and the Bay Classic, won the Brussels Cycling Classic and two stages at the Giro d'Italia. Ewan, who said he has more climbing ability to win uphill sprints, made his Tour de France debut in 2019.

Ewan won stage 11 at Toulouse beating Dylan Groenewegen in a tough sprint to the line, won stage 16 at Nimes and on the final stage up the Champs-Elysees, conquered the cobblestones to win from Groenewegen and Bonifazio and place second in the Tour de France sprint points classification. Ewan fought for position behind Lotto-Soudal's Roger Kluge and burst through the right-hand side for the win, SBS Cycling Central said.

In December 2019 Ewan was awarded the 'Oppy' Medal for the Cyclist of the Year. In early 2020 he was seventh in the Cadel Evans Great Ocean Road Race and won the points classification at the UAE Tour.

At the 2020 Tour de France Ewan won two stages with brilliant last-minute sprints on stage 3 and on stage 11, when the Lotto Soudal team was hit by crashes and down to just five riders. Ewan finished a close seventh on the final Champs-Elysees stage and was sixth in the sprint points classification.

Adam Hansen

Adam Hansen is from Queensland (born 1981). He rode for the Cairns Cycling Club and trained as an engineer. He won the national time trial championships in 2008, was second in the road championships in 2008 and also won the North Queensland eight-stage MTB classic the Crocodile Trophy in 2004-05.

Hansen competed in Europe from 2004 winning seven road races up to 2006 including Slovakia's Grand Prix Bradlo and in 2010 won the GC at the Netherlands' Ster Elecktrotoer tour. In 2008 he was second in Netherland's Hel van het Mergelland after turning professional in 2007, riding for T Mobile and Team Columbia-HTC.

Riding for Lotto-Belisol/Lotto Soudal teams from 2012 Hansen became the thirty-second cyclist to complete all three grand tours and the second Australian after Neil Stephens. He told velonation.com in September 2012 that, "I enjoy my career as a domestique. My victory is to have finished the Giro, the Tour and the Vuelta this year".

Hansen was Australia's iron man of Europe's gruelling grand tours. From 2007 to 2019 he rode in nine Tour de France, 11 Giro d'Italia, and nine Vuelta a Espana tours. He rode in 20 consecutive grand tours from the Vuelta a Espana in 2011 to the Giro d'Italia in 2018, beating the previous record of 12 consecutive tours held by Spain's Bernardo Ruiz and holds the record for the most starts by an Australian in the Giro d'Italia and the Vuelta a Espana.

At the Giro d'Italia grand tour in 2013, he won stage 7 in a solo breakaway to win by one minute at Pescara in the pouring rain. On stage 19 at the Vuelta a Espana in 2014 on a medium mountain stage, Hansen broke away from the peloton at four kilometres to go and held off a chase group for a clear win at Cangas de Morrazo.

Hansen, who lives in the Czech Republic, was 39 in 2019. He was in the final year of his contract with Lotto-Soudal in 2020 and said in October that he would switch to ironman events in 2021.

Luke Durbridge

Luke Durbridge (born 1991) came from Greenmount in Western Australia and took up triathlons at age 14. At the UCI junior track world championships, Durbridge won the team pursuit in 2008 and the madison in 2009 when he also won the junior road time trial. In 2011 he won gold in the team pursuit at the world track championships.

He won the national road time trial championship four times (2012-13, 2019-20) and the road race title in 2013.

Known as 'Turbo Durbo' for his powerful road time trial rides, he rode for GreenEDGE and Mitchelton-Scott teams from 2012. In 2010 he won Tasmania's Mersey Valley Tour, the Memorial Davide Fardelli race, and was third in France's Chrono Champenois time trial.

Durbridge also won the bronze medal in the road individual time trial at the Commonwealth Games in Delhi.

Other top results for Durbridge include winning the Duo Normand team time trial with Svein Tuft three times in 2012-13, 2016 and in 2012, GC wins in the Tour du Poitou Charentes and the Circuit Cycliste Sarthe, and in 2014, winning the Oceania road championships and a GC second at the VDK-Driedaagse De Panne-Koksijde; and in 2017, fourth in the Dwars door Vlaanderen, fourth in the BinckBank and sixth in the Strade Bianchi road classics.

He won silver in 2013-2014 and bronze in 2012 at the UCI world team time trial championships and competed in four Giro d'Italia and seven Tour de France grand tours for GreenEDGE and Mitchelton-Scott up to 2020, winning two stages at the Giro d'Italia. In 2019 the Sydney Morning Herald said that Durbridge "upset world champion Rohan Dennis to win a third Australian time trial championship".

In 2020 at the world individual time trial championships in Italy he put in a strong performance to finish 15th at 1min, 36.29secs. In January 2021 he won the GC at the Santos Festival of Cycling stage race.

Patrick Jonker

Patrick Jonker was born in Amsterdam in 1969 and went to high school in Adelaide and was an AIS scholarship holder. From 1992 rode for world road teams such as ONCE, Rabobank and U.S. Postal Service.

He competed in the Olympic Games at Barcelona in 1992. At Atlanta in 1996 he finished eighth in the individual time trial. From 1993 top results included third in the Teleflex Tour, second in the Circuit de la Sarhte tour in 1995, the GC at the Volta a Catalunya in 1996 and the GC at the Route du Sud in 1997. In 1998 he won the Dutch national road championship, in 1999 the Grand Prix de Wallonie and was second in the Route du Sud.

In 2001 Jonker placed second in the Tour de Limousin, third in the GP Ouest-France and fourth in the GP d'Isbergues one-day classics. He was third in the GC at the Tour Down Under in 2002 and in 2004 claimed the GC ahead of Robbie McEwen and Baden Cooke. Jonker competed in five Tour de France tours between 1994-99 with a best result a GC twelfth in 1996, the second highest place by an Australian. He rode in the Giro d'Italia in 1995 and the Vuelta a Espana in 1997. Jonker told Cyclist Magazine the Tour de France is the pinnacle of the sport: "To be just outside the top ten overall for me was probably one of my greatest achievements." He denied involvement in the U.S. Postal Service-Lance Armstrong EPO doping scandal in 2000 when riding for the team.

Cameron Meyer

Cameron (Cam) Meyer (born 1988) is from Western Australia and rode for the Mitchelton-Scott cycling team. From 2009, Meyer was a champion track cyclist and won nine gold medals and 18 medals overall to 2018 at the UCI track world championships (see track cycling). In 2007 he won the Tour of Tasmania and in 2008 claimed the GC at the Tour of Japan and third overall at the Tour of Oman.

Meyer won the national road time trial championship in 2010-2011 and the national criterium championship in 2013. He turned professional in 2009 and rode for Team Garmin and Orica GreenEDGE and showed his versatility on the road with GC wins in 2011 at the Tour Down Under and the Tour de Perth, in 2013 the Oceania road race championship, stage wins at the Tour de Suisse in 2013-14, and the GC at the Herald Sun Tour in 2015.

In 2017 Meyer posted third place in the Cadel Evans Great Ocean Road Race and won Belgium's Dwars door Vlaamse Ardennen one-day race. In 2018 he was second in the GC at the Herald Sun Tour and won a stage of the OVO Energy Tour of Britain. At the 2018 Gold Coast Commonwealth Games, Meyer won the road time trial in a time of 48:13.04 over a difficult 38.5km course.

In the grand tours he won stages at the Tour de France and the Giro d'Italia in the team time trial. In 2019 he claimed a GC second at the Herald Sun Tour. At the RoadNats in 2020 after many attempts, he won his first elite road championship from Lucas Hamilton and in February 2021 claimed his second national road championship title.

Damien Howson

Damien Howson (born 1992) comes from South Australia where he rode for Central Districts cycling club after being a state junior basketballer at 13. He came through the Australian Jayco-AIS development team and in 2011 won the Oceania under 23 road championship.

Howson showed his all-round and time trial ability in 2012 placing third in the under 23 world road time trial championship, second in the Memorial David Fardelli and fourth in the Chrono Champenois time trial. He won the time trial at the under 23 road world championships in 2013 and Oceania road and time trial championships.

From 2015 Howson rode in all three grand tours with a best placed 45th in the Vuelta a Espana in 2016. His top results include a win at the Trofero Alcide Degasperi in Italy; second in the Chrono Champenois; a GC third at the Thuringen Rundfahrt tour; at the Herald Sun Tour a GC third in 2016, a GC win in 2017 and GC third in 2018. In 2020 riding for Mitchelton-Scott, he won the GC at the Czech Cycling Tour and was third at the Tour of Hungary.

Jay McCarthy

Jay McCarthy (Born 1992) is from Maryborough, Queensland and took up road cycling as a teenager with the Fraser Coast cycling club. A top junior/under 19 road cyclist, McCarthy was seventh in the 2009 junior road world championship, won silver in the junior road worlds in 2010 and the under 19 national road championship.

McCarthy turned professional in 2010 and competing in Europe won the 3 Giorni Orobica road race in Italy and was second at the GP General Patton tour in France. In 2012 he rode for Australian teams UniSA-Australia and Jayco-AIS and had a GC win at New Zealand's Tour of Wellington. Top results included a win in Italy's Trofero Piva Banca Poplare race, second in the GP Capadarco, and eleventh in the Liege-Bastogne -Liege classic.

From 2013-14 McCarthy rode for Saxo-Tinkfoff and posted a GC third at the Tour of Turkey in 2015, a GC fourth at the Tour Down Under and rode in all three grand tours. In 2017 he joined Bora-Hansgrohe and placed third at the Santos Tour Down Under.

In 2018 McCarthy won the Cadel Evans road race and was second in the national road race championships. In 2020 he placed sixth in the Cadel Evans Great Ocean Road Race and rode in the European classics and tours.

Jack Haig

Jack Haig (born 1993) moved from Queensland to Bendigo, Victoria when quite young and started mountain bike racing, winning the under 23 MTB cross country title in 2013. He took up road cycling riding for the Tasmanian Avanti Racing Team and won two stages in the Tour of Bright, Victoria in 2012. In 2013 he won the GC at the Tour of Tasmania.

Haig rode in Europe with the Australian under 23 Jayco-AIS World Tour Academy Team in 2014-15 and was a GC second at the 2014 Herald Sun Tour, placed second in the Tour Alsace and third in the Tour de Korea. He joined Orica-GreenEDGE in 2015 and posted second places in the under 23 Tour de l'Avenir and GP Palio del Recioto.

In 2016 he was signed by Mitchelton-Scott for his climbing ability. He was fifth in the Herald Sun Tour and second at the Tour of Slovenia. In 2017 Haig placed third in the Tour of Slovenia, eighth in the Tour of Poland and was a credible 21st at the Vuelta a Espana. Haig's best result in 2018 was a GC third at the Tour of Utah. In 2019 Haig claimed third place in the Bretagne Classic Ouest-France, sixth in the Il Lombardia classic, third in the GP Bruno Bhegelli, and a GC fourth at the Paris-Nice tour.

In 2019 Haig claimed two second GC places riding in the

Vuelta a Andalucia and the Volta a la Comunitat Valenciana. He competed in all three grand tours up to 2019 with a best result of 19th in the Vuelta a Espana in 2018. In August 2019, Haig, now 26, signed with the Bahrain McLaren cycling team for 2020.

Lucas Hamilton

Lucas Hamilton comes from Ararat, Victoria (born 1996). He started cycling with the Ararat and Districts Cycling Club at 12 years and later joined the Victorian Institute of Sport Talent Program. He won the under 23 national road race championships in 2012, was second in the time trial and won the Oceania road championships.

He placed third in Ireland's An Post Ras tour in 2016, was second in the under 23 road championships and third in 2017. Other top results from 2017 were a win in the Oceania road championships; the GC at the Tour Alsace; GC second at the Giro Ciclistico d'Italia; and third at the under 23 Leige-Bastogne-Leige classic.

Hamilton signed with Mitchelton-Scott in 2018 for three years and claimed the GC at Italy's Settimana Internazionale Coppi e Bartali tour in 2019 for his first elite win, was a GC second at the Czech Cycling Tour and sixth in the Herald Sun Tour.

Riding in his first grand tour in the Giro d'Italia, Hamilton was 25th on debut and Mitchelton-Scott said he was one of Australia's best GC prospects in the grand tours. In 2020 he was second in the national road championships and a GC ninth at the Tour Down Under.

Jai Hindley

Jai Hindley comes from Perth, Western Australia (born 1996). His father was a cyclist and Jai took up track and road cycling when six and rode for the Midlands cycling club. Hindley placed second in the Oceania road cycling championships in 2013 and third in 2014. Hindley rode in Europe's under 23 races from 2015-16 for the Australian Cycling Academy team and Mitchelton-Scott from 2017. In 2016 he won Italy's GP Capodarco and claimed a GC second at Ireland's An Post Ras tour.

2017 was a breakthrough year at under 23 and elite tours with a GC second at the Herald Sun Tour, wins at the Toscana-Terra di Ciclismo and the Tour of Fuzhou, third in the Giro Ciclistico d'Italia, and second at the Trofero Citta di San Vendemiano road race. He signed for Team Sunweb for 2018 and came 32nd at the Vuelta a Espana grand tour. In 2019 Hindley claimed a GC second in the Tour de Pologne and was 35th in the Giro d'Italia.

In 2020, Hindley rode at the Tour Down Under with Team Sunweb and claimed a GC win at Victoria's 5-stage Herald Sun Tour, also winning the mountains classification. Hindley thanked his Team Sunweb teammates and told the Herald Sun newspaper: "Some big names and a lot of great riders have ridden this race. To etch my name on the trophy is pretty unreal."

He capped 2020 by claiming the GC second place at the Giro d'Italia in Italy after leading the race before the final time trial stage, becoming the highest placed Australian on the podium at Italy's grand tour.

Chapter 2
Australasian Cycling Year Book, 1937-38. 'Jack Parsons obituary', George Broadbent, Australian   Cycling and Motor Cycling, July 14, 1932. Australian Cyclist, 1898-1905. Grivell, H. Curly, Australian Cycling in The Golden Days, 1950. 'Dick Davis', The Carnavon Times newspaper, December 1888. 'Wally Kerr', The NSW Cyclist, September 1893. 'Ben Goodson', the NSW Cyclist's Union, 1892, 1889. 'Austral Wheel Notes', The Press, Christchurch, January 1898. '500 pounds Austral Wheel Race', The Referee, Sydney, November 30, 1927. 'Austral Wheel', The Sydney Mail, 1894, 1889. 'Sydney Thousand', Kalgoorlie Western Argus, March 21, 1905.

Chapter 3
Harold   K.   Smith   author   story,   National   Cycling,   September   1985. 'Interest in Warrnambool', Horsham Times, August 11, 1922. Melbourne to Warrnambool, race website. 'Warrnambool to Melbourne', The Age, September 27, 1897. 'J Beasley breaks world's record in Warrnambool', The Sporting Globe, October 31, 1923. 'Centenary Thousand', Dunlop-Perdriau Rubber Co., October 1934.

Chapter 4
'Pedals, Politics and People' (H. Opperman 1977), National Cycling series, John Drummond, 1980s. Jessop K. & Churchward M. (2008) Hubert Ferdinand Opperman, Cyclist & Politician in Museums Victoria Collections. The Sporting Globe newspaper, 1895-86, 1936. The Age newspaper, 1897, 1927. The Camperdown Chronicle, 1931.

Chapter 5
Author correspondence with Alf Goullet, January 1987. Harold K. Smith story, National Cycling, September 1985. Author story 'Alf Goullet and Harold Smith reunited', Australasian Cycling newspaper, March 1987. Author story 'The Grenda Saga', National Cycling, March 1985. 'Goullet – Australia's Greatest', John R. Crawford, The Australian Cyclist, April 1950. 'The Great Days of Bike Racing', Willie Ratner, the Newark Sunday News, January 29, 1968. 'Clarke vs Kramer', The New York Times, September 19, October 24, 1910. 'Alf Grenda, Australian cyclists at Newark', Newark Evening Star newspaper, May 1912, August 1912. 'Cecil Walker in America', Evening News, Sydney, January 1913. 'Cecil Walker unique cycling success', Sydney Morning Herald, October 16, 1930.

Chapter 6
Harold K. Smith story, National Cycling, 1985. Sharp M.P. Spears, Robert Adam (1893-1950), Australian Dictionary of Biography, Volume 12, (MUP), 1990. Bob Spears writing in Sports Novels Magazines, 1950s. 'Spears's Cycle Record', The New York Times, August 3, 1914.

Chapter 7
Danny Clark, author story Freewheeling magazine, 1987 and author communication July 2020. Australian Olympic Committee: 'Russell Mockridge' by Harry Gordon; 'Kevin Nicholls, Turtur, Grenda and Woods, Olympic gold medallists in the team pursuit'; 'Four-time Olympian' Gary Neiwand. Bates, Phill, 'Sutton Australia's most decorated cyclist', St George Cycling Club Facebook page. 'Billy Guyatt's Great Cycle Win', The Sporting Globe, October 9, 1954. 'Billy Guyatt Most Successful Rider', The Argus newspaper, May 4, 1939. Gordon Johnson – 1970 World Pro Sprint

Champion', Edmond Hood, velovertias.co.uk, July 24, 2020. Grivell, H. Curly, Australian Cycling in The Golden Days, 1950. Hazelhurst, Cameron, and Whitehead, Sally, Mockridge Edward Russell (1928-1958), Australian Dictionary of Biography, Volume 15 (MUP), 2000. 'Australian star of track and road – Dean Woods', by Edmond Hood, Pezcyclingnews.com, June 14, 2019. 'Remembering the king of the track Sid Patterson', The Advocate newspaper, December 3, 2008.

Chapter 8

'America's short, violent love affair with indoor track cycling', Nathalie Lagerfield, Atlas Obscura, September 27, 2016. Author story, 'Six-day bicycle racing', Push-On Cycling, 1983. Reg Arnold author story Freewheeling magazine, 1987. 'The extreme sport of six-day bicycle racing', pateblog.nma.gov.au/2013. 'Australian Six Day Races/Jack Rolfe', SixDay.Org. 'Velodrome d'Hiver', Ernest Hemingway, A Moveable Feast, Arrow Books, 2009. Jack Pollard, Sporting Life, September 1951.

Chapter 9

'A Lady Bicyclist, 600 miles on a safety', The Advertiser newspaper, October 3, 1894. Bootcov, Michelle Dr, The International Journal of the History of Sport (2019). 'Edna Sayers', The Truth newspaper September 17, 1933; 'Irene Pyle, Sydney to Melbourne ride' The Argus newspaper, November 2, 1938. 'Iris Bent (Dixon)', Monique Hanley, cyclingtips, 2016. 'Ladies Bicycle Club in Victoria', The Age newspaper, February 15, 1895. Langmore, Dianne, Biography – Maddock, Sarah (1860-1955), Australian Dictionary of Biography, Volume 10 (MUP), 1986. 'Sarah Maddock', The Bicycle and the Bush, Jim Fitzpatrick, Oxford University Press, 1980. 'Sydney Ladies Bicycle Club', Evening News, Sydney November 25, 1985. 'Billie Samuel women's record Sydney to Melbourne', The Sydney Morning Herald, July 5, 1934. Valda Unthank cycling records, the State Library of Victoria. 'Margaret McLachlan story', The Women's Weekly, May 1967. The National Pioneer Women's Hall of Fame.

Chapter 10

Christian Prudhomme, Amaury Sports Organisation, Le Telegramme newspaper, 'Women's Tour de France', April, July 2020. Grace Brown, 'Grace Brown shines of Leige-Bastone-Leige debut', SBS Cycling Central, October 5, 2020. Australian Olympic Committee, Sarah Carrigan by Harry Gordon, AOC historian. Gracie Elvin, 'Tour of Flanders', Mitchelton-Scott cycling, 2017. Chloe Hosking, athlete profile, Gold Coast CG2018. 'Chloe Hosking relishing mentor role at Rally UHC', Rally UHC team, December 5, 2019. 'Garfoot announces retirement', Commonwealth Games Australia, July 12, 2008. Tracey Gaudry, 'Women's Tour de France', ABC News, 2019. Olivia Gollan, 'Athens 2004', AOC. Rochelle Gilmore, 'Unbreakable Gilmore happy again after overcoming horrific injuries', Sydney Morning Herald, December 11, 2011. Elizabeth (Liz) Hepple, author communication. 'Australian pioneers', Cyclingnews, July 26, 2014. 'Queensland's Lucy Kennedy wins 2020 Women's Herald Sun Tour', www.heraldsuntour.com. Sara Roy, 'Clasica Femenina Navarra victory', Mitchelton-Scott cycling, 2019. Amanda Spratt, 'Spratt wins third Women's Tour Down Under', January 2019. Oenone Wood, author communication, August 2020. 'Wood turns full attention to family', Cyclingnews.com, September 2008. Anna Wilson, author communication.

Chapter 11

Ashlee Ankudinoff, Australian Olympic Committee (AOC), 2019. Katherine Bates, 'Former world champion Bates calls time on her career', Cyclingnews, 2015. Amy Cure, '2017 track world championships, Hong Kong', Cycling Australia.   Annette Edmondson, 'Track World Championships, 2015', AOC. Michelle Ferris, Atlanta Olympics, 1996, AOC. Ride Media interview, November 22, 2018. Katie Mactier, Athens Olympics, 2004, AOC. Anna Meares, the Queensland Sporting Hall of Fame, 2008. AOC historian Harry Gordon, London Olympics, 2012. Anna Meares Now, by Anna Meares, Stoke Hill Press, 2020. Kerrie Meares, the Commonwealth Games Association, August 2017. Kaarle McCulloch, Cycling Australia, 2019. Stephanie Morton, 'Stephanie Morton made history on several fronts', Commonwealth Games GC2018 report.   Julie Speight, Cyclingnews, November 2017. Kathy Watt, 1992 Olympic Games, AOC.

Chapter 12

Phil Anderson, ABC Radio, Tour de France Yellow Jersey, 1981. Author correspondence with Phil Anderson. "The Master Returns, no brass band for cycling hero,' John Drummond, National Cycling magazine, November 1985. Peter Besanko, The Standard newspaper, Warrnambool, September 2015. Commonwealth Bank Classic amateur cycling tour, National Cycling, 1985-86. Author correspondence with race organiser, Phill Bates. Jack Hoobin, Australian Cyclist magazine, August 21, 1950. Revolvery website. 'Russell Mockridge wins senior Australian Amateur Road Championship', The Argus newspaper, September 1, 1947. 'Cycling to Rowley', Keith Rowley, The Sunday Herald, 1950. Author correspondence with Clyde Sefton, 2020. Clyde Sefton, Cycling Victoria Hall of Fame, 2017. Barry Waddell, Herald Sun newspaper, February 11, 2011. Author correspondence with John Trevorrow.

Chapter 13

Brett Aitken and Scott McGrory, '2000 Sydney Olympic Games madison', The Australian Olympic Committee (AOC). Graeme Brown, Stuart O'Grady, 'O'Grady, Brown win madison gold', The Sydney Morning Herald, August 26, 2004. Ryan Bayley, 'Athens individual sprint 2004', Harry Gordon, historian, AOC. Matthew Glaetzer, '2018 world championships', AOC. Michael Hepburn, '2012 Olympic Games, London'. AOC. Darryn Hill, 'Olympic team sprint at the 2000 Sydney Olympics', AOC. Glen O'Shea, 'The 2012 world championships', AOC. Shane Kelly, 'A five-time Olympian', 1996, AOC. Cameron Meyer, Australian Cycling Team, Cycling Australia. Brad McGee, 'Individual pursuit medals at three Olympic Games', AOC. Chris Scott, 'the first Para-cyclist inducted into the Hall of Fame', Cycling Australia Hall of Fame. Scott Sunderland, 'Scott Sunderland wins one kilo time trial', ABC News, July 27, 2014. Sam Welsford, Porter, Howard and O'Brien. 'First team in history to break the three-minute and fifty second barrier', Australian Cycling Team.

Chapter 14

Allan Davis, 'Team aspect & of road cycling', Bikeexchange.com, June 2004. Cadel Evans, Aldo Sassi, The Art of Cycling, Cadel Evans, HarperCollinsPublishersAustralia, 2016. ABC News, January 31, 2015. The Herald Sun newspaper, July 25, 2011. Caleb Ewan, 'Ewan earns hat-trick on Champs-Elysses', SBS Cycling Central July 29, 2019.

Cycling Australia, Team of the Century, November 2014. Jai Hindley, 'Mountain stages launch Jai Hindley to greatest win of cycling career', Herald Sun newspaper, February 9, 2020. Michael Matthews, 'Change of team the key for Matthews race for Green Jersey', The Sydney Morning Herald, July 21, 2017. Robbie McEwen, 'Greatest road sprinters', Peleton magazine (USA), 2020. Stuart O'Grady, '2012 Olympic Games road race, London', Australian Olympic Committee. Matt Hayman, '2016 Paris Roubaix champion', Mitchelton-Scott cycling, September 2017. Ritchie Porte, 'Porte gets long-awaited podium', Trek-Segafredo website July 2020. 'This stage is not a procession', SBS Cycling Central, September 21, 2020. Patrick Jonker, Cyclist Magazine profiles. Michael Rogers, 'Rogers tactical mind, physical prowess', Ride Media/Ride Cycling Review, April 2016.

Other Sources/Cyclist Profiles

Ampol Australian Sporting Records, Budget Books, 1981. AusCycling Australia, Australian Cycling Team. Australian National Road Championships/National Road Series. Australian Olympic Committee website. The Cadel Evans Great Ocean Road Race. The Commonwealth Games website, www.thecgf.com.au. Cycling Australia Hall of Fame. Cyclingarchives.com.au. National Cycling magazine, 1979-1986. Procyclingstats.com. Sport Australia Hall of Fame. Tasmanian Sporting Hall of Fame. The Tour Down Under. Trove (nla.gov.au). The Union Cycliste Internationale (UCI).

ACKNOWLEDGEMENTS

Many thanks are due to the former editor-publisher of National Cycling magazine John Drummond for his total commitment to cycling sport. I worked with John on National Cycling magazine in 1985-86 as associate publisher and writer and it was an invaluable experience. Credit is due to the former cycling champions who made the time to tell their amazing stories and provide comments for the book; Rob Arnold of Ride Media Cycling Review for allowing me to quote from Ride's stories. And to the cycling photographers and photo providers: Ray Bowles from AusCycling Victoria for access to historical black and white photos and the AusCycling Victoria History Archive; Graham Watson, Alamy Australia, SWPix.com, Sara Cavallini photography, Velofocus, State Library of Victoria, Museums Victoria collections, Jim Fitzpatrick's The Bicycle and the Bush, Collection of the Queen Victoria Museum & Art Gallery, Launceston, Libraries Tasmania, City of Sydney, Harold K. Smith, Roger Arnold, and the Gallery of Sport, MCG.

DISCLAIMER

The author/publisher has taken all reasonable care in preparing this book and makes no warranty about the completeness of and accuracy in the contents of this book.

INDEX

Front cover top: Ritchie Porte on stage 20 of the Tour de France in 2020 when he rode a brilliant time trial to claim the GC third place. Photo by Alex Broadway, SWpix.com.

Front cover: Australia's gold medal winning women's team pursuit (Ashlee Ankudinoff, Amy Cure, Annette Edmondson, and Melissa Hoskins) on day 2, 2015 UCI track world championships, Saint Quentin-Yvelines, France. Photo by Adam Day, PA Images/Alamy Stock Photo.

Back cover main photo: Chloe Hosking wins the La Course by Le Tour one-day road race at Paris, July 24, 2016. Photo by Balant Hamvas @Velofocus.

Back cover top left: Cameron Meyer was Australia's most successful male track cyclist at the UCI track world championships to 2018, winning nine gold medals and 18 medals overall. Ray Bowles photo.

Back cover centre: Russell Mockridge took European track cycling by storm in 1952 by winning both the amateur and professional Grand Prix of Paris. Photo courtesy Cycling Victoria History Archive.

Back cover bottom: Shane Kelly riding in the kilo time trial at the 1995 UCI track cycling championships at Bogota, Colombia, when he won the gold medal for Australia.
Graham Watson photo.